PETER MAY

KNOCKOUT

FIRST CERTIFICATE

STUDENT'S BOOK

OXFORD
UNIVERSITY PRESS

Contents

Outline of the Examination page 6

	TOPICS	GRAMMAR	VOCABULARY	READING
UNIT 1 In fitness and in health page 8	Health and fitness	Present tenses Countable and uncountable nouns	Parts of the body	Multiple matching: summaries (Part 1) Gapped text: paragraphs (Part 3)
UNIT 2 Thrills and frights page 18	Cinema Personal experiences	Articles Participle adjectives	Collocations Phrasal verbs with *get* Films	Multiple matching: headings (Part 1) Multiple choice and global MCQs (Part 2) Gapped text: sentences (Part 3)
UNIT 3 Looking ahead page 28	Science and technology	The future *Make* and *do*	Affixes	Multiple matching (Part 4)
UNIT 4 Taking it easy page 38	Hobbies Music Expressing opinions	Frequency adverbs *Must / have to / should*, etc. Comparatives and superlatives	Hobbies and interests Reading	Multiple matching: headings (Part 1) Gapped text: sentences (Part 3)
UNIT 5 Home and away page 48	Living conditions	Past tenses Contrast links	Living conditions Phrasal verbs with *look*	Multiple choice (Part 2)
UNIT 6 If it tastes good page 58	Food and drink	Conditional 1 Conditional 2 *Unless / as long as / provided*	Food and cooking Smelling and tasting Phrasal verbs with *put*	Multiple matching: headings (Part 1)
UNIT 7 This sporting life page 68	Sports	*Can / could / may / might* Relative clauses Punctuation	Compound words Prepositional phrases with *in* Phrasal verbs with *give*	Multiple matching (Part 4)
UNIT 8 In the spotlight page 78	The arts and TV	Present perfect	The arts	Gapped text: sentences (Part 3)

WRITING	USE OF ENGLISH	LISTENING	SPEAKING	EXAM STUDY GUIDE	COMMON ERRORS
Transactional letter: formal (Part 1) Report (Part 2)	Key word transformations (Part 3)	Part 4: multiple choice	Part 1	Self-assessment	Present simple / continuous Indefinite article
Informal letter (Part 2)	Multiple-choice cloze (Part 1)	Part 2	Part 3	Listening Comprehension	Definite article
Discursive composition: for and against (Part 2)	Word formation (Part 5) Open cloze (Part 2)	Part 1 Part 3	Part 2		*Enough*
Article (Part 2)	Key word transformations (Part 3) Multiple choice cloze (Part 1)	Part 2	Part 3	Extensive reading	Modals without *to* Subject / object pronoun
Report (Part 2)	Open cloze (Part 2)	Part 3	Part 1		Present form of *used to* *Though / although*
Article (Part 2)	Word formation (Part 5) Key word transformations (Part 3)	Part 2 Part 4: yes / no	Part 3 Part 4	Checking for mistakes	*No matter*
Report (Part 2)	Error correction (Part 4)	Part 2 Part 4: true / false	Part 2	Extensive listening	*Whom* *At the end / in the end* Repetition of object
Transactional letter: formal / informal (Part 1) Composition (Part 2)	Word formation (Part 5)	Part 4: who said what? Part 1	Part 1	Speaking	*During / for*

	TOPICS	GRAMMAR	VOCABULARY	READING
UNIT 9 What happened next? page 88	Crime Transport	Past perfect Narrative time links *Wh-* questions	Crime Transport Phrasal verbs with *take*	Multiple matching: headings (Part 1)
UNIT 10 Appearances and reality page 98	Fashion Shopping and consumer goods Services	The passive The gerund *I-ing* form	Phrasal verbs with *bring* Describing appearance Shops Facilities and services	Multiple choice (Part 2)
UNIT 11 The place to go page 108	Travel and tourism	Reported speech The infinitive	Holidays and travel British and American English	Gapped text: paragraphs (Part 3) Gapped text: sentences (Part 3)
UNIT 12 Getting on well page 118	Social relations / family relationships	Conditional 0 Conditional 3 Mixed conditionals Short replies	Describing character	Gapped text: sentences (Part 3) Multiple choice (Part 2) Multiple matching: summaries (Part 1)
UNIT 13 Come rain or shine page 128	The weather Occupations	*So / such … that* Adjective order	The weather Phrasal verbs with *turn* Jobs	Multiple choice (Part 2) Multiple matching (Part 4)
UNIT 14 Making a better world page 138	The environment Animals	Past modals *Wish / if only*	The environment Animals	Multiple matching (Part 4)
UNIT 15 Doing your best page 148	Education, study and learning	Expressing purpose *Have something done*	Education First Certificate	Multiple matching: summaries (Part 1)

Exam revision section	page 158
Grammar reference	page 169
Irregular verbs	page 185
Index of phrasal verbs and multi-word verbs	page 187
Index of exam task-types and advice	page 189
Index of grammar and functions	page 190

WRITING	USE OF ENGLISH	LISTENING	SPEAKING	EXAM STUDY GUIDE	COMMON ERRORS
Narrative (Part 2)	Open cloze (Part 2)	Part 3 Part 4: multiple choice	Part 4	Reasons for mistakes	Past perfect / past simple *On / by*
Narrative: describing people (Part 2) Formal letter (Part 2)	Error correction (Part 4)	Part 1 Part 2	Part 2 Part 3	Vocabulary	Use of passive *Looking forward to + -ing*
Article: describing places (Part 2)	Key word transformations (Part 3) Error correction (Part 4)	Part 4: true / false	Part 2		Word order in reported questions *Make* + bare infinitive
Transactional letter: formal (Part 1) Report (Part 2)	Key word transformations (Part 3)	Part 1	Part 3		Future in *if* clauses Short replies using *so*
Formal letter: job application (Part 2)	Open cloze (Part 2) Error correction (Part 4)	Part 4: multiple choice	Part 4		*Have / be*
Discursive composition: opinion (Part 2) Transactional letter: informal (Part 1)	Multiple-choice cloze (Part 1)	Part 3 Part 1	Part 3	Revising	Question tags *It's time* + simple past
Set books (Part 2)	Key word transformations (Part 3) Word formation (Part 5)	Part 3 Part 2	Part 3 Part 4	Timing	Separable / non-separable phrasal verbs *If / in case*

Outline of the Examination

The Cambridge First Certificate in English Examination consists of five papers, each of which carries an equal number of marks. You can find detailed advice on how to approach each part of these papers by using the page references listed under *Guidance*.

PAPER 1 READING (1 HOUR 15 MINUTES)

Part 1 chiefly tests your understanding of the main points of the text, while Part 2 focuses on detail, Part 3 on text structure and Part 4 on specific information. You will find general advice about reading on page 39.

Part and task type	Questions	Task format	Guidance
1 Multiple matching	6 or 7	summaries	8 123 148
		headings	18 38 59 89
2 Multiple choice	7 or 8	four options	18 24 48 98 118 128
3 Gapped text	6 or 7	paragraphs	14 108
		sentences	24 44 78 114 118
4 Multiple matching	13–15	short texts / extracts	28 68 134 138

PAPER 2 WRITING (1 HOUR 30 MINUTES)

In Part 1 you show your ability to write a letter based on instructions and information, while in Part 2 you can choose from a number of different tasks. In both Parts 1 and 2 you write between 120 and 180 words. You will find general advice about writing on pages 63 and 97.

Part and task type	Questions	Task format	Guidance
1 Transactional letter	1, compulsory	combination of prompts	15 84 85 122 147
2 From six types:	Choose 1 of 4	context-based task	
article			45 62 117
letter			26 107 136
report			17 56 74
composition			35 87 142
short story			93 97 103
set books			152
(choice of two)			

PAPER 3 USE OF ENGLISH (1 HOUR 15 MINUTES)

While Parts 1 and 5 mainly test your vocabulary, Part 4 concentrates on grammar and Parts 2 and 3 focus on both vocabulary and grammar.

Part and task type	Questions	Task format	Guidance
1 Multiple-choice cloze	15	text with gaps: four options given	21 47 146
2 Open cloze	15	text with gaps	36 57 96 131
3 Key word transformations	10	rewriting sentences	11 41 65 111 126 151
4 Error correction	15	text with errors	75 107 117 137
5 Word formation	10	text with gaps: base word given	30 61 83 156

PAPER 4 LISTENING (40 MINUTES APPROX.)

Questions in Parts 1 and 3 test your understanding of gist, main points, detail, function, location, roles and relationships, mood, attitude, intention, feeling or opinion. Parts 2 and 4 focus on gist, main points, detail or specific information, or your ability to deduce meaning. You will find general advice about listening on pages 22 and 76.

Part and task type	Questions	Task format	Guidance
1 Multiple choice	8	eight unrelated short texts; three options given	32 86 102 124 144
2 Note taking / blank filling	10	one text; write in answers	22 42 62 72 104 154
3 Multiple matching	5	five related short texts; match with prompts	34 52 92 142 152
4 Selection from options	7	one text; two or three options given:	
		true / false	76 112
		yes / no	66
		multiple choice	13 94 132
		'who said what'	82

PAPER 5 SPEAKING (14 MINUTES APPROX.)

The examiner begins by asking you questions about yourself and then, in Part 2, gives you two pictures to compare and contrast. You also comment briefly on the other candidate's pictures.

In Part 3 you work in pairs, for example solving problems, making plans or taking decisions based on material such as pictures or diagrams. Finally, in Part 4, you discuss topics related to the theme of Part 3.

You will find general advice about speaking on page 87.

Part and task type	Time	Task format	Guidance
1 Interview	three minutes	talk to examiner	13 53 87
2 Individual long turn	four minutes	talk about pictures	33 77 112
3 Collaborative task	three minutes	talk to other candidate	23 43 66 105 125 145 155
4 Three-way discussion	four minutes	talk to other candidate and examiner	66 95 133 155

In fitness and in health

SPEAKING

1 Give the following a score of 1–5 for how good you think they are for your health (1 = not good, 5 = excellent).

> eating fruit   eating red meat   drinking lots of water
> taking vitamin pills   yoga   going on holiday
> visiting the doctor regularly   jogging   martial arts   football
> a good night's sleep

2 Can you add to the list? What advice would you give:

a a young child   b a teenager   c a pensioner

on how to stay fit and healthy?

READING: multiple matching

1 What is happening in the picture? What qualities do these people need? Use some of these words:

> fit   strength   jump   speed   react   practise   opponent   rules
> tough   train   attack   defend   self-control   skill   strike   kick   punch

2 Do you think these statements are true or false?

1   All martial arts started in China.
2   Taekwondo comes from Japan.
3   Only men can reach a high level.
4   Each coloured belt means something.
5   There are never any injuries in training.
6   When you reach Black Belt you know it all.

Now find the answers by quickly reading through the text.

3 1   In Reading Part 1 you match summary sentences or headings to paragraphs in a text. Look at the exam instructions and summary sentences opposite, but do not choose any summaries for the moment. Read these steps for doing this kind of task and then put them in the correct order.

1   When you have gone through all the paragraphs like this, have a last look at any you still haven't done. These might now be easier as there should be fewer summaries left.
2   Quickly read the whole text, including this example paragraph, to get the general idea. Don't worry too much about any difficult words or phrases.
3   Next, read the list of summaries to get an idea of the main points. Write the example heading at the top of paragraph 0.
4   Study the instructions, title and any pictures to form a first impression of what you are going to read.
5   If you really can't decide, guess and move on quickly to Part 2 of the test.
6   Go back to the beginning and look at the paragraphs you have not done, choosing from the remaining summaries. If you are not sure of any, leave a blank or put a question mark.
7   After you have read the text for the first time, look at the list of summaries again and cross out the example so you don't spend any more time on it. If you think you can match some of the summaries to paragraphs, write the letter for each on the question paper.
8   Each time you choose a summary, cross it off the list (lightly, in case you change your mind later and need to use it again).

2   For each step 1–8, underline one word or phrase that helped you decide where it should go.
Example: *1 – last*

④ Follow the exam instructions carefully.

You are going to read an article about Taekwondo. Choose from the list **A–H** the sentence which best summarizes each part (**1–6**) of the article. There is one extra sentence which you do not need to use. There is an example at the beginning (**0**).

A People take up Taekwondo for a variety of reasons.
B You should be careful when you are deciding where to learn it.
C Some people are changing to Taekwondo from another martial art.
D The colour for each grade has its own particular meaning.
E All students promise never to misuse what they learn.
F It is a safe activity if you take plenty of care.
G We are not certain where the art of self-defence began.
H It is a unique and increasingly popular activity.

◄ **HELP**

The key words in the summaries are underlined. Look for links with these as you read.

TAKING UP TAEKWONDO

0   H

Taekwondo is the Korean name for the 'art of foot and hand fighting'. There is no other martial art style like it and none is so enjoyable in its freedom of expression. Jumping and spinning in the air and striking out with
5 hands and feet are its special characteristics. These can be wonderful to perform and great to watch. Today there are more than twenty million practitioners of Taekwondo and the numbers are growing quickly.

1

The history of the martial arts is the subject of much
10 discussion and there are many theories concerning its origins. China, Japan, Korea and India all have strong claims to the beginnings of unarmed combat, while fighting skills were a natural development throughout the world for self-protection. Taekwondo itself began in Korea,
15 a country which has a tradition of martial arts that goes back more than two thousand years.

2

If you have visited a traditional Karate class and found it too formal or even military in its approach, you will recognize that Taekwondo is more modern in the way
20 things are done. None of the politeness or discipline you would expect in a martial arts club is missing, but there is an air of enjoyment. Many people who previously did Karate are now training in Taekwondo as it is in many ways more progressive, more dynamic, more exciting and more
25 entertaining.

3

Beginners are often attracted by what is an enjoyable, physical form of recreation with the added benefit of self-defence and increased self-confidence. For some the fascination of learning techniques and performing them to
30 exacting standards, combined with a high level of fitness, speed and strength, may be what appeals. Others enjoy being a part of a disciplined group of people of both sexes, of all ages and from many different backgrounds who can work together and help achieve their aims. It is not
35 unusual to find a 12-year-old girl or a 70-year-old man wearing a Black Belt.

4

To reach that level takes years of hard work. Your first belt is white, which shows the innocence of the student who has no previous knowledge of Taekwondo. If you pass
40 your first grading exam, you receive a yellow belt. This represents the Earth, where a plant takes root as the Taekwondo foundation is being laid. The next grade is green, symbolizing the plant's growth as skills begin to develop. This is followed by blue: the plant is now
45 maturing and growing towards heaven as training progresses. Then comes red, meaning danger, cautioning self-control to the student and warning the opponent to stay away. Finally there is black, meaning maturity and proficiency in Taekwondo. It also indicates the wearer's
50 conquest of darkness and fear.

5

The first thing to learn, though, is that Taekwondo is a martial art to be practised with control. Careless practice or fooling around can lead to injury. Strict rules of conduct and close attention to them will help keep injuries to a
55 minimum, particularly when you are training one-to-one with another student. In all combat situations like this you will have to wear thick gloves and padded boots to avoid damaging either yourself or your opponent, and – depending on the club you join – you may also need to
60 wear a helmet and a chest protector.

6

In a good club there should be a feeling of friendliness. The pace may be fast and the training might be tough at times, but nobody should be getting hurt. Sit in on a class, see if people are enjoying themselves and have a look at
65 who is there. If the club has been going for a few years there should be, apart from the instructor, some other high grades – Blue, Red and Black Belts – practising, because there is always more to learn. From Black Belt 1st Dan you can go further still, possibly reaching 5th, 6th or even
70 higher Dans after many years' training.

⑤ Would you like to learn Taekwondo, or any other martial art? Why? Why not?

GRAMMAR: present tenses

We use the present simple for:

a   things that happen repeatedly.
b   permanent situations.
c   natural or scientific laws.
d   future calendar or timetable events.
e   future meanings after *if, when, until,* etc.

We use the present continuous for:

f   something happening as you speak.
g   temporary situations in a given time period.
h   changes, development and progress.
i   definite intentions for the future.
j   irritating things that often happen.

Example: *We play matches on Saturdays. (a)*
We are training in the gym this week. (g)

1 Now match sentences 1–10 with uses a–j.

1   They start aerobics classes here in April.
2   Exercise like this makes the heart beat faster.
3   We're training here again next Thursday.
4   She runs round that track every morning.
5   We're working out specially hard this week.
6   Why are you always forgetting your trainers?
7   Our overall fitness level is improving quickly.
8   We practise over there, next to the indoor pool.
9   You'll be exhausted when you first try this.
10 Everyone in the main gym is going home now.

The speakers in 1–10 are all in the same place. Where?

COMMON ERRORS

'Where are you from, Nikos?'
'I'm coming from Athens.'
What is wrong with the answer? Why?
See the Grammar Reference on page 169.

2 *Health experts now believe it is safe. Many don't realize just how beneficial it is.*

Some verbs are not normally used in the continuous. Put the verbs in the box below into categories 1–5.

like hate believe hear belong dislike imagine love know seem suppose prefer taste possess realize admire keep need own see smell appear have understand want remember wish

1   Perception: *see,* ....
    ....
2   Appearance: *seem,* ....
    ....
3   Thinking: *realize,* ....
    ....
4   Likes and dislikes: *like,* ....
    ....
5   Possession: *own,* ....
    ....

3 Some of these verbs can be used in the continuous, but the meaning changes:

I'm seeing her at 9 o'clock. = I'm meeting her.
He's tasting the food. = He's trying it.

What do the underlined verbs mean in these sentences?

1   I'm thinking about joining a club.
2   People are having such a good time.
3   She was smelling the flowers.
4   I found it so I'm keeping it.

Which other verbs can be used in the continuous with a change in meaning?

4 For each of questions 1–6 choose a verb from this list. Use the same verb in both the present simple and present continuous.

go   ~~stretch~~   reach   start   try   think   help

Example:
I'm stretching this muscle here, as you can see.
I'll warm up before I stretch any muscles.

1   Exercising every day .... me work, eat and sleep better. The cooler weather this week .... me to do a little more.

2   I always .... to avoid training too soon after a meal. Some people .... always .... to show off.

3   I .... that this is by far the best way to build up strength. I .... of buying some equipment to use at home.

4   I .... the stage where I can lift twice as much as I could. I'll think about adding another 10 kg when I .... that level!

5   My session officially .... at seven thirty, so I'll have to wait. It's only seven but I .... to feel like exercising right now.

6   Sometimes I .... for a nice cold drink after I finish. This evening, though, I .... straight home after all that work!

What kind of training does the speaker do?

5 Look back at the sentences in 1–6 again. Match the uses of the verbs with a–j in activity 1.

1 Read the instructions for Use of English Part 3 and look at the example below.

Complete the second sentence so that it has a similar meaning to the first sentence, using the word given. **Do not change the word given**. You must use between two and five words, including the word given.

Example: We cannot make any exceptions, I am afraid.

impossible

I am afraid that it .... make any exceptions.

You should always try to include all the information from the first sentence in the second one. In this case, 1 mark would be given for *is impossible to*, but 2 marks for *is impossible for us to*.

2 Work in pairs, Student A and Student B.

Student A: Put a tick (✓) or a cross (✗) against each of statements 1–8. If you think a statement is wrong, correct it.

Example: *You must always use five words.* (✗) *a maximum of five words*

1 There are always ten key word transformation questions in the exam.   ( )
2 You can put six words if the extra word improves the grammar.   ( )
3 You must spell every word you use correctly.   ( )
4 You can cross out some of the words printed in the second sentence.   ( )
5 It is better to change the key word, or leave it out, than put nothing.   ( )
6 There are always two marks possible for the right answer.   ( )
7 Short forms (e.g. *won't, I've*) count as two words.   ( )
8 Words with possession apostrophes (e.g. *the man's foot*) count as two.   ( )

Now check your answers by asking Student B. Remember not to use the auxiliary *do* with the verb *be* or modals like *must* or *can*.

Example: *Do you always have to use five words?*

Student B: Read the information in the box on page 164 and then answer Student A's questions about it. Help him or her to correct any mistakes.

3 Do questions 1–10. Follow the instructions in activity 1 above and think about the statements in activity 2.

> ◀ **HELP**
>
> All the answers use a present tense. The number of words needed is given in brackets.

1 She owns all this land now.

   belongs

   All .... now. (5)

2 Alexis has decided that he'll go on Tuesday.

   planning

   Alexis .... go on Tuesday. (4)

3 Our neighbour says he definitely won't return the ball.

   keeping

   Our neighbour says he .... the ball. (3)

4 Organized activities don't interest Eva very much.

   interested

   Eva .... organized activities. (5)

5 Our plane's departure time is 10.00 am.

   takes

   Our plane .... 10.00 am. (3)

6 If you run every day, your breathing improves quickly.

   running

   Daily .... your breathing. (3)

7 Which games is she particularly good at, Mrs Kay?

   play

   Which games .... , Mrs Kay? (5)

8 I have arranged a brief meeting with him at 5 pm.

   seeing

   I .... at 5 pm. (4)

9 I'll finish this job and then I'll phone you back.

   soon

   I'll phone you back .... this job. (5)

10 Our team regularly loses matches here.

   losing

   Our team .... here. (4)

VOCABULARY: parts of the body

① Where are these parts of the body? Look at the picture. Identify the items in the box, then tell your partner which you have ever injured, and how.

> toes lips calf bones joints chest hips stomach / tummy ball of the foot elbow
> thigh wrist forehead thumb ankle shoulders chin throat waist
> Achilles' tendon

② Read the text below and then fill in gaps 1–10 by using each of these words once. There is an example at the beginning (0).

> skills strain breathe rhythm stiff loose co-ordination skipping ~~workout~~
> warm-up endurance

A (0) ..*workout*.. consists of doing hard physical training for a period of time. However, you must always start with a (1) .... by doing some gentle practice exercises. When you are doing these exercises your body should be (2) .... , not tense. Otherwise you might (3) .... a muscle or some other part of the body: in other words you might injure it by stretching too much.

Exercises may have different aims, such as to increase strength, suppleness or (4) .... , which is really another way of saying stamina. Others might develop particular (5) .... , like the ability to make muscles work together to perform particular actions. This is known as (6) .... One apparently simple activity that is particularly useful in this respect is (7) .... , for which of course you only need to borrow a rope from a younger member of the family.

When you are coming to the end of your training session, you should do some cooling-down exercises, which can help you avoid feeling (8) .... the next morning. It is often a good idea while you relax to (9) .... slowly and deeply, not from the chest but from the diaphragm. Do this for a few minutes, keeping up a steady (10) .... as the air flows smoothly in and out, your stomach rising and falling.

1 In the exam, you always hear every part of the Listening twice. This means that the first time you listen you have time to form a general impression and get used to the speakers' voices so that you always know who you are listening to. Follow these instructions for Listening Part 4:

▶ HELP

There are two speakers: Cheryl and Josephine. Cheryl gives the answers to all the questions except number 3. You will hear her speaking first.

You will hear a radio programme about skipping. For Questions 1–6, choose the best answer A, B or C.

1 Skipping is now becoming popular with
   A boxers.
   B children in school playgrounds.
   C people who want to get fit.   [1]

2 What was the first thing Cheryl did wrong?
   A She began skipping when she wasn't prepared.
   B She was not wearing good trainers.   [2]
   C She injured someone who was training near her.

3 People who have physical problems
   A will not be harmed by skipping.
   B can do a little light skipping.   [3]
   C should do no skipping at all.

4 Cheryl thinks that rhythm skipping is
   A simple to do.
   B harder than it looks.   [4]
   C easier for children than adults.

5 Cheryl felt much happier when she
   A stopped skipping.
   B started to laugh.   [5]
   C began to relax.

6 Cheryl says that you can skip
   A with a friend.
   B wherever you are.   [6]
   C while you watch TV.

2 Which parts of the body is skipping good for? Which parts can it damage?

1 Read this text about Speaking Part 1 and put examples A–G into the numbered spaces in brackets (1–7).

A When are you going to university?
B What do you usually do at the weekends?
C My house is just down the road, but I used to live near …
D How is your school work going?
E Yes, I'm hoping to work in tourism, so I need to be able to speak and write English well.
F Are you learning English for any special purpose?
G Where do you live?

In Part 1, an examiner will talk to you about yourself for three minutes. This will help you relax, as you will be talking about familiar things like your past experiences, your present life and your future plans. There may be questions about permanent situations (1 ………) or things that you often do (2 ………). To answer them you will probably use a combination of the present simple with past tenses when you give more information (3 ………). Other questions could be in the present continuous if they are about temporary situations (4 ………), plans (5 ………) or progress (6 ………). As always in the Speaking test, your answers should be longer than just *Yes* or *No*, for example, (7 ………).

2 Use these prompts to practise asking and answering questions with somebody else in the class. When it is your turn to answer, give as much information as you can.

- What / name and where / come from?
- Which part / town / live in?
- Where / studying? *or* Where / work?
- Why / preparing for First Certificate?
- How / usually spend / evenings?
- What / doing after / lesson?

3 If the examiner asks what you do in your free time, you may want to talk about how you keep fit, or about a hobby. Look at the answers (1–6) that someone who skips might give about what they do. For each one, write a suitable question.

Example: *To get fit and healthy. Why do you do it?*

1 In health clubs and gyms.
2 Just a rope and some music.
3 Anyone from age six to sixty.
4 You should warm up first.
5 It strengthens the whole body.
6 For two years.

Think about your questions and tell your partner about an activity you like doing.

READING: gapped text

1 Look at the instructions for Reading Part 3. First, read the text quickly for a general impression. Next, look for the main idea in each of the missing paragraphs and decide which part of the text the paragraph probably belongs to: the beginning, the middle or the end.

▼ HELP

The beginning (gaps 0 and 1) introduces the place and the health of its people. Two paragraphs, including the example, go there.
The middle (gaps 2, 3 and 4) gives a scientific explanation and describes new research. Three paragraphs go there.
The end (gaps 5 and 6) contrasts it with another diet and looks at how this could be improved. Two paragraphs go there.

You are going to read a newspaper article about healthy eating. Seven paragraphs have been removed from the article. Choose from the paragraphs **A–H** the one which fits each gap (**1–6**). There is one extra paragraph which you do not need to use. There is an example at the beginning (**0**).

LIVE LONGER WITH VIRGIN OIL FROM Crete

CRETE, that Greek island of olive trees and sunny beaches which was the home of the mythical Minotaur, now has another claim to fame. It has Europe's healthiest population.

0   **H**

The key to the Cretans' good health, say experts, lies in their diet. They have long been known to use far more extra virgin olive oil, flavoured with fresh herbs from the mountains, than other nationalities.

1

5 Experts believe the oil is so good for the health because it provides plenty of oleic acid. This is the kind of fat that is found in the purest olive oil.

2

Research has shown the benefits of this. When tests were carried out, replacing part of the animal fat content of the 10 north European diet with olive oil, it was found that olive oil can greatly reduce levels of the cholesterol that can clog the bloodstream and cause heart problems.

3

Research was conducted by Christine Williams, Professor of Food Studies at Reading University. She wanted to compare 15 a diet rich in animal fats with one that used olive oil.

4

The results showed that the oily simplicity of the Cretan diet is its strength. As the very essence of Mediterranean cooking, it lacks the piles of pasta favoured by the Italians, the grilled meats of southern France or the chorizo (spicy 20 sausages) of Spain.

5

Spreading mountains of butter on toast is equally foreign to them. The standard treatment for bread is to break it into lumps and dip them into a bowl of oil.

6

'I don't think we're going to get people eating a 25 Mediterranean diet here because we don't have the climate for it, but we could incorporate the benefits of olive oil into the foods we are used to,' she said. 'The scientific evidence is sufficient to justify a really major campaign.'

FIRST CERTIFICATE FACTS

The text in Reading Part 3 can have either sentences or paragraphs missing, but never a mixture of both in the same task.

A These scientists also say that the greener and more virgin the olive oil, the higher the level of flavonoid chemicals. These stop cholesterol deposits sticking to the artery walls.

B But whether this diet will catch on with Britons is uncertain. Williams believes it's unlikely that they will change their eating habits.

C A significant reduction in heart disease was noted when rationing limited people's choice of food during the Second World War and the years immediately afterwards. Once they returned to their usual diet the number of patients quickly rose again.

D In fact Cretans consume almost three times as much oil as northern Europeans, whose diets tend to be dominated by animal fats. The oil undoubtedly brings many benefits.

E Unilever, the food multinational, supplied her with a variety of apparently identical foods, including ready meals, puddings and cakes, for a seven-month

F experiment involving two groups of men aged 30 and 45. In half the meals the fat content was made up of animal products, the others contained olive oil instead.

This discovery is one reason why leading doctors and scientists recruited by the European Commission are finalizing a Cretan dietary factsheet. This will be circulated to all family doctors in the European Union, so everyone can benefit from the sun-kissed island's nutrition secrets.

G Unlike the British, the islanders have always had a low intake of meat and dairy products. Instead of decorating animal-based food with creamy sauces, they would much rather soak the local aubergines, tomatoes and courgettes with their precious olive oil.

H In a development that could create a new fashion for Cretan food, nutritionists have found that the islanders have rates of heart disease, obesity and cancer far below those of people in Britain. They are also much lower than in other European countries.

2 Is your diet more like the Cretan or the British? How do you think this affects your health?

WRITING: a transactional letter

1 In Writing Part 1 you read one or more texts and then write a letter based on the information given. You must read the instructions and texts very carefully, as they will tell you who you are writing to, why you are writing and what the main points in your letter should be.

Sentences 1–5 contain more advice. Fill in the gaps by using each of these words once only:

> copy   formal   addresses   unnecessary   ending

1 You don't have to write any .... or telephone numbers.
2 Use a proper beginning (e.g. *Dear John,*) and .... (e.g. *Best wishes,*).
3 You shouldn't .... whole sections from the text.
4 You can add sensible ideas, but not .... information.
5 Your style needn't be very .... , even in a letter to a company.

2 Read the instructions and information below and discuss your ideas with your partner. First look at Question 1 on p159 for an example of how to answer this type of exam task.

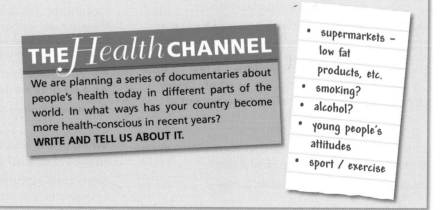

You have read this advertisement placed by a television company and you have decided to reply. You've made some notes on what you want to say.

Look at your notes. Then write to the TV company telling them about your country's attitude to health. Write a **letter** of between **120–180** words in an appropriate style. Do not write any addresses.

THE *Health* CHANNEL

We are planning a series of documentaries about people's health today in different parts of the world. In what ways has your country become more health-conscious in recent years? **WRITE AND TELL US ABOUT IT.**

- supermarkets – low fat products, etc.
- smoking?
- alcohol?
- young people's attitudes
- sport / exercise

3 Start writing. Here are some suggestions:

- Base the content on the ideas in the notes. You should try to use your own words, but you can take some expressions from the notes.
- Use the present simple for permanent situations, repeated events and natural / scientific laws. Use the present continuous for temporary situations, changes and annoying things.

GRAMMAR: countable and uncountable nouns

1 Two of these sentences are correct but eight of them are wrong (or unlikely). Find and correct the mistakes, discussing with your partner any misunderstandings they could cause.

1　People is becoming more and more concerned about pollution.
2　I'm on a diet so I had a very light lunch: just a turkey with a little salad.
3　We did much hard exercise as we realize that intensive training is essential.
4　She spent several days in bed with flu, so she's quite weak.
5　He enjoys playing cards, especially poker, but he always seems to have a bad luck.
6　I saw an interesting news about gymnastics on television last night.
7　There was such a bad behaviour by a few youths that the place closed down.
8　Little players turned up for the basketball game so it was cancelled.
9　Safety is the absolute priority when using equipment such as this.
10　He says he speaks a very good English but I have my doubts.

2 Countable nouns have both a singular and plural form, for example *tree* and *trees*. They are marked [C] in most dictionaries. Uncountable nouns have no plural form. They are marked [U] in most dictionaries.

Which of these words from the Reading text are countable, and which uncountable?

island [ ]　beaches [ ]　health [ ]　diet [ ]
herbs [ ]　pasta [ ]　toast [ ]　bread [ ]　bowl [ ]
evidence [ ]　butter [ ]　cakes [ ]　cancer [ ]
secrets [ ]

3 Study the expressions below and decide which ones are used with:

a　countable nouns only.
b　uncountable nouns only.
c　either countable or uncountable nouns.

Which of them are used in questions and negative statements, but not often in positive statements?

a / an　much　many　few　little　a few　a little
a large number of　each　all　a lot of　every
plenty of　a great deal of　a large amount of
lots of　large amounts of

Choose from these expressions to form a short phrase with at least ten of the nouns in 2 above.

Examples: *a few islands, a little butter*

COMMON ERRORS

We have a lovely weather in my country.
What is wrong with this sentence? Why?
See the Grammar Reference on page 170.

4 Some uncountable nouns have different meanings when they are used as countables:

The bowl was made of glass. (the material)
Have a glass of water. (to drink from)

What is the difference in meaning between the two uses of each of these nouns?

1　We've got plenty of time. It was the last time I tried it.
2　She likes eating fish. They caught a huge fish in their net.
3　He has lovely dark hair. There's a hair on your jacket.
4　We use a lot of oil. There are lots of bath oils to choose from.
5　They're in business together. He runs a small business.
6　There's not enough room here. The flat has four rooms.
7　I really hate the cold. She caught a bad cold at school.
8　The bridge was made of iron. Use an iron on those clothes.
9　Put some wood on the fire. I went for a walk in the woods.
10　Tin is a soft, light-coloured metal. Can you buy a tin of tomatoes?

5 To talk about an uncountable in the singular we sometimes use a different noun, such as *an experiment* instead of *research* in the Reading text on page 14, line 13. For each of the uncountable nouns in list A choose a countable in list B which you could use for a single example.

Example: *music – a song*

A (uncountables)			
information	shopping	education	medicine
scenery	~~music~~	traffic	advice	luggage
cash	travel	vocabulary	homework	work
accommodation			

B (countables)			
a vehicle	a word	a suggestion	a room
a suitcase	a coin	an exercise	a job
a purchase	a pill	a report	a view	~~a song~~
a course	a journey		

6 With some uncountables we can also use *a piece of*, *a bit of* or *an item of*.

Examples: *a piece of evidence, a bit of fun, an item of news*

Which of the words in list A can be used with one of these expressions?

Look again at the nouns in list A and at the uncountables in activity 2. Do any of them have countable equivalents in your first language? Make a special note of any that do.

For questions a and b, put a tick (✓) in the appropriate place for each paper.

		Reading	Writing	Use of English	Listening	Speaking
a	Rank your performance in each paper.	GOOD				
		AVERAGE				
		BELOW AVERAGE				
b	How do you find the materials that you are using?	HARD				
		AVERAGE				
		EASY				

c   How many hours per week do you spend practising for each paper?

d   Write down six mistakes you are always making when you speak English.

_____

_____

_____

_____

_____

_____

When you next do a Speaking activity, look at these mistakes before you begin.

STUDY CHECK

1. Ask your partner if he or she:
   - normally feels healthy.
   - has any unhealthy habits such as smoking.
   - usually eats healthy or unhealthy food.
   - does much exercise.
   - is making any changes in his or her lifestyle.

   Are there any kinds of exercise or food that you could recommend to your partner?

2. Read these instructions:

   A doctor wants to know about your lifestyle so that she can offer you some advice on healthier living. Write a **report** about yourself in **120–180** words.

   Before you start writing, ask yourself the questions in activity 1 above and note down the answers.

   When you write, remember these points:

   Style: • Avoid expressions that are too informal.

   Content: • Begin by describing your general state of health and any possible risks.
   • Continue by saying what you eat and drink, and how you get exercise.
   • Finish by talking about changes to your lifestyle now and in the future.

   Language: • Use the present simple for permanent situations, things you often or usually do and the results of changes (after *when, if,* etc.).
   • Use the present continuous for temporary situations, changes you are making at present and any annoying things that are always happening.
   • Use appropriate expressions like *not many* and *a little* with countable and uncountable nouns associated with food, exercise and health in general.

2 Thrills and frights

SPEAKING

1. Look at the pictures opposite.

1 Which of these are you afraid of? Why? Which of them are not really dangerous?
2 In pairs, see if you can agree on an order: from the least to the most frightening.
3 Which of these fears have special names?

2. According to a survey carried out in the USA, people there fear these five things most:

1 public speaking   2 heights   3 insects   4 financial problems   5 deep water

Do any of these scare you? What advice would you give to someone who was afraid of any of 1–5?

3. People sometimes enjoy being scared, for example at a funfair. Why? Which rides at the funfair are frightening?

> **HELP**
>
> In this text the information that will help you is underlined.

READING: multiple matching and multiple choice

1. Follow these instructions for Reading Part 1:

You are going to read an article about a new ride at a theme park. Choose the most suitable heading from the list A–I for each part (1–7) of the article. There is one extra heading which you do not need to use. There is an example at the beginning (0).

A Going underground
B A shorter ride than it seems
C Spinning round and round
D Nothing below you
E A big investment
F Hitting the water
G Not just height and speed
H The latest technology
I Where it is

ALL ABOARD FOR A RIDE INTO TERROR

REPORT BY CHRISTOPHER LLOYD

0 | I

In the depths of The Forbidden Valley, at Alton Towers, in the Midlands, stands a new generation 21st-century rollercoaster. It is the most terrifying ride in Europe and possibly the world.

1

Already famous for such rollercoaster rides as 'The Corkscrew', which throws its riders upside-down in barrel loops, Alton Towers spent more than £10m and two years building what it claims is one of the most innovative and best-designed rollercoasters in the world. It is also one of the most frightening ever built.

2

'Nemesis' – a monster buried in the earth – is a completely new kind of rollercoaster, says John Wardley, the ride's designer. 'The most obvious difference between this and other rollercoasters is that people are not housed in a train with the track reassuringly beneath them. Instead they hang on a series of chairs, like chair lifts above a ski-slope, that are suspended from rails above. This means there is no solid structure underneath and it gives you a very precarious feeling.'

3

Nemesis is the first rollercoaster to send its riders on the outside of a loop-the-loop. The ride, which starts and finishes at the centre of a trapped alien, has four key features: the barrel roll; the zero-gravity roll (when riders experience four seconds of weightlessness); the outside vertical loop (four times the force of gravity) and the stall turn.

4

Modern rollercoasters are designed using sophisticated computer software. However, the builder of Nemesis developed a new way of joining tube tracks together and bending them, so there is no rocking in the ride. 'This technique has more benefits than just giving you the smoothest of rides,' says Wardley. 'It means the trucks travel further and faster for a given amount of energy.'

5

Nemesis has tried to avoid the design of traditional Big Dippers, says Wardley. 'Anyone can build a rollercoaster that goes high and drops low, throwing people down very fast. But we are looking for emotion and you can be far more effective without straight pieces of track. Instead, we have designed a ball of twisted metal that gives a really merciless ride.'

6

The only time people know where they are in relation to their surroundings is when they are briefly hanging upside-down. For those already scared out of their minds this may be one of the worst moments of a ninety-second ride that feels as though it is going on forever.

7

Nemesis is also the first rollercoaster to plunge down a 30ft cavern blasted out of rock. As the rider rushes into tunnels and is taken perilously close to the ground and the cavern walls, an 'added amount of terror' is given to the ride.

2 Now, as in Reading Part 2, choose the answer (A, B, C or D) which you think fits best according to the text.

⚠ HELP

You will find the answers to the questions in these parts of the text:

Question 1: paragraph 2
Question 2: paragraph 3
Question 3: paragraph 4
Question 4: paragraph 5
Question 5: paragraph 6
Question 6: paragraph 7

1 The newest ride is called
   A The Forbidden Valley.
   B Alton Towers.
   C The Corkscrew.
   D Nemesis.

2 The ride begins inside a
   A monster.
   B house.
   C computer.
   D spaceship.

3 Why is the ride so smooth?
   A The track is made in a special way.
   B It is longer than other rollercoasters.
   C It goes so quickly.
   D The plans were drawn by computer.

4 The ride is exciting because
   A it twists a lot.
   B it climbs very high.
   C it goes very straight.
   D it is very steep.

5 The riders' feet are above their heads for
   A a minute and a half.
   B most of the ride.
   C part of the ride.
   D an hour.

6 Riders will
   A hear explosions close to the track.
   B almost touch the sides of the tunnel.
   C almost be hit by falling rocks.
   D get very wet.

3 1 Would you like to go on 'Nemesis'?
  2 What is the most frightening ride you have ever been on?
  3 Is there another ride you would like to try?
  4 How else do people intentionally scare themselves for fun?

GRAMMAR: the indefinite and definite article

1 1 Match rules 1–4 for using the indefinite article, *a*, with examples a–d.

1	the first time a countable noun is mentioned	a	Lloyd is a reporter.
2	to classify or describe, often with an adjective	b	I won a thousand pounds.
3	with people's jobs	c	The ride is a new experience.
4	in some expressions with numbers	d	There is a monster in the earth.

2 When do we use *an*? Is it: **a** before a vowel, or **b** before a vowel sound? Put *a* or *an* in front of each of these: .... umpire, ... hobby, ... MA, ... honour, ... uniform, ... honest answer.

2 Match rules 1–9 for using the definite article, *the*, with examples a–i.

1	when a person or thing is mentioned again	a	We'll meet at the usual place.
2	when there is only one	b	The eagle dives much faster, in fact.
3	with superlatives	c	I think I'd rather take the bus.
4	when others know what we are referring to	d	The nervous are advised to stay away.
5	with musical instruments	e	There's a loop and a roll. The roll is better.
6	with means of transport	f	Something heavy fell to the ground.
7	with inventions	g	It is the most terrifying ride in Europe.
8	with adjectives used as a noun, like *the old*	h	She plays the saxophone all the time.
9	with species of animal	i	The computer has changed its design.

COMMON ERRORS

The thief was sent to the prison for ten years.
What is wrong with this sentence? Why? See the Grammar Reference on page 171.

3 Match the rules for using no article with the examples.

1	with plural countable nouns used in a general sense	a	We are looking for emotion.
2	with abstract nouns used in a general sense	b	Alton Towers is in England.
3	with most streets, cities and countries	c	The wheels are made of rubber.
4	with uncountable nouns used in a general sense	d	Modern rides are smoother.

4 Correct these sentences and in each one say which rules have been broken.

Example:
Kangaroo lives in the Australia. The (rule 2.9) *kangaroo lives in* (rule 3.3) *Australia.*

1 I think most exciting game in world is the cricket.
2 He is working as shop assistant in the Oxford Street.
3 Everyone just wants to have the fun at seaside.
4 Train from Madrid to Seville travels at nearly 200 miles hour.
5 She's doing MA in modern languages at well-known university.
6 You don't often hear bands playing violin at the rock concerts.
7 She reckons parachute was best thing ever invented.
8 Some say it is expensive sport, but an equipment can be cheap.
9 We were hit by storm and floods. Two days later a storm ended.
10 To go to a same place it happened would be bad mistake.

5 Fill in each of gaps 1–20 in this text with *a, an* or *the*, or leave it blank if no article is needed.

Disneyland Paris may not be on anything like the scale of Disneyworld near (1) .... Orlando, but (2) .... technology here is a lot more advanced. Go on (3) .... weekday, when there are not so many (4) .... schoolkids and the waiting does not require such a lot of (5) .... patience. The queues do in fact get shorter after about (6) .... five o'clock and it's often (7) .... good idea to leave (8) .... best rides until quite late. If you must go in (9) .... morning, though, do the rides anti-clockwise. In other words go (10) .... opposite way to (11) .... crowds so that for at least some of the rides you won't face (12) .... hour-long wait. But however long (13) .... wait is, don't miss (14) .... Big Thunder Mountain rollercoaster. It's by far (15) .... most exciting ride: very bumpy with marvellous robot animals alongside (16) .... track. If (17) .... frightening things are what you really want, then check out Phantom Manor. This is (18) .... haunted house that's got (19) .... really stunning special effects, and everyone gets (20) .... good fright before they leave!

USE OF ENGLISH: multiple-choice cloze

1 Most of the questions in Use of English Part 1 test your vocabulary. Some might focus on phrasal verbs, but many are likely to be *collocations*, which are words that usually go together, for example, a *long way*, a *great idea*.

These are adjective + noun collocations, which are very common, but you will see other kinds:

- noun + verb (or verb + noun) collocation: BBC *television showed* the rescue.
- preposition collocation: He survived *thanks to* his dog.
- adverb + verb collocation: They could have been *seriously hurt*.

In sentences 1–8, choose the correct word to complete the collocation.

1 He's interested *at / in / to* anything which involves speed and danger.
2 The best memory is of *driving / riding / piloting* a motorbike from coast to coast.
3 After we came to the end of the road we continued *by / with / on* foot.
4 People's interest didn't last *much / long / many*, so the park soon closed down.
5 The report criticizes the *low / weak / bad* safety standards at the centre.
6 She *owns / manages / holds* the world record for the voyage.
7 The journey consists *in / to / of* four stages, each of them harder than the last.
8 I'm planning to *give / take / make* First Certificate in June, just before my school exams.

HELP

Ten collocations are underlined, including the example.

2 1 Without attempting to fill in any of the spaces, read the text below in no more than two minutes. Say where you think it is taken from and suggest a title for it.

2 Now read the text more carefully and follow the exam instructions:

For Questions **1–15**, read the text below and decide which answer **A**, **B**, **C** or **D** best fits each space. There is an example at the beginning (**0**).

Example:

0   **A** concern   **B** fear   **C** worry   (**D**) doubt

Canada is a massive country full of wide-open spaces. With scenery that is truly magnificent, it is <u>without (**0**) ....</u> one of the great unspoilt areas of the world. If you <u>have the (**1**) ....</u>, make sure you go to Niagara Falls, which are the top attraction in North America and one of the most spectacular (**2**) .... anywhere. Visitors who are not <u>easily (**3**) ....</u> can take a boat ride to the edge of the roaring falls, almost <u>right (**4**) ....</u> the massive torrent of white water. Or walk through rock-cut tunnels for a terrific close-up look from behind the falls, a view familiar from the many film (**5**) .... taken there.

These tunnels are as near as anyone is likely to want to (**6**) .... to Niagara Falls. In 1960 a seven-year-old boy (**7**) <u>.... holiday</u> a little way upstream was playing happily in the water when he suddenly found himself (**8**) <u>.... difficulties</u>. There had been (**9**) <u>.... rain</u> and the river was very full, but nobody noticed that he was (**10**) <u>.... danger</u> until it was too late. Onlookers watched helplessly as he was swept (**11**) .... the Horseshoe fall. But despite being thrown down the 48-metre drop he miraculously came through the experience with no (**12**) .... at all. Such (**13**) <u>.... escapes</u> are the exception <u>rather (**14**) ....</u> the rule, however, and visitors are (**15**) .... not to try this for themselves!

		A		B		C		D
1	**A**	occasion	**B**	chance	**C**	success	**D**	fortune
2	**A**	visions	**B**	sights	**C**	looks	**D**	scenes
3	**A**	scared	**B**	feared	**C**	thrown	**D**	shocked
4	**A**	down	**B**	beneath	**C**	low	**D**	further
5	**A**	pictures	**B**	photos	**C**	images	**D**	shots
6	**A**	get	**B**	arrive	**C**	reach	**D**	land
7	**A**	in	**B**	on	**C**	at	**D**	of
8	**A**	with	**B**	in	**C**	by	**D**	on
9	**A**	hard	**B**	strong	**C**	deep	**D**	heavy
10	**A**	in	**B**	on	**C**	into	**D**	with
11	**A**	straight	**B**	towards	**C**	for	**D**	in
12	**A**	injury	**B**	hurt	**C**	blow	**D**	wound
13	**A**	slim	**B**	narrow	**C**	tight	**D**	close
14	**A**	than	**B**	of	**C**	that	**D**	by
15	**A**	suggested	**B**	warned	**C**	informed	**D**	demanded

When you practise listening comprehension, which of these are good ideas and which are not? Why? If an idea is bad, write what you should do next to it.

a   Read the introduction and think about the topic before you listen.

_____

_____

b   Study the questions in all four parts before the first part begins.

_____

_____

c   Try to predict the content of the listening text from the questions.

_____

_____

d   Try to translate every word as you listen.

_____

_____

e   If you find the text hard, stop listening and wait for it to be played again.

_____

_____

LISTENING

1 Quickly write down all the words you associate with this subject:

pot holing *n* [U] *(sport)* exploring deep holes in rocks and caves

2 You are going to hear an interview with a pot holer who has just come out of a cave. Think about what you already know about the subject and look at Questions 1–10. Before you listen, answer these questions:

How many speakers do you think there will be?

How do you think the pot holer feels when she is underground?

What kinds of details are needed to answer Questions 4, 9 and 10?

3 Now follow these Listening Part 2 instructions:

You will hear a radio interview with a pot holer. For Questions **1–10**, complete the sentences.

Karen used to go rock climbing in her _____ **1**
She is afraid of _____ **2**
In a deep cave there isn't enough light to see the _____ **3**
The maximum distance for using a ladder is _____ **4**
Underground you can only hear _____ **5**
She says it is exciting to go through a cave full of _____ **6**
The water level can rise if there is a change in the _____ **7**
You should tell somebody when you expect to be _____ **8**
The cave she most wants to explore is in _____ **9**
Its depth is _____ **10**

4 Discuss these questions:

1   Has Karen convinced you that pot holing is both safe and good fun? Why? Why not?

2   Have you ever done – or would you like to do – any dangerous or unusual sports?

In Speaking Part 3, the examiner gives you something visual (such as a map or diagram) to discuss with another candidate. You might have to solve a problem or plan something. Normally, the examiner does not take part, but he or she will tell you at the beginning whether you must both agree on what to do. Now practise by imagining you are in this situation:

You and your partner are on a survival course. You have to get from the camp (X) to the safety of the village (Y) as quickly as possible and there are only two possible routes: over the top of the mountain, or underground through the caves. Now it has started to snow heavily. This means that soon it will be very difficult to cross the mountain, while the caves lower down will start to fill up with water. For safety reasons it is important that you stay together, so you must agree on which route to take. You have about 3 minutes.

1 Take turns giving information and opinions, try to talk for about the same time as your partner and listen closely to what he or she says.

2 Talk about the advantages and disadvantages of both routes, in particular:

- the dangers shown in the picture
- how they could be overcome
- how the weather might affect them
- any special fears you have (such as heights, water, cold or enclosed spaces)
- any experience or knowledge you have that could help

3 Make a decision based on all the points you discuss.

PHRASAL VERBS: *get*

We use phrasal verbs more often when we are talking informally than when, for instance, we are making speeches, writing job applications, etc. In these more formal kinds of language, we may use other (usually longer) words with similar meanings.

For example, the interviewer in the Listening activity on page 22 asks Karen:

And how exactly do you <u>get down</u> that far?
And, perhaps more importantly, how do you <u>get back up</u> again?

We could replace *get down* with 'descend' and *get back up* with 'return to the surface', but this would not really sound appropriate in a relaxed conversation between two young people.

Practise using less formal verbs by replacing the expression in italics in 1–10 with the correct form of *get* plus one of the following:

up off on by over into through together away with up to

1 Somebody *managed to enter* the studio and stole all the sound equipment.
2 It is unusual for him to *rise* before noon when he's on holiday.
3 Please do not *leave* the ride until it has come to a complete stop.
4 I hope we'll *reach* the next unit before the end of the week.
5 After a few problems at first, she's *progressing* well at her new school.
6 Let's *all meet* after the film for a couple of drinks.
7 The cameras filmed them breaking the windows, but they *were not punished for* it.
8 He had a moment of panic, but soon *recovered from* it when the interview started.
9 We're sure that you will *be successful in* your exam.
10 I *manage to survive* on very little money when I am on holiday.

VOCABULARY: films

These words are all associated with films. Complete sentences 1–13 using each once only.

reviews script suspense ~~certificate~~ audience performance casting scene shot
release plot pictures screen edit

Example: *It was given a PG ..certificate.. , which stands for 'parental guidance'.*

1 Americans usually talk about going to 'the movies' rather than 'the cinema' or 'the
   .... '.
2 Her outstanding acting .... will surely win her one of this year's Oscars.
3 Best of all is the .... where, just for a second, he sees Callahan waiting on the bridge.
4 She's not really a film critic but she often does the MTV film .... on Fridays.
5 The chase through San Francisco is a thrilling .... It seems to go on forever.
6 One of the jobs of a film studio is to .... a film by putting together different parts of
   it.
7 The .... is a written version of what people say, sometimes called the 'screenplay'.
8 The connected events in a film – the story – is often called the ....
9 Spectacular films like that are so much better on a big .... than shrunk onto TV.
10 We didn't know whether she would escape till the last moment: the .... was
   incredible.
11 Her latest film is due for .... in May and should reach local cinemas by the summer.
12 At the end of the film's premiere, many people in the .... stood and applauded.
13 Choosing the right actors to play the right parts is known as .... , which needs skill.

READING: multiple choice and gapped text

① Think of your ten favourite films.

1 Now put them in order – your own top ten movies.

2 Compare your list with your partner's. Tell each other why you liked some of these films.
You could talk, for example, about the casting, the acting performances, the script, the plot,
the photography, the music and particular scenes or shots.

② In Reading Part 2 (and possibly Part 4) you may be asked about the source and author of
a text. Read the text opposite (without filling in any of the gaps), answer these questions and
in each case note down the reasons for your choice.

1 The text is probably taken from
   A a sensationalist newspaper.
   B a film script.
   C a 'serious' newspaper.
   D an advertisement for a film.
   Reason: ....

2 Which would be the best title for it?
   A 'Old films are better than new ones'
   B 'My favourite science-fiction film'
   C 'New films are better than old ones'
   D 'Science-fiction is never convincing'
   Reason: ....

3 Which, according to the text, is
   old-fashioned?
   A *Alien*
   B *Blade Runner*
   C *Star Wars*
   D *Jurassic Park*
   Reason: ....

4 The text is probably by
   A the director of *Alien*.
   B another film director.
   C a film critic.
   D a schoolboy.
   Reason: ....

③ Now follow these Reading Part 3 instructions:

You are going to read an article about a film. Seven
sentences have been removed from the article.
Choose from the sentences **A–H** the one which fits
each gap (**1–6**). There is one extra sentence which
you do not need to use.

HELP

To show you the kinds of expression you need to find, there is a clue in red for each gap. Match these clues to seven of sentences A–H to help you find the correct answers.

Example: *0H: the photo-book→before video recorders*

Chris Jones remembers being fascinated at the age of 13 by a film that he still admires,

ALIEN

You have to understand the way I first saw *Alien*. When it was released I was 12 or 13 and it had an 'X' certificate, as it was then. My brother saw it and came home and told me the story, which I thought was terrific, and then I got **the photo-book** and fell in love with **the pictures.** | 0 | H |

It was the first film I saw in Dolby stereo. I knew a lot of time and care had been taken to give it that strange sound that you find even more in *Blade Runner*, the film Ridley Scott made after *Alien*. It was just lovely to hear the sound of next-millennium machinery in space.

Every science-fiction film that has come after it seems to have **that dirty, wet, steamy look,** that kind of blue light and green darkness. It has totally changed this type of movie, when you consider that only two or three years previously *Star Wars* was it as far as sci-fi was concerned. | 1 | | Without doubt, it has to be the most influential film of my life.

There's one scene in particular where I thought: I wish I had shot that. They're hunting down the alien after it's got away – they believe it's only the size of a small dog at that point. They send Harry Dean Stanton off on his own to look for the ship's cat, and we all know that in the meantime the alien has got a lot bigger ...

The bit that for me was really dramatic is where Harry Dean Stanton is leaning down to pick up the cat, and **the alien's tail just drops down** into view. | 2 | | And it's so understated: you know just from the tail that this creature has immense power and is going to get him.

There was no attempt to shock, no violence. The audience knows something bad is going to happen and everyone is expecting the alien to jump into the shot in some way, but it does the opposite: **it moves slowly and smoothly in.** | 3 | |

It was the first time I'd ever seen on film a creature that was a real killer. It's purely a special effect, nothing that couldn't have been done before with just a little technical knowledge: there's no *Jurassic Park*-style computer graphics. But up until then, whenever I saw a movie monster, it would be a guy in a rubber suit; it would always have that falseness about it. Or the film-maker would rely on editing but **you would never really see the creature** | 4 | | Even though we couldn't quite make out what it was, which added to the terror. That in itself was very interesting.

One of the other things that's really effective is **the teeth** of the alien. | 5 | | When it opened its mouth there was another mouth inside it, which was a **stroke of genius by H.R. Giger – his** design is genuinely shocking and inventive. | 6 | | That may be true, but I also think that the director realized that no matter how good your special effects are, if you leave them too long on screen, people will spot that they're not real. Fortunately, that didn't happen in *Alien*.

A However, in this scene the alien moved like a cat that was hunting, and we *could* see it.
B It's a shame that when they show *Alien* on television you miss it because it's on the edge of the wide screen.
C I think seventy per cent of *Alien*'s success is owed to him, even though he complained to Twentieth Century Fox that all the best shots of the alien were eventually left out of the film.
D And the look has stuck; it's even got into *Star Trek: The Next Generation*.

E It seemed to have so many.
F It was just the first of many battles with the creature.
G It's like ballet.
H This was in the days before video-recorders, so I was a serious fan of *Alien* for probably three or four years before I even saw it.

④ The verbs in italics in 1–8 are all used in the text. Match them with expressions a–h.

1 The police will *hunt down* the killers, wherever they may be.
2 The legend says he was the only prisoner to *get away*.
3 The director liked to *send* people *off* to find what he wanted.
4 We saw her *pick up* the phone and talk to someone.
5 You can always *rely on* Disney to make successful cartoons.
6 In the darkness, we could just *make out* the figure of a man.
7 To *add to* their worries, there was also a thunderstorm.
8 It would be a pity to *leave out* the best part of the story.

a not include
b have confidence in
c see with difficulty
d tell someone to go and do something
e look for until they find
f increase
g escape
h take hold of and lift

⑤ Do you like this kind of film? Why? Why not?

GRAMMAR: participle adjectives

1 Many verbs can form adjectives both from their present and past participles.

Adjectives ending in *-ed* describe how people feel:

Some people felt <u>terrified</u> during the film. I was quite <u>frightened</u> too.

Adjectives ending in *-ing* describe the cause of those feelings:

It is the most <u>terrifying</u> ride in Europe. It is also one of the most <u>frightening</u> ever built.

Write down the two participle adjectives from each of the verbs below.

Example: *alarm – alarmed, alarming.*

> ~~alarm~~ amaze astonish bore disappoint excite fascinate interest reassure
> shock surprise thrill tire

2 Choose a word from 1 above to form a word that fits into each space, as in the example (0).

> By far the most (0) ..*interesting*.. ride is the Pirate's Cave. Though maybe not quite as
> (1) .... as the Vertical Plunge or as (2) .... as the Water Jump, there are nonetheless
> plenty of (3) .... special effects as you are taken on this (4) .... journey. Visitors to
> this immense theme park, (5) .... and perhaps even a little (6) .... after a long day
> on the rides, may be (7) .... to discover just how (8) .... this underground world
> really is. Take a boat round the mysterious channels. You won't be (9) .... when you see
> the pirate ships, and some of the island scenes are truly (10) ....

3 Write a paragraph about an exciting place you have been to. Say how you felt **a** before
you went, **b** while you were there, **c** afterwards. You could choose from the words in activity
1 and from these: *relax, confuse, horrify, embarrass, exhaust, refresh, threaten, tempt.*

WRITING: an informal letter

1 In Writing Part 2 you might have the option to write a letter to an English-speaking
friend. In this kind of letter we may use:

- a friendly and personal tone
- contracted verb forms like *I'm* and *hasn't*
- phrasal verbs
- informal expressions such as *a bit* (for 'a little')
- fewer polite expressions like *I would be most grateful if you would ...*
  (we would probably say *Could you ...* or *Will you ...* instead)
- fewer passive verb forms

Can you think of anything else to add to this list?

2 Study these instructions. Then read the sample letter. Find and correct six mistakes.

> You have recently done an exciting sports or leisure activity for the first time. Write to an English-speaking penfriend, describing what you did and how you felt. Write your **letter** in 120–180 words in an appropriate style. Do not write any addresses.

....

I must tell you about a really amazed experience I had yesterday. It was our
day off so we went to an old airfield near Oxford and flew in a microlight!

I was with Jane, who is very friendly instructor. First we went across grass
very quickly, shaking a lot. Then we were in the air with only the noise of the
engine and I thought 'I hope this thing doesn't stop' because when I looked
down I saw it was a long way.

After that we flew over some trees and suddenly we started to drop. Jane
said it was because the air was colder there and it always happened like that,
but I was terrifying and at that moment I wished I had stayed on ground.

At last we came down. Our landing was hard but the first thing I said when
I got out was 'When can I do this again?'. It was the wonderful fun.

Please write soon to tell me your news.

....

3 Read the letter again. Which words or sentences:

a   say why the sender is writing?
b   tell you the order in which things happened?
c   ask for a reply?

4 Put an English name and other details in the spaces in the letter in activity 2 opposite. For the beginning and ending, choose from these:

> Dear Sir,   Dear Mr / Ms / Mrs / Miss (surname),   Dear (first name),   Yours faithfully,
> Yours sincerely,   Yours,   Best wishes,   Regards,   Love,

When would the others be appropriate?

5 Look at expressions a–h and match them with purposes 1–8.

a   That reminds me,   1   to finish the letter
b   I'm really sorry I   2   to ask for information
c   I'd better close now   3   to comment on good news
d   Please let me know   4   to change the subject
e   why don't you   5   to ask for a reply
f   I'm glad to hear that   6   to apologize
g   I look forward to hearing from you   7   to thank them for writing
h   Many thanks for your letter   8   to suggest or invite

6 Read through this extract from an informal letter. Then fill in each of the gaps with one of expressions a–h above.

1 .... , which arrived this morning just when I was thinking of you! 2 ....
haven't written sooner, but there have been so many things to catch up on since I got back.

3 .... you're keeping well, and I hope that by the time this quick note gets there you will have
sorted out that problem you talked about. 4 .... if there's any way I can help.

Life here goes on very much as always, though my exams are getting alarmingly close! 5 .... , how
are your First Certificate studies going? What do you find easy and what's not so easy? Doing an advanced course here in
the UK next summer sounds like a great idea. If you have any time off, 6 .... come and stay with me
for a few days?

Anyway, 7 .... as I've got a mountain of work to do and it's getting a bit late, so I'll say 'bye' for
the moment and 8 .... soon.

7 Write a reply to the sender of the letter in activity 6 in 120–180 words. Follow this plan:

- Use an appropriate beginning from activity 4.
- Thank your friend for writing, apologize for taking a long time to reply and say why.
- Ask how he / she is and say how you are.
- Thank him / her for the offer of help and say if you need it or not.
- Talk about your First Certificate studies. Be honest in your answers!
- Thank him / her for the invitation and say if you can accept or not.
- Explain why you have to stop writing now and say when you hope to see him / her again.
- Close with an appropriate ending from activity 4.

STUDY CHECK

1 Work in pairs. You have recently seen a film or television programme that scared you, or else you think it would scare other people. Describe it to your partner and say how you felt when you were watching it, and how other people might feel.

2 Write to your teacher asking at least three questions about what you have studied in this Unit. These questions could, for example, be about vocabulary, grammar – or letter writing! Before you begin, check with your teacher what kind of beginning (*Dear ...*) and ending is appropriate. Write your letter using a separate paragraph for each question.

3 Looking ahead

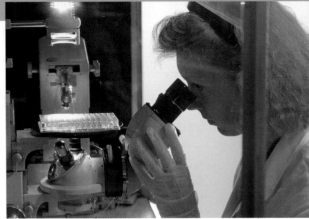

SPEAKING

1 Look at the pictures. Compare the places, the objects and the people.

2 Think about scientists in films and TV programmes that you have seen. Tell your partner about one that you particularly remember.

READING: multiple matching

1 Look at the title of the text opposite and the three lines below it. Think about the topic and try to form an impression of what you are going read. Then answer these questions:

1 Where do you think this text is taken from?
2 How do you think real scientists feel about the way they are portrayed by the media?

2 Follow these instructions as in Reading Part 4:

You are going to read a magazine article about scientists in the cinema and on television. For Questions **1–13**, choose from the films and programmes **A–G** in the box. The letters may be chosen more than once. When more than one answer is required, these may be given in any order. There is an example at the beginning (**0**).

> A Frankenstein
> B Dr Cyclops
> C It Conquered the World
> D Them!
> E Back to the Future
> F Apollo 13
> G The Dean

FIRST CERTIFICATE FACTS

Paper 1 Reading texts can be from advertisements, correspondence, fiction, informational material (brochures, guides, manuals, etc.), messages, newspaper and magazine articles or reports.

In which film or TV programme:

does a scientist invent a new kind of vehicle?	0	E
do scientists use difficult language?	1	
does the scientist make people smaller?	2	
do scientists make insects bigger?	3	
is the scientist eaten by a plant?	4	
do scientists often find out new things?	5	
does a scientist create something from pieces?	6	
is the scientist well-intentioned but dangerous?	7	8
is science portrayed realistically?	9	
is the figure of the mad scientist established?	10	
did people find the scientist funny?	11	
does a very clever scientist do great harm?	12	13

▶ **HELP**

To show you the kind of information you need to find, a clue to each of the answers is underlined in the text. For example, the clue to Question 0 is *time machine car*, so the answer is E (*Back to the Future*).

CAN SCIENTISTS SHAKE OFF THEIR MAD MEDIA IMAGE?

American physicists are campaigning to change the way they are portrayed on screen, but **Geoff Brown** believes the absent-minded professor is here to stay.

Professor Robert Park of the University of Maryland has launched an attack on the popular image of scientists as shown by movies and television. Scientists, he says, are generally portrayed as forgetful, short-sighted and even
5 crazy.

The professor is right, of course. Though there have been a few serious attempts to treat scientists with respect, the model for most movie scientists remains the screen version of Mary Shelley's **Frankenstein.** Brilliant man, of
10 course, but so obsessed with making a monstrous Boris Karloff from spare body parts that he seems quite unconcerned by what his awful creation is likely to get up to.

Frankenstein had even madder movie contemporaries. There was Dr Moreau, whose speciality was genetics: his
15 laboratory was an island of creatures that were half animal and half human. Or how about Dr Alexander Thorkel as a role model? In **Dr Cyclops** he might be the world's greatest biologist, but his fondness for shrinking people to the size of chickens does not suggest a candidate for the Nobel Prize.

20 Postwar movie scientists were mainly of a different sort. They worked on top-secret government jobs and usually wanted to do good – though their mental stability was still questionable. Science in the 1950s was widely accepted as the new frontier, but this was also a time of fear and
25 paranoia, and some scientists wanted to push the boundaries too far, threatening both national security and themselves. Men like Lee Van Cleef in **It Conquered the World**: he regarded the 'it' as a close personal friend, and ended up as a meal for this large vegetable from Venus.

30 Film after film repeated the conflict: the men with guns keen to shoot down the alien; the scientists eager to learn from a superior civilization. Science-fiction films of the Fifties also reflected the suspicion that scientists were taking too many chances with nature. They may genuinely have
35 believed that atomic power was a safe, clean energy source but people were starting to have their doubts. So many nuclear tests took place in New Mexico that the result, in **Them!**, was an army of giant ants.

Once horror and science-fiction films had established
40 the stereotype of the mad or absent-minded scientist, comedies began to spread it around. Youngsters in the 1960s delighted in a Disney comedy about the distracted inventor of 'flubber', or flying rubber. Twenty-five years later, a different generation had a great laugh watching Christopher
45 Lloyd's crazed inventor of the time machine car in **Back to the Future**.

A serious scientist, all scriptwriters know, is a boring one. True, the moment of breakthrough might produce high drama; but how do you handle the years of research, the
50 false trails, the midnight hours hunched over keyboards and test-tubes?

The language of science is another problem. Either scriptwriters fool the general audience with meaningless nonsense, or an expert is hired to teach everyone the
55 authentic technical terms. Film-makers want words to match the reality of their sets and special effects, with the result that half the talk in **Apollo 13** is right over people's heads. At least Professor Park recognizes the problem. 'We cannot seem to free ourselves of the jargon which we use,' he
60 says. 'Our families have got used to it, but not the public.'

So when will there be a television series about scientists? The American Association for the Advancement of Science has been helping to explore the possibilities. The result is **The Dean**, a projected show about a research centre where
65 scientists regularly make exciting discoveries. British producer Adrian Malone has been given the job of selling the idea to US television. The only rules, he says, are not to tell lies about science and never to bore people. Some contradiction, surely?

3 Look again at the way these expressions are used in the text and complete definitions 1–7.

> unconcerned (line 12)   genetics (line 14)
> absent-minded (line 40)   breakthrough (line 48)
> research (line 49)   authentic (line 55)
> jargon (line 59)

1 An .... document is known to be genuine and original.

2 .... is the study of how characteristics pass from one generation to the next.

3 A .... is an important advance or discovery, especially in science.

4 .... people are forgetful and do not pay attention to what they are doing.

5 .... means not to be worried about something, when maybe you should be.

6 .... is technical or specialized language.

7 .... is the study or investigation of a subject in order to discover new facts.

4 Do you prefer serious or light-hearted science-fiction films? Why?

USE OF ENGLISH: word formation

1 *Brilliant man, of course, but <u>mis</u>guided.*
The world's greatest biolog<u>ist</u>.

The prefix *mis-* gives a negative meaning, while the suffix *-ist* is often used to indicate a person.

Look at these words from the Reading text. What meaning does the suffix or prefix give?

meaning<u>less</u>   <u>post</u>war   <u>non</u>sense   invent<u>or</u>

2 Put the underlined affixes into sets 1–5. The number to go into each set is given in brackets.

<u>un</u>fair   <u>out</u>grow   <u>dis</u>prove   <u>pre</u>war   <u>anti</u>nuclear <u>il</u>logical   <u>under</u>estimate   <u>in</u>complete <u>micro</u>processor   employ<u>ee</u>   <u>over</u>load   <u>ir</u>regular <u>hyper</u>active   teenag<u>er</u>   <u>trans</u>plant   <u>post</u>mortem <u>super</u>sonic   <u>inter</u>net   <u>mega</u>star   engin<u>eer</u> <u>im</u>patient

1 Negative (7): ....
2 Size or amount (7): ....
3 People (3): ....
4 Time (2): ....
5 Positions (2): ....

3 Follow the exam instructions for Use of English Part 5:

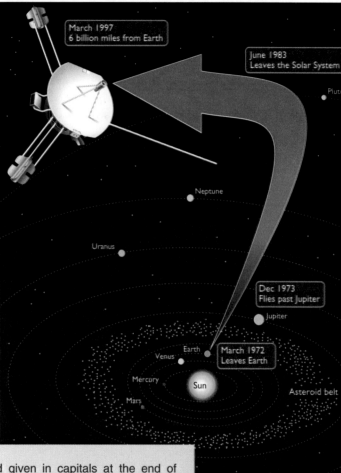

March 1997
6 billion miles from Earth

June 1983
Leaves the Solar System

Pluto

Neptune

Uranus

Dec 1973
Flies past Jupiter

Jupiter

Earth   March 1972
Leaves Earth

Venus

Mercury

Sun

Mars

Asteroid belt

Saturn

For Questions **1–10**, read the text below. Use the word given in capitals at the end of each line to form a word that fits in the space in the same line. There is an example at the beginning **(0)**.

> **HELP**
>
> The letter p (prefix) or s (suffix) in each space indicates which you need to use, although in some cases you will also need to make grammatical changes.

Journey into space

Pioneer 10 left Earth in 1972 and began to cross the **(0)** ..p..*unexplored*...   **EXPLORE**
asteroid belt four months later. Some people said it would be **(1)** ...p... to   **POSSIBLE**
find a way through the dust and **(2)** ...s... millions of rocks that lie beyond   **COUNT**
the inner planets; but despite its very **(3)** ...s... technology, Pioneer made a   **BASE**
(4) ...s... crossing and went on to carry out its first mission: to study Jupiter.   **SUCCESS**

It continued past the **(5)** ...s... planets until 1983, crossing the paths of Saturn,   **OUT**
Uranus and Pluto before finally entering the vast **(6)** ...p... area outside our solar   **KNOW**
system. There it will maintain course on its **(7)** ...s... journey, passing close to   **END**
Proxima Centauri in 70,000 years' time. Eventually, **(8)** ...s... believe, in the safe   **SCIENCE**
vacuum of deep space, it may even **(9)** ...p... the Earth, which in five billion years   **LIVE**
will **(10)** ...p... as the Sun grows ever bigger and swallows up our tiny planet.   **APPEAR**

GRAMMAR: the future

There it will maintain course.
We shall see.
I'll look forward to that.

Apart from using the *will / shall / 'll* future, we can also talk about the future by using:

- the present simple
- *going to* future
- the future perfect
- the present continuous
- the future continuous
- the future perfect continuous

1 **1** Look at 1–9 and in each case say which tense is being used about future time.

1 At this time next Monday I'll be working in the laboratory.
2 No, I'm sorry. I'm staying at home on Friday night.
3 I had no idea you were waiting for me. I'll be there in five minutes.
4 By 2010 scientists will have found a cure for flu.
5 Data collected so far indicate there is going to be an earthquake.
6 I suggest you read the report when you have the time.
7 We take our physics exam on Tuesday, which is the 13th.
8 I reckon there'll be no more wars anywhere in the world.
9 By June we'll have been working on this project for a year.

2 Now match 1–9 with descriptions a–i.

Example:
At this time next Monday I'll be working in the laboratory. Answer: c

a Something that will happen before a definite time in the future.
b Definite arrangements for the future.
c Something that will be happening at a future point in time.
d Future calendar or timetable events.
e Future meanings after time or conditional conjunctions.
f A decision you take when you are actually speaking.
g A prediction based on present evidence.
h Something that will continue for some time before a future point in time.
i A prediction made without any present evidence.

2 Nine of these ten sentences contain an error. Find and correct each one.

1 I'm going to go out with you on Saturday if you'd like me to.
2 By the time you learn how to use this model, new ones are appearing in the shops.
3 After you'll have finished work we can go for a quick drink.
4 As you can see on your ticket, your flight is going to leave at 17.35 on Sunday.
5 I buy some new batteries for the remote control tomorrow.

6 By the summer I'll have been at university for two years.
7 Mobile phones will work better when communications satellites will be in lower orbit.
8 At this time on Thursday I'm using the newest scientific equipment in the country.
9 I don't think he's trying that experiment again after what happened last time.
10 I'm sorry but I can't see you tonight because I'll wash my hair.

3 Complete the second sentence so that it has a similar meaning to the first sentence, using the word given. **Do not change the word given.** You must use between two and five words, including the word given. In this activity, all the answers refer to future time.

1 It's Linda's sixteenth birthday on Wednesday.
will
Linda .... Wednesday.
2 Have you got any plans for tonight?
planning
Are .... tonight?
3 I'll talk to the others and then I'll have a word with you.
after
I'll have a word with .... to the others.
4 I expect them to be arriving at half past six.
think
I .... at half past six.
5 We won't see an eclipse like that again until 2020.
before
It will .... an eclipse like that again.
6 He'll probably be studying that problem for a week before he solves it.
been
By the time he solves that problem he'll probably .... for a week.

4 What would you say in these situations? Use verb forms from activity 1 to talk about the future.
1 You ring up National Rail Enquiries. Ask for details about train times to a city you want to visit.
2 You've been given a day off work, university or school. Describe what you'll be doing while everyone else is hard at work.
3 Somebody phones to invite you out next Saturday night, but you don't really want to go out with him or her. Make an excuse.
4 You've discovered the perfect way to spend a summer's day. Describe your plans for the next sunny day.
5 You've decided that you want to get married and buy a house. Tell your parents about your plans.
6 You are drawing up a 'life map' and are thinking about your future. Say what you think you will have achieved in one, three, five and ten years' time.

VOCABULARY: affixes

All these words are used in the Listening text below.

1 Say what part of speech each of these is and form at least one other word from it.

Example: *educational: adjective – educate, educated, education, educationally.*

1 electrical industrial visual technological
2 employment environment equipment
3 apparently automatically particularly
4 powerful

2 Work out the meanings of these using the underlined prefixes and suffixes as clues:

<u>bio</u>chemistry fault<u>y</u> <u>micro</u>computer port<u>able</u> <u>under</u>powered

LISTENING

In Listening Part 1 there are eight questions and eight texts, in each of which one or two people talk for about thirty seconds. As it is the beginning of the test, this part is specially designed to help you relax!

- You can both hear and read the questions, so you have more time to choose your answers.
- The eight texts are separate, so if you have trouble with one question it doesn't affect the next one.
- An introductory sentence before every question describes the situation.

1 Read the exam instructions below and think about suggestions 1–7. Which two should you do *before* you listen and which five *while* you listen?

1 Make sure you always know which number text you are listening to.
2 As you listen, imagine the place, the people and what they are doing.
3 Don't worry about understanding every word you hear.
4 Study the introduction and question to form an idea of what you will hear.
5 Don't assume that if you hear a word from an answer, then that is the right answer.
6 Be prepared to change your mind about which is the correct answer while you listen.
7 Look at options A, B and C and think of words that you associate with them.

2 Now do the activity. This is like the exam task except that:

- the topics all have a connection with science.
- you are listening for factual information only, not attitudes, feelings, etc.
- there are six questions instead of eight.

You will hear people talking in six different situations. For Questions **1–6**, choose the best answer, **A, B** or **C**.

1 You hear a radio programme about modern technology.
What is the woman describing?
A a microcomputer
B a portable TV   [1]
C a mobile phone

2 You hear someone from an employment agency describing a job.
What is it?
A doctor
B writer   [2]
C lecturer

3 You hear an extract from a radio science programme.
What is it about?
A going to sleep
B dreaming   [3]
C waking up

4 You hear a man talking about working on railway journeys.
What does he use to do his work?
A a pen
B a typewriter   [4]
C a computer

5 You hear a conversation in an audio-visual shop.
What does the man want to clean?
A a video recorder
B a television   [5]
C a CD player

6 You hear a man giving a warning about technology.
Who or what, according to him, could it harm?
A the environment
B people with computers   [6]
C poor people

In Speaking Part 2 the examiner will give you two photos. First you talk about the pictures and ideas connected with them; then the other candidate will be asked to comment briefly. The other candidate talks about two different pictures and then it is your turn to make brief comments.

1 Work in pairs, following steps 1 – 6.

1 Decide who is going to speak first.
2 Look at pictures a and b.
3 Compare and contrast the two pictures.
4 Say which is more likely to be the workplace of the future.
5 Say how you would feel working in each of those situations.
6 Your partner says which he or she would prefer to work in.

Here is some advice on the kind of things to say:

- At step 3, first say what the similarities are, for example:
  In both pictures there's somebody doing some work on a PC and …
  Then say what the differences are, for instance:
  She's working at home but / while / whereas they're …
  The house will be much quieter than / not so noisy as …
  Working there would be a bit lonely compared with …
- At step 4, say what *is going to* happen (if you are sure), what you think *will probably* happen and what people *will be doing* in the future.
- At step 5, talk about any advantages or disadvantages you can think of, such as the surroundings and the other people, the travelling and the working hours.

2 Change roles with your partner and look at pictures c and d. Compare and contrast them, saying which is more likely to be the city of the future, and why. Then say what you think life in both would be like. Finally, your partner compares them to present-day cities, including those in his or her own country.

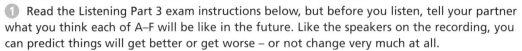

LISTENING

1 Read the Listening Part 3 exam instructions below, but before you listen, tell your partner what you think each of A–F will be like in the future. Like the speakers on the recording, you can predict things will get better or get worse – or not change very much at all.

Example:

(A) *'In my opinion there'll be longer and longer traffic jams to get into the car parks of bigger and bigger out-of-town shopping centres.'*

2 Now do the exam task.

> You will hear five people talking about the future.
> For Questions **1–5**, choose which of **A–F** each speaker is talking about.
> Use the letters only once. There is an extra letter which you do not need to use.
>
> | | | |
> |---|---|---|
> | A shopping | Speaker 1 | 1 |
> | B houses | Speaker 2 | 2 |
> | C communications | Speaker 3 | 3 |
> | D clothes | Speaker 4 | 4 |
> | E working | Speaker 5 | 5 |
> | F cooking | | |

3 Work in pairs. Did any of the speakers make similar predictions to yours? Which of their predictions do you agree with, which do you disagree with, and why?

VOCABULARY: suffixes

1 Write down the name for a person who specializes in each of 1–10.

Select from these suffixes: *-ian, -er, -eer, -ic, -ist.*

1	biology	6	mathematics
2	chemistry	7	astronomy
3	physics	8	engineering
4	geology	9	mechanics
5	ecology	10	computer science

2 Choose three of the subjects 1–10. What developments do you think there will be in the future? Make notes of the ideas you have.

WRITING: a discursive composition

1. In Writing Part 2 there is sometimes a discursive composition, in which you give information and your own opinions in a fairly formal way. Look at Question 5 on page 163 for an example of how to answer this type of exam task. The text below gives some advice on answering this type of question, but three sentences have been removed. Choose from the sentences A–C the one which fits each gap 1–3.

In Part 2, you may be asked to express your ideas in a discursive composition. This could be in the form of giving your opinion or writing a balanced discussion, for example giving the advantages and disadvantages of something. This may mean you have to write arguments you do not necessarily agree with. 1 ....

One way of organizing this kind of composition is to give reasons for and against each point in turn. 2 .... For most people a better way is to divide your composition into four parts, beginning with an introduction to the topic. Start with a short, interesting sentence. 3 .... In the second paragraph, give the points on one side, with reasons and possibly examples. Then, in the third, do the same with the points on the other side. Finally, write a brief concluding paragraph, summarizing your opinions.

A   This will attract the reader's attention and should make him or her want to read on.
B   If you find this difficult, note down your opinion about a point and then imagine what someone who disagrees with you might say, and note that down too.
C   The problem with this kind of organization is that you may end up writing very long and complicated sentences, which is not a good idea unless your level is very high.

2. Read these exam instructions. Then follow some of the suggestions in 1 and those below.

The class has been talking about developments in science and technology, and whether these will affect us positively or negatively. For homework, your teacher has asked you to write this composition:

Will the advances in science and technology being made at present improve our everyday lives?

Write your **composition** in **120–180** words.

- Note down as many ideas as you can.
- Put your best points together in two groups so that you can organize them into paragraphs.
- You could begin the introductory paragraph with a sentence such as *We are going to see the fastest changes in history.*
- The second paragraph should start with something like *On the positive side, ... , Progress will bring many benefits, such as ... ,* or *Some might say that ...* (or start with the points against).
- Link your points with expressions like *to begin with, firstly, first of all, secondly, finally, besides (that), in addition to (this), as well as, another point / reason / advantage is that ...*
- The next paragraph might begin with *On the other hand, ... ,* or *There are, however, some risks such as ... ,* or *Others might argue that ... .*
- Write in a semi-formal or formal style.
- You could begin the final paragraph with *On balance, ... To sum up, ...* or *In conclusion, ...*
- Check for correct length, appropriate style, clear organization, good paragraphing, relevance of points, linking expressions, grammar (especially verb tenses and agreement), correct use of affixes, spelling and punctuation.

COMMON ERRORS

I think the future will be enough different.
What is wrong with this sentence? Why?
See the Grammar Reference on page 172.

GRAMMAR: *make and do*

① *I enjoyed <u>making model planes</u> when I was a child.*
<u>Make the tea</u>, will you, while I <u>do the washing-up</u>.

There is no rule which says when to use *make* and when to use *do*, but if you look at the expressions above you should be able to complete these guidelines with one word or the other:

1   We often use .... to talk about work.
2   We often use .... to talk about constructing or creating something.

② Would scientists *do* or *make* the following? Write the correct word in front of each one.

BANX

.... a discovery
.... harm
.... a promise
.... certain
.... damage
.... an attempt
.... a plan
.... an excuse
.... better
.... their best
.... an experiment
.... a choice
.... a suggestion
.... progress
.... notes
.... an effort

③ Write a short sentence about yourself using a form of *do* or *make* with each of the expressions below.

Example: *I did my homework last night.*

~~homework~~   some mistakes   well at school   me angry   a noise   friends with somebody   nothing at all   some housework   everyone laugh   sure   an exercise   a phone call   the First Certificate exam

④ What do these verbs mean: *overdo, redo, outdo, undo*? Think of a sentence with each.

USE OF ENGLISH: open cloze

① In Use of English Part 2 you have to think of a word to fit each of the gaps in a text.

Match these questions about the open cloze with their answers.

Example *1–C.*

1	How many questions are there?	A	Yes, correct spelling is essential.
2	How long is the text?	B	Work out what part of speech it needs.
3	What should you do before you fill in any gaps?	C	There are always 15, plus an example.
4	Is the open cloze a test of vocabulary?	D	Read the whole text for gist.
5	Is it better to leave a blank than make a mistake?	E	Normally between 200 and 250 words.
6	What should you do if you're stuck on a gap?	F	The answer is never a contracted form.
7	Does spelling matter?	G	No, it is more a test of grammar.
8	Can a gap have two possible answers?	H	No, you should always put something.
9	Does *I'm* count as one word or two?	I	No, the answers are never hyphenated.
10	Can you join two words to make one, like *part-time*?	J	Yes, but you should only fill in one word.

② Look at the title and the first sentence of the text in activity 3 opposite. Then answer these questions: What is its general topic? What kinds of things might be 'a little late'?

3 Follow these exam instructions. For each answer, write in what part of speech it is, too.

For Questions **1–15**, read the text below and think of the word which best fits each space. Use only **one** word in each space. There is an example at the beginning (**0**).

◀ HELP

Here are the answers in jumbled order:

~~make~~ too away to it more will into the until according on least out which however

Tomorrow's world will be a little late

In a report for the US magazine *Wired*, a large number of academics, writers and experts were invited to (**0**) ..*make*.. (verb) their predictions for the future. In some respects they are quite cautious, ruling (**1**) .... ideas that they believe belong (**2**) .... science fiction more than to practical reality, at (**3**) .... in the next half-century or so. In other areas, (**4**) .... , they foresee changes before too long.

On the roads, self-driving taxis and cars, in (**5**) .... satellites guide the vehicle from office to home, or to holiday destinations, could arrive by 2019, (**6**) .... to the experts. By 2034, (**7**) .... than 50 per cent of people in industrialized countries, (**8**) .... is forecast, will drive clean electric vehicles.

In space, a landing of humans (**9**) .... Mars could be the highlight of 2020, say writers and scientists at NASA. Aliens may be contacted in 2025, but even 2050 is (**10**) .... soon for androids like C-3PO in *Star Wars*.

On the James Bond-style personal jetpack, Noah Rifkin, director of technology deployment at (**11**) .... United States's Department of Transportation, said that companies are unlikely to put enough money (**12**) .... research and development (**13**) .... they know how many people might want to buy it.

At work, all the technologies needed to do (**14**) .... with the need for paper have already been invented, yet Don Norman at Apple Computer forecasts that people (**15**) .... always want paper, although society may be 80 per cent paperless in 2009.

STUDY CHECK

1 Work in pairs, Student A and Student B.

Student A:

Ask your partner about things he or she:
- is definitely doing, or not doing, tonight.
- is going to make or would like to make.
- will have done by the end of the year.

Student B:

Ask your partner about things he or she:
- is or isn't going to do in the holidays.
- will do when he / she passes FCE.
- will still be doing in five years' time.

2 Think back over the topics you have looked at in this Unit.

1   With your partner, decide which are the six biggest problems the world will face in the future, for example: *hunger*. Make a list, without discussing them yet.

2   Choose the problem that interests you most; your partner can choose the same one or another of the six. Now discuss the problem(s) as Student A and Student B.

Student A:
You are an optimist. You believe that the problem, although it is very serious, will be solved in the end.

Student B:
You are a pessimist. You believe that the problem is so serious that it will never be solved.

3 Choose one of the topics from activity 2.1 and write it in the gap below.

Will the problem of .... get better or worse in the future?

Write your composition, using both optimistic and pessimistic arguments.

4 Taking it easy

SPEAKING AND VOCABULARY

1 Discuss the following questions.

1 Approximately how many hours' free time do you have each week?
2 About how many hours per week do you spend:
   a watching television? b reading? c doing hobbies? d doing nothing?
3 For each of a, b, c and d, how many days per year is that? (For a rough estimate, multiply the number of hours by 2.)

2 In groups, make a list of hobbies and interests that are popular in your country in each of these categories:

1 arts and crafts (e.g. *drawing*)	4 books	7 card games
2 music	5 keeping pets	8 electronic games
3 outdoor activities	6 board games	

Which is the most popular in each category in your group?

3 Look at the different kinds of reading material in the box.

1 In pairs, think of an example of as many of these kinds of reading as you can.

Example: *newspapers – the Independent*

~~newspapers~~ science fiction comics romantic novels language studies thrillers poetry biographies history humour encyclopaedias plays magazines travel

2 Which three kinds do you like most and which three do you like least? Note down your answers. Are there any other kinds of reading that you like?
3 In pairs, compare answers. Try to persuade your partner that he or she would enjoy reading the same kinds.

READING: multiple matching

1 Find out where and when your partner normally reads. Then ask about the last book he or she read: its title, the author, your partner's reason for reading it and whether he or she would recommend it to you.

2 Look at the Reading Part 1 instructions opposite. As you read the article, write your own heading or summary sentence for each paragraph.
Then, when you have finished, try to match your headings or sentences with those your teacher will provide.

You are going to read an article about reading. Choose the most suitable heading from the list **A–I** for each part (**1–7**) of the article. There is one extra heading which you do not need to use. There is an example at the beginning (**0**).

TURNING OVER
a new leaf

Do you only ever read on holiday? David Mills tells infrequent page-turners how to keep going all year.

| **0** | **I** | The importance of reading |

Nobody would argue that reading books is a bad thing. We may feel that Arnold Bennett was going slightly over the top when he said that the man who does not read books 'is merely not born. He can't see; he can't hear; he
5 can't feel, in any full sense. He can only eat his dinner', but more often than not, we would agree, reading a book is normally better than watching television. So, most of us would really quite like to read.

| **1** | |

A recent government survey of what we *actually* do
10 revealed that the average woman spends the equivalent of only five days a year reading (the average man four days), compared to 56 days watching television. Cutting down on time spent in front of the box should give you some spare hours, and if you are male you're even luckier.
15 The same survey also discovered that the average man spends 17 days a year 'doing nothing at all'.

| **2** | |

If you examine your day for reading opportunities, you will discover lots of free time. Standing at the bus stop, travelling by train, over lunch, in the dentist's waiting
20 room, queuing up for things: the occasional 10–20 minutes here and there quickly add up. But the time will fly if you always have your book with you.

| **3** | |

Books are there to be read. You can generally buy classics for £1, so don't be overprotective with them. Read in the
25 bath (in the shower may not be such a good idea). I once found myself with 75 pages of a Dickens novel left to read, and a plane to catch. Rather than spend a two-week holiday lumbered with a 900-page book I pulled the last 100 pages out and took them with me.

| **4** | |

30 There are 106,000 books published in Britain every year. The best of seven centuries worth of literature is published in paperback. There *has* to be something you would like. Identifying it may take time. Be guided by what you have enjoyed in the past and branch out
35 from there: Roald Dahl? Then try R.L. Stine. Stephen King? Then try Clive Barker. Agatha Christie? Then try Patricia Highsmith or Ruth Rendell.

| **5** | |

If you are not particularly enjoying a book, you are guaranteed to find 143 other things to do instead of
40 reading. Consequently, it will take months to finish and put you off picking up another. When you find this happening, stop reading this book and start another immediately.

| **6** | |

Most people usually go to bed because they are tired.
45 Why then do so many of them also think it would be the ideal time to read? Reading is tiring – it is mental exercise. Either you will fall asleep after two pages, or your brain will become so stimulated you will have insomnia.

| **7** | |

If you want to be part of 3,000 years of civilization (and
50 speculation about what happened before that) then get reading. Otherwise, stick to eating dinner.

3 Some people believe that electronic media will eventually replace books. Do you agree?

GRAMMAR: frequency adverbs

reading a book is <u>normally</u> better
if you <u>always</u> have your book
you can <u>generally</u> buy classics
people <u>usually</u> go to bed

1 Look at these examples from the Reading text and decide which is usually the best place in the sentence for the frequency adverb with:

1 main verbs
2 the verb *to be*
3 modal verbs like *can* and *must*

2 Put the adverbs below on the scale in order of frequency.

The number of spaces tells you how many there should be at each level.

generally   hardly ever   sometimes   rarely
nearly always   occasionally   usually   often
regularly   seldom   almost never   normally
frequently

- **ALWAYS**
- ....
- ....
- ....
- ....
- ....
- ....
- **NEVER**

3 Put the adverb in brackets into the best position in each sentence. What game do 1–9 describe?

1 The player with the white pieces starts. (always)
2 The first piece to move is a pawn, but it could be a knight. (usually)
3 White begins by attacking the black king. (sometimes)
4 Black may reply by bringing its queen into play. (sometimes)
5 The player that loses their queen wins the game. (seldom)
6 After the queen, the strongest piece is the rook, or 'castle'. (generally)
7 The bishop can move sideways, only diagonally. (never)
8 When pieces threaten the king, the attacker must say 'check'. (always)
9 A king in a weak position escapes 'checkmate' against a good player. (rarely)

GRAMMAR: *must, have to* and *should*

a *you <u>have to</u> start with an ace*
b *you <u>must</u> pay attention*
c *you <u>should</u> keep your best cards*
d *you <u>mustn't</u> start with a king*
e *you <u>don't have to</u> play if you don't want to*
f *you <u>mustn't</u> look at my cards*
g *you <u>shouldn't</u> tell others what you have*

1 Match each of the underlined modal verbs (a–g) with one of these descriptions:

1 A strong obligation imposed by the speaker.
2 A strong obligation imposed by somebody other than the speaker, by rules or by laws.
3 A strong suggestion or some advice.
4 A prohibition imposed by the speaker.
5 A strong suggestion or some advice not to do something.
6 A lack of necessity or obligation.
7 A prohibition imposed by somebody other than the speaker, by rules or by laws.

2 The following can be used instead of some of the above:

you needn't   you've got to   you don't need to
you ought to   you haven't got to

Fill in the alternatives in these sentences (there are three possibilities in **3**).

1 I think you should / .... practise a little more to improve your game.
2 Rule 5 says that you have to / .... take a card when it is your turn.
3 Surely you don't have to / .... / .... / .... start all over again?

3 Write a reply to each of the comments below, using the modal verb in brackets.

1 'How can I learn to play the piano?' (should)
2 'Can you play chess on your own?' (have got to)
3 'I've got no money left.' (shouldn't)
4 'I'm bored – I just don't know what to do in the holidays.' (ought to)
5 'I'd like to grow plants but we haven't got a garden.' (don't have to)
6 'I'm going to hit him if he does that again!' (mustn't)
7 'Is it true that in Britain you need a television licence?' (have to)
8 'Is it only worth collecting stamps if they are very old?' (don't need to)
9 'I'm sorry but I've lost the pen you gave me.' (must)
10 'I'll never be a brilliant artist so I've given up painting.' (haven't got to)

4 Tell your partner about each of the following:

Example:
- *Three things you have to do early every morning.*
I have to make my bed.

- Three things you shouldn't, or mustn't, do in class.
- Three things you should, or must, do after the lesson.
- Three things you don't have to do at the weekend!

COMMON ERRORS

Must you to go so soon?
What is wrong with this sentence? Why?
See Grammar Reference on page 172.

Part 3 of Use of English often tests modals like *should* and *mustn't*, as well as frequency adverbs. Follow these exam instructions:

Complete the second sentence so that it has a similar meaning to the first sentence, using the word given. **Do not change the word given.** You must use between two and five words, including the word given.

◀ HELP

The questions are grouped according to the form you need to use:

- Questions 1–5 use a frequency adverb.
- Questions 6–9 require a modal verb of obligation.
- Question 10 needs both!

1 It's not common for women to be racing drivers.

   seldom

   Racing drivers ………………………………… women.

2 Well-known artists are regular visitors to his workshop.

   visit

   Well-known artists………………………………… workshop.

3 It's unusual for Jane to lose at backgammon.

   hardly

   Jane ………………………………… at backgammon.

4 It's rare for my sister to take a holiday.

   goes

   My sister ………………………………… holiday.

5 There are few weekends when Steve isn't fishing.

   always

   Steve ………………………………… at weekends.

6 It'd be a good idea for you to come with us next Sunday.

   ought

   Next Sunday ………………………………… with us.

7 Photography is not allowed in the museum.

   photographs

   You ………………………………… in the museum.

8 Is leaving everything here really necessary?

   left

   Does everything ………………………………… here?

9 There's no need for you to do any work if you don't feel like it.

   have

   If you don't feel like it ………………………………… do any work.

10 It isn't always necessary to be a member of the club.

   need

   You ………………………………… be a member of the club.

FIRST CERTIFICATE FACTS

If you change, or don't use, the word given in a key word transformation, you won't get any marks for that question.

LISTENING

1 In Listening Part 2 you have to take notes or fill in blanks while you listen to the recording. Study points 1–12 and at the end of each line write one of the following:

before you listen   while you listen   after you listen

1   Write quickly so that you are ready to hear the next point. ....

2   Read all the questions to form an idea of what you will hear.
....

3   Check your answers are grammatically correct: number, tense and so on.
....

4   For each question, think about the kind of information you should listen for.
....

5   Underline key words in the questions that you might hear on the recording.
....

6   When you hear key words from the questions, pay special attention.
....

7   Write what you hear (you won't be asked to rephrase). ....

8   Listen for the information you need in the same order as the questions.
....

9   You normally need to write no more than three words. ....

10 Check your spelling (though if the meaning is clear, you'll get the mark).
....

11 Even if you can think of two good answers, only put one. ....

12 Don't miss information by spending too long thinking about one question.
....

2 The recording you are going to hear is about music. Put this vocabulary taken from the text into three groups:

1   kinds of music, e.g. *jazz*
2   words used in music, e.g. *melody*
3   equipment, e.g. *stereo*

pop   notes   opera   ~~melody~~   cassette-recorder   techno   tune   reggae   symphony rhythm   classical   chant   chord   rock   CD player   ~~jazz~~   ~~stereo~~

3 Follow the exam instructions.

▶ HELP

The key expression for each question is underlined. When you hear it (or a form of it), you should get ready to listen for the answer to that question. You should have stopped thinking about that question by the time you hear the next key expression.

You will hear part of a radio discussion about music. For Questions **1–10**, complete the sentences.

The music <u>industry</u> creates a lot of employment for [**1**] people.

Music has <u>now</u> split into a wide range of [**2**]

<u>Supermarkets</u> know how to make people [**3**]

There <u>isn't anything new</u> about using music to make work seem less [**4**]

The aim of <u>football</u> songs is to encourage players to [**5**]

<u>Before games</u>, players try to sing [**6**] than their opponents.

<u>Concentration</u> can be helped by the sound of certain [**7**]

People <u>choose</u> some forms of music in order to change their [**8**]

When you <u>put on</u> a record, the beginning can immediately affect [**9**]

<u>Memories</u> may be brought back by songs you heard over [**10**] ago.

---

4 Can you think of a song that makes you particularly sad or happy?
Tell your partner about it.

1 In pairs, make a list of all the places and situations where you hear – or listen to – music. Then for each one, decide which kind of music you associate with it, and what effect it has on you.

2 Look at these exam hints for Speaking Part 3 and write *should*, *shouldn't* or *don't have to* in the gap. In each case say why, and where the missing word is *shouldn't*, suggest an alternative.

1	Before you start the task you .... study the material carefully.
2	If you're not sure what you have to do, you .... ask the examiner.
3	Once you have started, you .... expect the examiner to take part in the conversation.
4	You .... talk about something else just because you don't like the task.
5	You and your partner .... take turns, speaking for about the same length of time.
6	You .... reply to your partner, not the examiner.
7	You .... ask your partner questions which only need a one-word answer.
8	You .... talk quietly in the hope that the examiners won't hear your mistakes.
9	If your partner is looking for a word or phrase, you .... help him or her.
10	You .... agree with everything your partner says.
11	If you can't think of a word, you .... ask the examiner for a translation.
12	You ....encourage your partner to keep talking as you would in real life.
13	If your partner is talking too much you .... politely interrupt.
14	You .... leave periods of silence in the conversation.
15	You .... speak for the whole time without making any mistakes!

3 Read these exam instructions. Think about the points in activity 2 and follow the advice below.

Imagine that you are in a music store. You and your partner have been given some money to buy what you like there. Decide what you would both enjoy listening to while doing any **four** of the things mentioned. Give reasons for your choices.

- travelling by car
- dancing
- exercising
- relaxing at home
- studying
- sunbathing
- spending an evening with friends

Discuss what you like and what you should buy. Take turns and help your partner as suggested in activity 2 above. While you are talking:

- say why some kinds of music would be more suitable for one activity than others.
- decide whether you prefer singles, albums by one artist or compilations.
- mention the titles of particular artists, albums and songs (but don't just give a list).
- say why you particularly like these.
- talk about any that have a special meaning to you personally.

4

1 Discuss these questions in pairs:
1 Who are the people in the pictures opposite?
2 When did they first become famous?
3 What do they look like these days?
4 Has their music changed and who listens to it?

2 Ask each other Questions 2–4 about older pop singers and rock bands from your country.

3 Study the instructions below for Reading Part 3. The sentences directly before and after a gap often provide useful information. They may use the same or similar structures as in the missing sentence, or contain the same vocabulary. There might also be clues such as result links (*therefore, consequently*), sequence links (*secondly, the other*) or contrast links (*however, on the other hand*).

For example, look at gap 0 and the sentence before it. In the correct answer (I), *But here they are, still …* contrasts with … *their time had passed*. Now do the exam task.

HELP

There is a clue in brackets after each question.

You are going to read a newspaper article about older pop singers. Eight sentences have been removed from the article. Choose from the sentences **A–I** the one which fits each gap (**1–7**). There is one extra sentence which you do not need to use. There is an example at the beginning (**0**).

A Now they are old and balding, fat and slow-moving.
B Neither of them have had anything new to say for a quarter of a century.
C But this is how Dinosaur Rock deceives the world; everything seems bigger than it really is.
D So they use their experience, their influence, their managers and lawyers, their multinational record companies and their contacts to push themselves on us again and again.
E Will this new generation of Rock Dinosaurs realize how ridiculous they seem?
F And so, once more, we must endure their uninteresting views in endless boring interviews and hear the same old stories told all over again.
G Another prepares for a world tour, which of course is front page news.
H It makes no difference that their very existence goes against the ideals of their own youth.
I But here they are, still behaving as they always did, refusing to accept that they are history.

SMASH HITS OF THE SIXTIES
MEGABORES TODAY

How can we escape from these singing prehistoric creatures? We made the mistake of thinking their time had passed, that they were extinct. **0** **I** (contrast) We are fascinated by the terrible noise they make. They are the dominant species of pop culture: the Dinosaurs of Rock.

They are Mick Jagger, Paul McCartney, Bob Dylan, Phil Collins, Pete Townshend, Robert Plant, Bruce Springsteen, Rod Stewart, etc. Most of the time, they grow old alone in luxury, distant from the complexities of post-modern pop, untroubled by doubts about their values and opinions. It doesn't matter that for anyone under 25 their music is almost certainly irrelevant. **1** (same / similar structure)

Every once in a while, these beasts of beat feel the need to get some exercise. And so they do an *MTV Unplugged* performance, a world tour, a new sponsorship deal with a car manufacturer or a soft drinks company, TV chat shows. **2** (same / similar structure)

Astonishingly, the Dinosaurs of Rock were once young and healthy. They were slim and danced around the stage waving microphone stands, all hair and flared trousers; their music echoing out across the world: *Brown Sugar, Whole Lotta Love, Stay With Me.* They once had youthful attitudes and their songs made the young feel the world was changing, perhaps for the better. **3** (contrast)

But they have enormous appetites and monstrous egos that must be satisfied. **4** (result) They have nothing to say, but with all the power they have, they force the world to listen.

And so they turn up everywhere. One of them reaches 50 (or 60) and this achievement is seen as a major cultural event, to be greeted by article after article full of praise and celebration. **5** (sequence) Occasionally a single is released to show their commitment to good causes and everyone on TV applauds. Meanwhile, however, the real singing is done by cash registers.

Though nothing really happens in the virtual Jurassic Park where the Dinosaurs exist, it always looks busy, even important. **6** (contrast) Because size is important. Worse, a new breed of Dinosaurs is appearing. Slimmer and fitter, but just as greedy: Sting, Bono, Mick Hucknall, Jon Bon Jovi and, by far the worst of all, Axl Rose.

So it looks as if we will continue to have these monsters of rock with us for ages to come. No matter how far other species leave them behind, these ancient brutes are likely to keep making their unwelcome appearances. Will they ever die out? **7** (same / similar structure) Will they even care any more?

4 Look at these headings for the eight paragraphs of the text. Five are matched with the correct paragraph and three are not. Which three? Where should they go?

Paragraph 0: What they are
Paragraph 1: The future
Paragraph 2: What they do
Paragraph 3: Then and now

Paragraph 4: Making people listen
Paragraph 5: Who they are
Paragraph 6: Appearances and reality
Paragraph 7: The media love them

5 How far do you agree with the writer's opinions? Are there any arguments *for* these older rock stars? What do you think today's singers will do when they get older?

WRITING: an article

1 Look back at the Reading text and think about the following:

- Beginning: What is the form of the first sentence? Why is this used?
- Organization: Look at the headings in activity 4 above. What is the purpose of paragraphs?
- Style: What does the use of *And* and *But* to begin sentences tell you about the article?
- Ending: What is the form of the last three sentences? Why is this used?

2 Read these Writing Part 2 instructions and decide who you are going to write about.

An international music magazine for young people has invited readers to write contributions called *The best in the world*. Write a short **article** in **120–180** words for this magazine, based on what you know about your favourite pop group or singer.

3 Make notes based on the following. First look at Question 2 on page 160 for an example of how to answer this type of exam task.

- kind of music?
- where from?
- most famous songs?
- videos?
- their background?
- why are they the best?
- future career?

4 Make a plan. Think about these questions (and your answers in activity 1 above):

What kind of publication are you writing for? Who is going to read your article? Can you think of a title to attract the reader's (and the editor's) attention? How can you involve the reader from the beginning? What are you going to put in each paragraph? What style are you going to write in? How are you going to finish and make the reader think?

5 Write your article. Before you give it in, let your partner check it for mistakes.

GRAMMAR: comparative and superlative forms

1 Look at the phrases in the box below. Then complete rules 1–6. In each case add two of these expressions as examples. The first one has already been done for you.

> the finer points   the easiest one
> ~~the greatest band on earth~~   slimmer and fitter
> their latest hits   choose the most suitable heading
> more complex and challenging   the worst of all
> CDs are better than records   you're even luckier
> the biggest stars   ~~older pop singers~~

1   Regular one-syllable adjectives like *young* and *loud* form their comparative (*younger, louder.*) by adding *-er.* and their superlative (*the youngest, the loudest.*) by adding *-est*.
Examples: *older pop singers; the greatest band on earth.*

2   One-syllable adjectives that end in -e, like *pale* and *large*, form the comparative (.........., ...) by adding .... and the superlative (........., ...) by adding ....
Examples: ....

3   One-syllable adjectives ending in a vowel plus consonant, like *hot* and *flat*, may add -er / -est and double the .... to form the comparative (........., ...) and the superlative (........, ...).
Examples: ....

4   Adjectives that end in a consonant followed by a *y*, like *dry* and *busy*, may change the *y* to an .... and then add -er / -est to form the comparative (........, ...) and the superlative (........, ...).
Examples: ....

5   Regular adjectives (and adverbs) with two or more syllables, like *fantastic* and *beautiful*, add the word .... to form the comparative (............, ...) and the word ...... to form the superlative (............, ...).
Examples: ....

6   Irregular adverbs, like *little* and *much* use different words to form the comparative (........., ...) and the superlative (........., ...). The adverbs *well* and *badly* use the same forms as the adjectives *good* and *bad* to form the comparative (........, ...) and the superlative (........, ...).
Examples: ....

To say one thing or person has a quality to the same extent as another, we use the structure *as* + adjective / adverb + *as*. In the negative, the form is *not so / as* + adjective / adverb + *as*.

Examples:
She's as famous as her sister now.
They aren't so inventive as they were.

We can add words like *almost, nearly* or *quite* + *as* if one thing or person has a little less or more of a quality. *They're almost as big as The Beatles.*

We can also use expressions like *twice* or *five times* + *as much as / as many as* when we mean 'a lot more'.

He's earning twice times as much as he was before.

Another way to say that something has less of a quality than another is to use *less* + adjective / adverb + *than*:

The play was less enjoyable than the last one I went to.

The superlative is also possible:
It was the least enjoyable play I've ever been to.

To say that something has more of a quality, we use *more* and *most* in the same way.

We can qualify comparisons by adding *a little, a bit, slightly, rather, much, a lot, far* or *even*.

Examples:
If you're male, you're even luckier.
They're a bit less selfish than other bands.

COMMON ERRORS

You're a better musician than I.
What is wrong with this sentence? Why?
See the Grammar Reference on page 173.

2 Complete the second sentence so that it has a similar meaning to the first sentence, using the word given. **Do not change the word given.** You must use between two and five words, including the word given. All the answers require the use of a comparative or superlative form.

1   This is the best concert I've ever been to.
better
I've never been .... this.

2   The video we saw last week was better than this one.
good
This video .... the one we saw last week.

3   Cassettes are a lot cheaper than CDs.
far
CDs are .... cassettes.

4   Their last album was slightly more creative than this one.
quite
This album .... as that one.

3 Quickly make a list of ten rock bands or singers you know of. Then choose from your list to complete sentences 1–6, using forms of these words:

> cool   noisy   good   ugly   attractive   awful
> brilliant   creative   boring   bad   popular

1   ... is / are far more ... than ...
2   ... is / are much less ... than ...
3   ... is / are as ... as ... but not ... as ...
4   ... is / are ... than ... but less ... than ...
5   ... is / are ten times as ... as ...
6   ... is / are the ... on earth!

1 Look at the Use of English Part 1 instructions and the title of the text in activity 2 below. What do you know about MTV?

2 Before you do the exercise, look at the example (0) and the words underlined next to it. The correct answer is B, which completes the collocation *better known as*.

> **HELP**
>
> Eight collocations are underlined.

For Questions **1–15**, read the text below and decide which answer **A**, **B**, **C** or **D** best fits each space. There is an example at the beginning (**0**).

Example:

0 **A** good **(B)** better **C** more **D** most

MTV HITS THE SCREEN

A major chapter in the history of rock began on 1 August 1981, when Music Television, (**0**) ... known as MTV, first started broadcasting. Aimed at (**1**) ... aged between twelve and thirty-five, its appearance coincided with the (**2**)... of what was then a relatively new art form: the rock video.

Filmed sequences of rock music were, of course, (**3**) ... new. Since the 1960s major bands (**4**) ... as the Beatles and the Rolling Stones had made short movies to promote their (**5**) ... singles. What really helped MTV take (**6**) ... , though, was its clever idea of asking the record companies to let it use videos free of (**7**) ... , arguing that videos were promotional materials and that by showing them the new (**8**) ... would be giving both companies and musicians free advertising. (**9**)... the end all the main record labels agreed.

The only problem was that in those early years, before videos became as essential (**10**) ... they are now for any band or singer with serious (**11**) ... of success, the playlist tended to be dominated by big bands that were already (**12**) ... with sophisticated videos. But this did not seem to (**13**) ... much harm. In (**14**) ..., within two years of its launch MTV was being shown by nearly two thousand cable television (**15**) ... in the United States and would soon also be broadcasting from the UK in the form of MTV Europe.

1 **A** observers	**B** spectators	**C** viewers	**D** listeners
2 **A** climb	**B** lift	**C** increase	**D** rise
3 **A** nothing	**B** anything	**C** none	**D** no
4 **A** like	**B** kind	**C** so	**D** such
5 **A** freshest	**B** youngest	**C** latest	**D** soonest
6 **A** away	**B** up	**C** on	**D** off
7 **A** money	**B** charge	**C** payment	**D** fee
8 **A** channel	**B** producer	**C** speaker	**D** publication
9 **A** In	**B** At	**C** By	**D** To
10 **A** as	**B** so	**C** than	**D** that
11 **A** wishes	**B** hopes	**C** wants	**D** needs
12 **A** exploring	**B** examining	**C** experiencing	**D** experimenting
13 **A** make	**B** do	**C** give	**D** lead
14 **A** fact	**B** event	**C** point	**D** actual
15 **A** societies	**B** unions	**C** companies	**D** programmers

STUDY CHECK

1 **1** Look at the list of hobbies in Speaking 2 on page 38 and think about how often, if ever, you do them. Choose three and write a sentence for each, using frequency adverbs from page 40.

2 Tell your partner how to do one of the hobbies. Use expressions like *should, shouldn't, must, mustn't, have to* and *don't have to*.

2 Read these instructions and the points opposite:

> An English-language magazine for visitors to your country has asked you to write about this topic: *National or international music – which do you prefer?* Write a short **article** in **120–180** words for this magazine comparing the music (and musicians) in your country with music from abroad.

- You can choose to write about pop or any other kind of music.
- Compare the quality of the music from home and abroad.
- Consider how relevant the lyrics of the songs are and how easy it is to understand them.
- Use as many of the comparative and superlative forms from these pages as you can.

5 Home and away

VOCABULARY: living conditions

1. Note down as many words as you can in each of these categories in five minutes:

1 Places to live, e.g. *house*
2 Parts of the house, e.g. *hall*
3 Items in the house, e.g. *cooker*

Put the following expressions into category 1, 2 or 3.

landing   airing cupboard   mattress   freezer   detached house   terraced house   villa
cottage   semi-detached house   apartment   ceiling

2. What is the difference in meaning between these words?

homework   housework   household

3. What do these words have in common?

owner   rent   landlord / landlady   deposit   tenant   bills

The people in the picture pay money every month to live there. Which word do we use for them, what do they pay and who receives the money?

READING: multiple choice

1. When you do a Part 2 multiple-choice exercise, start by reading the whole text through quickly. Don't worry about any difficult words, as your aim at this stage is just to form a general impression – and you might waste time on parts of the text that are not even tested.

Read the text opposite in no more than two minutes, and think of an alternative title for it.

⊽ HELP

The parts of the text which are not tested are in brackets.

2. Follow these exam instructions:

You are going to read a newspaper article about sharing flats. For Questions **1–8**, choose the answer (**A, B, C** or **D**) which you think fits best according to the text.

3. Which would you prefer: sharing a flat or living in a place of your own? Why?

• ROOM TO LET •

You might think that sharing a flat with other young people is a good idea. But there is one major problem: how to choose the right people? I've had at least 25 flatmates, so I should know. It seemed the sensible thing to do when I moved to London. Missing my old friends and worried about feeling lonely, I moved in with 13 other people so that I would always have someone to talk to. I did – my bed was on the landing.

[Eventually I was promoted to a room with a door – the airing cupboard. It was just big enough for a single mattress and I had to leave the door open so I could breathe.] Then there was the bathroom rota. Accommodating 14 people before breakfast needed a military-style operation. We started taking turns at 5.30 and the last person to join the household got the first turn. The only advantage was that he or she also got all the hot water.

Sadly, the owners threw us out and I had to find a new home fast, which is why I ended up with Gina the circus performer. When I first met her, she was hanging upside-down above the stairs. She seemed nice though, and the elegant old building was ideal. While we were sipping herbal tea and she was questioning me about my diet and political beliefs, I noticed she had lots of great books I wanted to read. However, things went sour the day I moved in when Gina refused to let me get rid of an army of ants that had moved into my room. She said that killing was against her religion. So was cleaning the bath. As if that wasn't enough, she left a note on the fridge, where we usually left messages about phone calls and milk, stating her intention to murder me with poison. I moved out in the middle of the night.

[After that I ended up with some student doctors and was happy enough until we all caught a mysterious illness.]

It was at this point I broke my self-made rule. After sharing a student house with two friends in Oxford – a period that ended in a fist-fight over fruit juice – I had decided I would never again put a friendship to the phone-bill test. But of course I couldn't afford a one-bedroom flat in central London so I agreed to get a place with a very neat and tidy friend from school.

The house we found had three bedrooms, a washing-machine and a nice little garden. We moved in at once. I got the smallest bedroom because I wasn't going out with anyone, but my new flatmates promised we would swap round within six months. That was 18 months ago. I'm still in the small room and my belongings are still in boxes on the landing, though one of the original girls has been replaced by a banker.

What we had advertised for was a female non-smoking professional, but anyone who looked even slightly interesting had always found a better place by the time we decided that they wouldn't steal our boyfriends. The banker got in by promising that being male hadn't made him incapable of washing dishes and cleaning. He lied, of course.

[There are, though, advantages to the flat-sharing life. If you can forgive them for drinking the last of your milk, you get captive shoulders to cry on.] If you can forget about the ring around the bath, your CD collection instantly gets three times bigger – though you won't want to listen to most of it. You get three minds to remember to put out the rubbish. Three ways to split the rent. And, unlike a partner, your flatmates won't care if you wear those old clothes all weekend.

In fact, on a good day I wouldn't be without mine. Unless I could afford a place of my own.

---

1   Why did the writer share a flat when she moved to London?
   A   She went there with friends.
   B   She wanted to have company.
   C   There were twenty-five people to talk to.
   D   She had a big room all to herself.

2   The newest person in the flat had to
   A   get up very early.
   B   wash with cold water.
   C   go without breakfast.
   D   wash after breakfast.

3   She moved in with Gina because
   A   she wanted to live in a modern flat.
   B   she was in a hurry to find somewhere to live.
   C   Gina worked in a circus.
   D   Gina did not ask her any personal questions.

4   She moved out because Gina
   A   refused to pay the telephone bill.
   B   was cruel to animals.
   C   was always cleaning the bath.
   D   threatened to kill her.

5   Why did she move in with her friend?
   A   Living alone would be too expensive.
   B   The one-bedroom flat was big enough for two.
   C   They had already shared a flat in Oxford.
   D   She had decided only to live with friends.

6   Why is she still in the smallest bedroom?
   A   Her flatmates broke their promise.
   B   It is part of the agreement she made.
   C   She now has a boyfriend.
   D   It is big enough for her and her things.

7   Why did they let the banker move in?
   A   He was the kind of person they had advertised for.
   B   He was the writer's boyfriend.
   C   He had a lot of money.
   D   He said he would do housework.

8   One reason she likes flat sharing is that
   A   it is better than owning a flat.
   B   someone else will clean the bath.
   C   it is much cheaper than living alone.
   D   flatmates encourage each other to dress well.

GRAMMAR: past tenses

1 1 Match these examples of the past simple from the Reading text with uses a, b and c.

a Actions or events in the past.
b Habits in the past.
c Situations in the past.

I moved to London.
My bed was on the landing.
We usually left messages on the fridge.

COMMON ERRORS

These days, I use to stay with friends. What is wrong with this sentence? Why? See the Grammar Reference on page 173.

2 To refer to a past habit, we could also use the modal *used to*:
We used to leave messages.

What is the negative of this phrase? What is the interrogative?

3 Match these examples of the past continuous from the Reading text with uses a, b and c below:

a Temporary actions or situations in the past.
b Simultaneous continuous actions or situations in the past
c Past actions in progress when something else happened.

When I first met her, she was hanging upside-down above the stairs.
While we were sipping herbal tea and she was questioning me ...
I got the smallest bedroom because I wasn't going out with anyone.

For past habits we do not use the past continuous, but we sometimes use *would* – especially in written language. For example, we could write *We would leave messages.* Note that we do not use *would* to describe past states.

2 Read through this text without filling in any gaps.

1 Give two reasons why it is called *Deep Sleep*.

2 Fill in gaps 1–20 with a suitable past tense form of the verb in brackets.

DEEP SLEEP

I was spending the night a hundred feet below ground. I had paid my £17 to the club known as Spice (Special Programme of Initiative, Challenge and Excitement) to try a sleep-enriching night deep in the Earth.

The intense darkness (1) .... (mean) that no clue of the time would stop me getting the amount of sleep my body (2) .... (need), rather than the amount the alarm clock or the early morning sunshine (3) .... (allow).

Before I (4) .... (go) underground, experienced deep sleepers had told me that two things you need for a good night's rest, warmth and comfort, (5) .... (be) missing at that depth, and that the sheer density of that darkness (6) .... (create) anxiety, making sleep difficult for some. As it happened, warmth was not a problem. Whatever the weather outside, the temperature in the cave (7) .... (remain) at 54°F – cold and damp enough to make your breath steamy but not freezing.

Comfort, though, was a different matter. To get into the cave, I (8) .... (have to) crawl headfirst through a 2ft-wide tunnel. Inside, the ceiling height (9) .... (vary) from 3ft to 12ft, making a protective helmet essential when I (10) .... (walk) or standing up.

Even the combined effects of a plastic groundsheet, rubber mat and thick sleeping-bag (11) .... (can) not make the rocky cave floor comfortable. The drips of water from the roof were an added nuisance – wet when they (12) .... (hit) your face, loud when they landed on the groundsheet. Balanced against this, though, was the fact that, when lit with candles, the cave walls (13) .... (become) the perfect colour of rest: somewhere between warm baby pink and peach. At least to start with, that is. By 4.30am the last few flames (14) .... (go out), and that, unfortunately, was when I (15) .... (wake up).

Suddenly, the friendly peach shapes on the ceiling (16) .... (turn into) threatening black shadows; the rocks started to look terrifying and, all the time, the way out (17) .... (shrink) in my imagination to an impossibly dark, tight little tunnel.

For me, the whole experience was far too much like those childhood nights when you (18) .... (be) so afraid of the dark you didn't even have the courage to get up and turn on the light. Nevertheless, in one way the hours I (19) .... (spend) underground were a success. The next night, back home in my own bed, I (20) .... (sleep) better than I had done for years.

3 Complete the second sentence so that it has a similar meaning to the first sentence, using the word given. **Do not change the word given**. You must use between two and five words, including the word given. All the answers require the use of a past tense.

1   She doesn't live there any more, I believe.
    used
    She .... , I believe.

2   Whenever I told her that story she always laughed a lot.
    would
    I used to tell her that story and .... a lot.

3   Is that the place where you lived before?
    use
    Did you .... place?

4   I had no plans for Friday.
    planning
    I .... anything for Friday.

5   Our conversation was interrupted by a phone call.
    while
    A phone call interrupted us .... a conversation.

6   Before I moved in I had no one to talk to.
    use
    Before I moved in I .... anyone to talk to.

4 Think of a place where you lived, or somewhere that you often visited when you were younger, which was special to you in some way. Write sentences about what you used to do and how you used to feel when you were there.

5 Imagine you have moved into a house where everything is going wrong. Tell your partner what happened and what you were doing at the time.

Example:
The television screen went blank.
I was watching my favourite programme when the television screen went blank.

1   All the lights suddenly went out.   5   The phone went dead.
2   The bath water overflowed.   6   A frying pan caught fire.
3   The smoke alarm went off.   7   A mouse appeared on the stairs.
4   The microwave exploded.   8   A mirror came off the wall.

Now think of three real-life events of this kind that have occurred at home. Tell your partner about them, saying what you, or other people, were doing at the time.

PHRASAL VERBS: *look*

1 Without filling in any gaps, quickly read through sentences 1–9 below and answer this question:

Which of A, B, C or D are the speakers planning to do?

A sell a house   B buy a house   C rent a house   D rent a holiday flat

2 Fill in the gaps in sentences 1–9 by using each of these words once only:

after	into	forward	over	through	~~at~~	for	up	out

Then write one of these meanings after each sentence, as in the example:

*investigate   take care of   ~~consider~~   try to find   examine one by one
search for information   anticipate with pleasure   be careful to avoid   inspect*

1   We had already looked ....*at*... a few places but none of
    them quite suited us.   .... *consider* ....
2   We were looking .... the ads in the property section
    when we saw this one.   ....
3   It gave the owner's name so we looked .... her number
    in the phone book.   ....
4   We'd been looking .... somewhere with three bedrooms
    for quite a while.   ....
5   The surveyor looked it .... and said everything was in
    good condition.   ....
6   We've asked our lawyer to look .... any possible legal
    risks in the purchase.   ....
7   Our bank manager is looking .... the financial side,
    which will save us time.   ....
8   We've got a mortgage and we're looking .... to moving
    in as soon as possible.   ....
9   But we'll have to look .... for any extra costs which
    nobody told us about.   ....

LISTENING

1 Work in pairs, Student A and Student B.

Student A: Read the text and fill in as many of gaps 1–15 as you can, using these words:

introduction	vocabulary	therefore	might	end	hand	same	different	one	~~five~~
six	second	twice	function	connection	predict				

The first one has been done as an example.

> Part 3 of First Certificate Listening is a multiple-matching task. There are five questions and
> you also hear (0) ..*five*.. short extracts. They are all spoken by (1) .... people but, unlike
> in Part 1, there is some kind of (2) .... between these extracts. For example, the
> speakers (3) .... be talking about different aspects of the (4) .... topic, such as
> 'flatmates'. On the other (5) .... , they could be connected by the same language
> (6) .... , like asking for help, making suggestions or expressing disagreement. On the
> question paper there are (7) .... possible answers which you have to match to the
> extracts you hear, so you will not need to use (8) .... of the answers. Both the (9) ....
> to the questions and the possible answers give clues. You may find it useful to think about
> the topic and to (10) .... what the speakers will say and what (11) .... they might
> use. The recording is played (12) .... , but as in Part 2 you hear all the extracts once and
> then the recording is repeated from beginning to (13) .... , rather than playing each
> extract twice before moving on to the next one, as in Part 1. It is best, (14) .... , to leave
> your final choice of answers until you have heard everything for a (15) .... time.

Now go through the text with Student B and discuss your answers.

Student B: Read the information about multiple matching on page 166 and then discuss each
of Student A's answers to Questions 1–15 above. Help him or her to correct any mistakes.

2 Discuss these questions:

1 What can arguments between neighbours lead to?
2 What would you do if you had very noisy neighbours?
3 What can, or should, the local council or police do about them?
4 If you are looking for a quiet house, what kinds of places should you avoid?
5 Who could tell you whether a neighbourhood is quiet or not?
6 What places should you avoid if you are going to live in the country?

3 Follow the exam instructions.

You will hear five people talking about problems with noisy neighbours. For Questions **1–5**, choose from the list **A–F** what they are describing. Use the letters only once. There is an extra letter which you do not need to use.

A	using music to stop the noise		
B	how the authorities can stop it	Speaker 1	1
C	the ideal neighbours	Speaker 2	2
D	noise in the country	Speaker 3	3
E	noise in the city	Speaker 4	4
F	recent noise-related incidents	Speaker 5	5

4 What similarities / differences were there between your answers in activity 2 and what the speakers said?

5 What are your neighbours like? Are you a good neighbour?

SPEAKING

1 Look at these figures for British attitudes towards their neighbours. Do any of them surprise you? Talk about your experiences with your partner.

Know immediate neighbours well / they are personal friends:	34%
Immediate neighbours are pleasant and friendly:	90%
Immediate neighbours have strange habits or hobbies:	10%
Sometimes pop into the neighbours' house for a drink and a chat:	49%
Neighbours water your plants when you are away:	38%
Neighbours sometimes inflict loud stereo or radio music on you:	20%
Have had a terrible argument with a neighbour:	20%
Have reported a neighbour to the police:	7%

2 In Speaking Part 1, the examiner might ask you about your neighbourhood. Practise by asking your partner about the following:

1 Which part of … your partner lives in.
2 How long they have lived there.
3 What it is like living there.
4 What the houses and the people are like.
5 What young people can do there.
6 How easy it is to get to other places.
7 Whether he or she has ever lived anywhere else.
8 Where he or she would most like to live, and why.

READING: multiple choice

1 Sometimes Reading Part 2 is an extract from a book. Where this is the case, you need to form a picture in your mind of the situation as quickly as you can. Read through this text in no more than two minutes and think of a suitable title.

2 Follow the exam instructions.

You are going to read an extract from a novel. For Questions **1–6**, choose the answer (**A**, **B**, **C** or **D**) which you think fits best according to the text.

Here and there groups sat and drank in narrow passages between the market stalls. Ringling pushed his way through one of these, and Houston saw that behind lay a line of tall houses built of rough stone, several storeys high. People were leaning out of the glassless windows in the warm evening, and behind them oil lamps shone in the crude rooms. From one end to the other, this side of the street seemed to be lined with flickering stone chambers, and Houston saw that these must be the cheap doss-houses that the boy had mentioned.

A stream of people was being turned away from the first doorway, and they had to carry the baggage up and down the exhausting, noisy street for over an hour before they could find somewhere to stay. The room they were given, with two other men and a woman, was on the fifth floor, and they struggled, weighed down by their baggage, up a narrow, tunnel-like staircase which smelt horribly of hot oil from the lamps lining the walls.

The landings ran off into a confusing series of narrow corridors, brilliant and choking with the smoking oil; and in each was a series of tiny stone rooms. The young Tibetan who had led the way showed them into one, and left, and Houston looked at his three new companions. They were little, graceful people who had talked and laughed all the way up through the building, and they were still at it as they came into the room.

There were five straw mattresses on the stone floor, and a big leather bucket in the corner; this seemed to be the only furniture. A heavy cover was fastened over the window and the tiny room stank even worse than the corridor. One of the men removed the cover and hung out of the window, singing, while the other, with the woman, began preparing a meal on the floor with a small burner unpacked from the baggage.

Houston lay back on the filthy mattress and closed his eyes and mouth while Ringling unpacked their own kit. He had never in his life come across such an overpoweringly evil stench, and his head was swimming with the noise and the bright light. The noise in the street seemed if anything to be louder now that they were above it, and the people in the room were shouting to make themselves heard. Ringling was shouting as loudly as any of them, quite happy and quite unaffected by the confusion.

Houston again closed his eyes and tried to shut out the room and the yellow smoking glare, and succeeded for some minutes, till the boy shook him and he sat up and saw that the woman had prepared a large bowl of some soup-like substance and all were sitting round eating.

'Eat now,' the boy said loudly in Tibetan, grinning at him. 'Eat. Good to eat.'

Houston looked at the bowl and saw something swimming in it, and in a careless moment breathed through his nose, and he was struggling to his feet, about to be sick. He didn't know where to go, and the boy was quickly beside him, and he hung, trembling, over the bucket, and saw that it had not been empty even to begin with, and spewed, and leaned on the greasy rim some time longer, with his knees trembling and eyes watering.

He turned, smiling apologetically to the people round the bowl, and they smiled back at him, in no way disturbed and still enjoying their meal.

They went out after that, for he couldn't bear to stay in the same room with the food and bucket; but out in the street found himself suddenly hungry, and they ate.

1 Why did Ringling and Houston take that room?
   A They had already booked it.
   B They thought it was the most comfortable one.
   C It was the only one that was vacant.
   D It was in the first building they came to.

2 How many people were going to stay in the room?
   A three
   B four
   C five
   D six

3 What does 'it' in line 25 refer to?
   A looking at their new companions
   B talking and laughing
   C the way
   D the building

4 The people in the room were shouting because
   A they were trying to speak to people in the street.
   B it was difficult for them to hear each other.
   C they liked the sound of their own voices.
   D Ringling was starting to get angry.

5 Why was Houston sick?
   A He had tasted the food.
   B He had smelt the food.
   C He knew what it was made of.
   D The others were sick, too.

6 What is the main information in this extract?
   A The conditions in which some people lived.
   B Why Ringling and Houston were in a place like that.
   C How badly some friends of theirs were living.
   D Solutions to the problem of bad living conditions.

③ 1 Use the context to work out the meanings of these nouns:

passages (line 1)   chambers (line 8)   doss-houses (line 9)   burner (line 33)

2 Now do the same with these verbs:

struggled (line 16)   spewed (line 55)   couldn't bear (line 61)

3 What do the words in each of a–e have in common?

a   rough (line 4)   crude (line 6)
b   storeys (line 4)   floor (line 15)
c   stank (line 30)   stench (line 37)
d   brilliant (line 20)   glare (line 44)
e   filthy (line 34)   greasy (line 56)

④ How did you feel as you read this extract? How can people end up living in conditions like those described in the text? What should be done to prevent this happening?

GRAMMAR: contrasting ideas

① Read through 1–4 and fill in the gaps using the expressions in bold in these examples:

> He couldn't bear to stay in the same room with the food and bucket; **but** out in the street found himself suddenly hungry, and they ate.
>
> We paid to stay near the market, *despite* **in spite of** our experiences the night before.
>
> There was a basin in the corner. When she tried the taps, **however**, not a drop of water came out.
>
> There was some bed linen, **although** the pillowcases were dirty and the sheets stained.

1 The simplest way to contrast two ideas is to use the conjunction .... , for example: *Rents are going up .... benefits are coming down.*

2 You can also use the conjunction .... , followed by a subject and verb: *I managed to sleep .... the room was freezing.*

The order of the clauses can change: .... *the room was freezing, I managed to sleep.*

In both cases you could use *though* or the more emphatic *even though*.

3 Another way is to use the preposition .... , followed by a noun or gerund: *He bought a house .... his low income.*

Again, the order of the clauses can change: .... *his low income he bought a house.*

Alternatively, you can use the shorter *despite*: *We slept rough despite the cold. We slept rough despite feeling cold.*

To ensure these prepositions are followed by a noun, you can add *the fact that*: *We rented the place despite (or ....) the fact that it was so expensive.*

4 To contrast ideas in two sentences you can use .... , followed by a comma: *We wanted a reduction in the price. The seller, ... , did not agree.*

Sometimes it begins the second sentence: *We wanted a reduction in the price. .... , the seller did not agree.*

② Choose the best ending (a–f) for each of 1–6.

1 She used to live in that tiny bedsit, in spite of	a	the dangers they face there.
2 At first I liked living near to the main road, but	b	I soon found she was very selfish.
3 Even though we put a huge ad in the paper,	c	in the end the traffic got me down.
4 Young people still run away to London, despite	d	I didn't get on with them very well.
5 I moved in with Clarissa. However,	e	having two children with her.
6 We were staying with my in-laws, although	f	nobody answered it.

③ You have been travelling and staying in conditions like those in the Reading text on page 54. Your mother is worried about you. Try to convince her that things are not as bad as they seem. Write sentences using forms from 2–4 in activity 1 above.

Example: *Although there are lots of people staying here …*

COMMON ERRORS

She was late. So was I, although.

What is wrong with this sentence? Why? See the Grammar Reference on page 174.

WRITING: a report

1 In Writing Part 2 you could be asked to write a report. Below is a list of common report-writing techniques. Look at Question 3 on page 161 and put a tick (✔) against those which are used.

1   The title is factual and gives an indication of the content.   ....
2   Each section deals with a different aspect of the topic.   ....
3   The headings show clearly what each section is about.   ....
4   An introduction says what the purpose of the report is.   ....
5   The introduction gives an outline of the content.   ....
6   Facts and figures are given.   ....
7   The style is quite formal.   ....
8   Complete sentences are used, even where points are listed.   ....
9   The aim throughout is to be objective, not subjective.   ....
10 The text aims to give information, not to entertain.   ....
11 A final section summarizes what has been stated.   ....
12 The final section makes a recommendation.   ....

2 Look at these exam instructions:

> An international magazine is publishing a special edition about the living conditions of young people in your country and has invited contributions in English. Write your **report** in **120–180** words in an appropriate style.

First, ask yourself these questions and note down your answers:

• Who is going to read your report and what will they want to learn from it?
• Do young people usually have their own rooms? What might they have to share?
• What size, usually, is their room? What furniture does it normally have?
• Do they have peace and quiet in their rooms? Can they study there?
• What possessions do most young people have (own TV, stereo, PC, etc.)?
• How much pocket money do they usually get?
• How does their life differ in the city and in the country, and between regions?

3 1   Divide your report into sections.
    2   Decide on the best order for the sections.
    3   Group the points you have thought of under the headings you have chosen.
    4   Look at the techniques in activity 1 above. All of them are useful, although you are not expected to use detailed facts and figures (point 6). First Certificate is not a test of your general knowledge!

4 Write your report. Use, where appropriate:

• *although*, *despite*, *however*, etc. to contrast ideas.
• other links such as *in other words*, *while* and *therefore*.

Instead of statistics, you can use approximate expressions such as these:

at least   nearly all   hardly any   almost everyone   practically no one   up to   over
under   on the whole   roughly   at the most   something like   around

1 Read the text without filling in any of the gaps and give short answers to these questions:

1 Why, according to the writer, are people homeless?
2 Why does her attitude change?

2 Read the Use of English Part 2 instructions:

For Questions **1–15**, read the text below and think of the word which best fits each space. Use only **one** word in each space. There is an example at the beginning (**0**).

HOMELESSNESS CAN HAPPEN TO ANYONE

I can hardly pay my bills every month. I am living from pay cheque (**0**) ...*to*... pay cheque, and the amount of money I make (**1**) .... hour is insufficient for me to save anything. (**2**) .... , I am lucky enough to come from a family who worked hard to pay (**3**) .... my education and who will help me out (**4**) .... anything at all should happen to me. The irony is that without (**5**) .... a generous family and without a strong belief in myself, I too could be homeless.

Instead, I, along with most people, walk quickly past those who appear less fortunate (**6**) .... ourselves. Every day I see homeless people, (**7**) .... usually the most attention I might give them is a 'how sad' look. I sometimes get angry with myself for (**8**) .... so selfish, and I justify my fears by saying, 'They (**9**) .... get a job.' Unfortunately, the reality is: who would hire someone (**10**) .... is untidy and doesn't have a contact address or phone?

(**11**) .... I am ashamed for feeling the way I do, I know that it is not uncommon. One day I decided to experience the feelings associated with homelessness and understand those who might not have (**12**) .... to go. So, I got myself a pair of torn jeans, packed a bag, took off my make-up, and put (**13**) .... a very old sweater. Then I walked downtown and sat next to two homeless men.

It was freezing cold and during that day I learned more about people than I (**14**) .... had before. All I needed to do (**15**) .... to open my mind.

1 Make a list of the advantages and disadvantages of each of the following:

a living alone
b living with parents
c living with boyfriend / girlfriend
d sharing a flat or house with friends

Now write two pairs of sentences about each of a–d using contrast links.

Example: *Although living alone is expensive, you can always do what you want.*

2 Think back to when you were a few years younger and note down some of the things you did then but don't do now. Then tell your partner what you used to do and didn't use to do. Then ask what he or she used to do at the same age.

3 You work for an agency that helps people in different countries exchange their houses or flats for a few weeks in the holidays. Your job is to write reports on homes which might be attractive to people from abroad. Imagine that the agency has sent you to look at your own home. Write your report, as objectively as you can. You may want to think about the following:

Location and local facilities / type of building / number of floors / external appearance / number and types of rooms / garden / terrace / garage / features: quiet or noisy, light or dark, warm or cool, comfort, decoration, view from windows, security / items of furniture in each room.

6 If it tastes good

SPEAKING

Answer questions 1–5 below by putting ticks (✓) in the appropriate boxes. You can tick more than one box for each question, or no boxes at all. Then compare your answers with other students in your group.

1 Which of these restaurants have you eaten in?
McDonald's ☐ Burger King ☐ Pizza Hut ☐ Kentucky Fried Chicken ☐ Other fast food ☐
2 How often do you eat in a fast-food restaurant?
Never ☐ Rarely ☐ From time to time ☐ Quite often ☐ All the time! ☐
3 Why do you eat there (or not eat there)?
The place ☐ The food ☐ The drinks ☐ The people you meet there ☐ Other reasons ☐
4 What do you most often eat there?
Burgers ☐ Chips (French fries) ☐ Pizza ☐ Chicken ☐ Other ☐
5 When do you usually go there?
Daytime ☐ Evening ☐ Weekends ☐ Special occasions ☐ Never ☐

Do you think the food and drinks they sell are: good for your health? good value for money?

VOCABULARY: food and cooking

1 What do these expressions have in common?

fast food   a snack   convenience food   junk food   a bite to eat

Think of as many examples of these as you can.

2 What do these verbs have in common? What is the difference between them?

boil   fry   grill   roast   bake   steam

Make a list of foods you associate with each.

1 Look at the title of the text. In which of Britain, Germany, France, Spain or Italy do you think people spend most on fast food? Where do they spend least? How do you think your own country compares?

Now quickly read through the text and find the answers to the first two questions.

2 Study these Reading Part 1 instructions.

You are going to read a newspaper article about fast food. Choose the most suitable heading from the list **A–I** for each part (**1–7**) of the article. There is one extra heading which you do not need to use. There is an example at the beginning (**0**).

◀ HELP

Look at the question word in each heading (*What / Which* or *Why*). Which is more likely to go with a paragraph that contains:
a reasons?
b lots of figures and statistics?

A What the British often eat
B Why the burger never changes
C Why prices are lower in the UK
D What other Europeans spend
E Why sales are going up
F What the companies want to do
G What the Americans spend
H Which food in which country
I What the British spend

THE FAST-FOOD CAPITAL OF EUROPE

0 | **I**

Britain spends more on fast food than any of the other main western European countries, according to a market research report. Mintel, who carried out the study, estimates that Britons will spend almost £2.5 billion on hamburgers, pizza and chicken meals sold through fast-food chains this year, an average of £41 per head.

1

Hamburgers dominate the fast-food market, particularly in France, where they account for 88 per cent of fast-food sales. The proportion is only marginally smaller in Italy and Germany (86 per cent and 85 per cent respectively). In Britain and Spain sales are more evenly divided between hamburgers and pizzas, while chicken takes a minor share. In Italy sales of fast-food chicken are almost non-existent.

2

The survey's findings equate to the average Briton eating a hamburger every five days, or two pieces of fried chicken every three weeks, the researchers say. They also point out that if UK consumption continues to grow at present rates it will soon approach per capita American levels.

3

Hamburgers are relatively cheaper in Britain than any of the other countries surveyed, with McDonald's and the British firm Burger King competing aggressively for market share. Food prices and other costs also tend not to be so high as on the Continent.

4

This may help to explain why the figures for people in mainland Europe are much lower. The estimated expenditure is £29 per head in France, £20 in Germany and £11 in Spain. The Italians come bottom of the fast-food league, spending only £3 per head.

5

The big corporations, however, are set to expand dramatically everywhere, with thousands of new restaurants opening each year. One chain plans to open a new one every three hours, most of them outside the US and many of them in Europe.

6

Chris Butcher, Mintel's leisure analyst, said yesterday: 'Fast food is benefiting from the increasing trend towards snacking and convenience foods. Britain is the fast-food capital of Europe. The success of fast food in general lies in the standardized menus, where quality, quantity and price are guaranteed.'

7

Standardized the food certainly is. Company rule books spell out exactly how to grill or fry, as well as precise cooking times and temperatures. The burger, like other kinds of fast food, is a simple product and appeals because there is only one way to prepare it. No matter where you buy one, what you get will be basically the same thing.

3 Discuss these questions in groups.

Do you think the increase in fast-food restaurants has a good effect or a bad effect on: young people's social life? the environment? the culture and traditions of your country?

GRAMMAR: conditionals (1 and 2)

1 Look at these examples:

1 *If UK consumption continues to grow at present rates it will soon approach per capita American levels.*
2 *If you were in New York now, what would you have for lunch?*
3 *If I ate five hamburgers, I would feel sick.*

Match each of examples 1–3 with a, b and c.

a Something in the future that is likely or probable
b Something that is possible but not probable
c Something that is unreal or imaginary

Which forms of the verb are used in each case?

What is the name for each of these kinds of conditional sentence?

2 Five of these sentences are correct and five contain an error. Tick (✓) the sentences that are correct and find the mistake in those that are wrong.

1 I'll bring two takeaways if the shop's still open at midnight. ....
2 If I were you, I'd try to eat a little less junk food. ....
3 If we'll arrive early it will be easy to get a table for six. ....
4 I'd tell you the recipe if I knew it, but I'm afraid I don't. ....
5 If I had a million pounds I'll buy myself a restaurant. *would* ....
6 I'd probably enjoy eating that if I weren't a vegetarian. ....
7 I'll make big changes if I were in charge of the kitchens. *would* ....
8 If we didn't have to go I'd be happy to stay for a drink. ....
9 I'd eat there if they keep the place a little cleaner. *kept* ....
10 This salad would taste better if it would be fresher. *were* ....

3 Here is some advice about food safety. Look at the 'germometer' opposite and match 1–4 with A–D.

1 If you heat food above 72°C,
2 If you freeze food,
3 If you kept food at body temperature,
4 If you heated a liquid to 132°C,

A you would kill all the bacteria.
B some of the bacteria will start to die.
C the bacteria will become dormant.
D the bacteria would become very active.

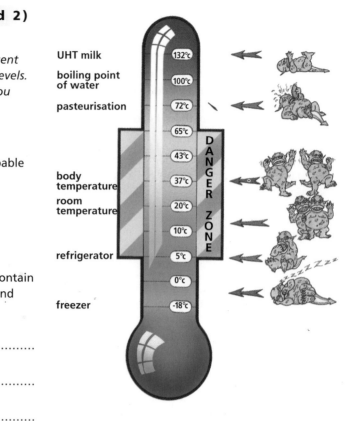

UHT milk — 132°c
boiling point of water — 100°c
pasteurisation — 72°c
— 65°c
— 43°c
body temperature — 37°c
room temperature — 20°c
— 10°c
refrigerator — 5°c
— 0°c
freezer — -18°c

DANGER ZONE

4 Your partner is going to stay with a family who do not eat very well. Ask what he or she will do if:

• the coffee is horrible.
• there is no fresh fruit.
• the food is mostly tinned or frozen.
• dinner is at 5.30 pm.
• the only drink is tap water.
• he or she is hungry in the evening.

5 Complete these sentences using the second conditional.

1 If I ate too much .... , I ....
2 If I ate too many .... , I ....
3 If I ate too little .... , I ....
4 If I didn't eat any .... , I ....
5 If I didn't drink any .... , I ....
6 If I drank too much .... , I ....
7 If I ate .... between meals, I ....
8 If I ate .... too quickly, I ....

6 Ask the others in your group what they would eat and drink a lot of if they:

1 lived alone.
2 were on holiday in another country.
3 were North American.
4 were British.

USE OF ENGLISH: word formation

1) In Use of English Part 5, there is a short text with ten gaps in it, as in activity 4 below. At the end of each line is a word in capitals (the 'base word'), from which you have to form a new word to fill in the gap. This could mean forming a noun or adjective from a verb, an adverb from a noun or adjective, a verb from an adjective or some similar change.

Study 1–8 and decide which of them you think you should do:

a first   b second   c next to last   d last

1   Check that all your answers make sense in relation to the ideas in the whole text.
2   Decide what kind of word is missing. Is it a verb, noun, adjective or adverb?
3   Note down all the other possible forms of the word that you can think of.
4   If you really aren't sure, make a guess from among the words you noted down.
5   Read the text through quickly to get the general idea.
6   Decide whether the context requires a negative form (e.g. un- or -less) of the word.
7   Make any necessary spelling changes if you add an ending (e.g. lie – lying).
8   When you have looked at the text once, write in any words that you know.

2) 1   Look at some of the words we can form from a base word, e.g. succeed. For each line write in the part of speech, as in the example.

succeed   (..verb.)   successful   unsuccessful   (.adj...)
success   (...n....)   successfully   unsuccessfully   (.adv.)

2   Now do the same with the base word care, starting with the verb.

3) Look at the underlined word in each line of the text and answer these questions:

1   How has the spelling changed from that of the word in capitals?
2   What, if any, has been the change in part of speech?

Diet, germs and the rise in asthma

A germ-free lifestyle and the Western diet share the **(0)** <u>responsibility</u> for a 300% increase in child asthma cases during the past 30 years, say **(1)** <u>environmental</u> medicine specialists.

   Infections in early **(2)** <u>childhood</u> may build immunity to asthma, whereas a diet rich in fats could increase the **(3)** <u>production</u> of the antibody that causes allergy. Low levels of fruit and vegetable **(4)** <u>intake</u> mean that people absorb too little vitamin C and E, weakening their **(5)** <u>resistance</u> to irritants that they breathe in.

   Research shows that the risk of hay fever in children drops **(6)** <u>considerably</u> with increasing family size. **(7)** <u>Apparently</u> the higher rate of infections among children in larger families acts as a **(8)** <u>defence</u> against asthma and hay fever because it encourages the **(9)** <u>development</u> of anti-infection cells and slows production of the asthma inflammation cell. **(10)** <u>Disagreements</u> about the causes of asthma, however, seem likely to continue for many years.

RESPONSE	
ENVIRONMENT	
CHILD	
PRODUCE	
TAKE	
RESIST	
CONSIDER	
APPEAR	
DEFEND	
DEVELOP	
AGREE	

4) For this text, follow the exam instructions.

● HELP

The part of speech of the missing word is given in brackets.

For Questions **1–10**, read the text below. Use the word given in capitals at the end of each line to form a word that fits in the space in the same line. There is an example at the beginning (0).

Eating to the music

Fast music can make you fat, **(0)** .researchers. (noun) have discovered. The quicker the beat, the more you eat, **(1)** .... (adverb) if the dining room is painted in bright colours. Any tune with a **(2)** .... (adjective) beat, from polka to pop, is all that is needed. Diners chew in time with the music, eating five forkfuls a minute. They **(3)** .... (adverb) feel the need for a second **(4)** .... (noun) because, by the time the plate is empty, their stomachs have not had time to register that they are full. Without any **(5)** .... (adjective) accompaniment, however, the average diner swallows four **(6)** .... (noun) of food a minute. The rate is cut to just three if a slow melody is playing in the **(7)** .... (noun). Special occasions are another **(8)** .... (adjective) time. Chatter with family or friends means people stay at the table longer and pay less **(9)** .... (noun) to the natural body **(10)** .... (noun) that the stomach is full.

RESEARCH
SPECIAL
LIFE
FREQUENCY
HELP
MUSIC
MOUTH
BACK
DANGER
ATTEND
WARN

VOCABULARY: smelling and tasting

1 Put these words into two groups, those you associate with:

a the mouth
b the nose

lécher   avaler   gorgée

| tongue smell bite flavour lick odour swallow sip aroma |
| fragrance chew taste sniff texture |

odorant   mâcher

Which of them are nouns, which are verbs and which can be both?

2 Make a list of the foods and drinks you like a lot, and those you don't like at all. Using words from activity 1 above, tell your partner why in each case. Use adjectives like *sweet, sour, bitter, spicy, salty, refreshing, light, bland, crunchy, creamy*; or expressions such as *It tastes / smells like …*

LISTENING

1 What happens to your sense of taste when you have a cold? Why? What does this tell us about the real meaning of the word 'flavour'?

2 Read these Listening Part 2 instructions:

You will hear a scientist describing experiments involving taste and smell. For Questions **1–10**, complete the notes.

First experiment

Amount of green peas: [   ] **1** (noun phrase)
Kind of green peas: [   ] **2** (adjective)
Kind of sugar: [   ] **3** (adjective)
Amount of sugar: [   ] **4** (noun phrase)
First, [   ] **5** the apple. (verb)
Next, [   ] **6** all the ingredients. (verb)
Then, [   ] **7** the cup. (verb)
Second experiment
First, [   ] **8** the rest of the fruit. (verb)
Then, with your tongue, see if it tastes [   ] **9** (adjective)
Third experiment
Cut a different fruit into a number of [   ] **10** (noun)

WRITING: an article

1 Read these instructions for Writing Part 2 and decide:

1 why you will be writing.   2 what you will be writing.   3 who will be reading it.

International Cooking Monthly
We would like to hear from our readers about tasty dishes for a future series of articles called *Meals around the world*. The best articles will be selected for publication.
Your **article**, of between **120–180** words, should say what is needed for one such dish, give instructions on how to make it and suggest how to serve it. It could be a dish from your own country or from any other part of the world.

2 You could plan your article as follows. Do not write the name of the dish at this stage.

1 Introduction: How long does it take to prepare and cook? How many does it serve?

2 Ingredients: What do you need to make it? How much of each item do you need?

Choose from these measures:

spoonful packet tin loaf lump pinch quarter third litre (l) gram (g) kilogram (kg) millilitre (ml)

3 Preparation: What do you associate with each of these verbs?

peel grate melt pour slice shred beat stir spread drain mash

4 Cooking: Choose from the verbs on page 58 plus these.

heat microwave stew simmer toast leave cool remove return

Also say what temperature the dish should be cooked at, e.g. *medium, 180°C.*

5 Serving: How will you serve it? (hot or cold, on a plate or in a bowl, etc.) What will it be served with? (salad, rice, bread, etc.) With which drinks? (fruit juice, mineral water, wine, etc.)

When you have finished your plan, show it to another student. He or she should try to guess what the dish is.

3 Write your article. Try to do the following:

• Think about your answers to the questions in activity 1 opposite.
• Use quite short sentences, but link them together with expressions like *first, next* and *then.*
• If you don't remember the exact measures you need to use, say *a little, some* or *plenty of.*
• Use the imperative form of verbs when you give instructions, e.g. *Cook the greens, add ... .*
• Use adverbs to say how to cook, e.g. *wash thoroughly, warm gently, spread thickly.*
• Use conditional forms, for example *if they are fresh, if it's too hot, if you don't ... .*

4 Check your completed article for mistakes (see below).

EXAM STUDY GUIDE

When you have completed a writing task, you should check your work for the following:

1	Vocabulary	6	Register / style
2	Forms and use of verbs	7	Spelling
3	Word order	8	Use of linking words
4	Agreement (number and person)	9	Use of articles
5	Prepositions	10	Punctuation and capitalization

Here are ten mistakes made by students. Match them with categories 1–10 and then correct them.

A	I slept when you phoned me.	F	I won't tell you who am I.
B	I stay in the bed late on Sundays.	G	I saw it last night in TV.
C	She's happy although all her problems.	H	I wish to dance with you, Alex.
D	You can buy that book in the library.	I	She's greek and he's spanish, I think.
E	This last two weeks have been wonderful.	J	Please tell me were she is.

Before the next lesson, look back at your written work since you began studying for First Certificate and make a list of your six most common mistakes. Keep this list handy when you are writing and check your work for all six when you have finished.

PHRASAL VERBS: *put*

1 Decide whether **a** or **b** is the better meaning for the phrasal verbs in italics.

1 You should *put on* the electric oven for 15 minutes to warm it up.
   a cause to start working   b place it over something
2 After you have finished using the oil and spices, *put* them *away*.
   a throw them in the bin   b return them to where they are kept
3 Could you *put* me *through* to the hotel restaurant, please?
   a let me speak by telephone   b go with me
4 We knew the bill would be a lot, but ordering another bottle *put* it *up* even more.
   a increased it   b delayed it
5 An overheated chip pan caught fire, but we *put* it *out* quickly and safely.
   a stopped it burning   b threw it through the window
6 After six months of working in a pub, he was starting to *put on* weight.
   a reduce (his)   b increase (his)
7 We're going to *put off* the celebrations until the summer.
   a postpone   b discourage
8 People nowadays refuse to *put up with* bad food when they eat out.
   a complain about   b accept
9 You have to *put on* a jacket in order to eat in this restaurant.
   a clothe yourself in   b carry over your shoulder
10 Don't let one spoilt meal *put* you *off* cooking forever!
   a stop you wanting to do   b stop other people wanting you to do

2 Reply to these questions using a form of the phrasal verb in capitals. Notice that the verb and adverb in each of 1–8 can all be separated by an object.

Example:

It's freezing in here! Can't you do something about it?   PUT ON
I'll <u>put on</u> the heating if you like. OR *I'll put the heating <u>on</u> if you like.*

1   Where's that bottle-opener you had a minute ago?   PUT AWAY
2   Do you think she's been eating a lot recently?   PUT ON
3   Aren't you going to have the party on Friday?   PUT OFF
4   Have you got an apron I can use while I'm cooking?   PUT ON
5   I'm afraid this is a no-smoking restaurant, Madam.   PUT OUT
6   Didn't that cost only £9 a bottle last Christmas?   PUT UP
7   Why don't you like the burgers they sell in the street?   PUT OFF
8   Hello, 345 5698? I'd like to speak to the manager.   PUT THROUGH
9   Are you really going to let him speak to you like that?   PUT UP WITH

3 Tell your partner what you do in a typical day, using as many phrasal verbs with *put* as you can.
Example: *As soon as I wake up I <u>put on</u> the light.*

GRAMMAR: *unless, as long as, provided*

1 Look at these sentences:

1 *I like this soup unless it's cold.*
2 *I like this soup as long as it's cold.*
3 *I like this soup provided (or providing) it's cold.*

For each of examples 1–3, decide which is the meaning, **a** or **b**:

a   If it is cold, I like this soup.   b   If it is not cold, I like this soup.

2 Complete these conditional sentences as in the example.
Example:
As long as ....<u>it is served</u>............ cold, cider is very refreshing.

1   Unless .... very little, coffee will keep you awake at night.
2   As long as .... mind, we'll stay at home for dinner.
3   Provided .... guest, meals will be charged to your hotel bill.
4   I think .... fish, as long as there are lots of chips with it.
5   Dinner .... at 8.30, provided that guests can arrive by that time.
6   Eating .... your teeth, unless you add sugar.

> **COMMON ERRORS**
>
> *No matter if I eat a lot, I'm always hungry.*
> What is wrong with this sentence? Why?
> See the Grammar Reference on page 175.

3 Work in pairs, Student A and Student B.

Student A:
You have invited your partner out
for a meal but he or she is not very keen.
Try to persuade him or her to go.

Student B:
You don't really want to go.
Try to make as many conditions as possible.
You may use a maximum of five from the list
below.
Use *unless, as long as, provided.*

Example: A *Go on – you'll have a really good time.*
B *All right, I'll go as long as it's not too noisy.*
A *Oh I'm sure it'll be very quiet.*

- it mustn't be too noisy
- it has to be near where you live
- it mustn't be too formal
- you don't want to wait for a table
- the service must be good

- it has to be a no-smoking restaurant
- they must serve the drinks ice-cold
- your favourite meal must be on the menu
- the surroundings have to be attractive
- your partner must pay the bill!

Now change: Student A becomes Student B, and vice versa. The new Student B chooses from
the five remaining conditions above before thinking of more.

USE OF ENGLISH: key word transformations

Use of English Part 3 often tests conditionals, but with basic first and second conditional
forms (*I'll do; if I had,* etc.) the questions often test something else, too. So to get both marks
you may also need to make another change, which may be grammatical or lexical (such as
changes in the part of speech and phrasal verbs). Follow these exam instructions:

Complete the second sentence so that it has a similar meaning to the first sentence, using the
word given. **Do not change the word given**. You must use between two and five words,
including the word given.

1 I won't stay if you don't apologize immediately.

long

I'll only .... apologize immediately.

2 You can eat sweets but you must always brush your teeth afterwards.

provided

You can eat sweets .... your teeth afterwards.

3 If you don't get dressed right away we'll go without you.

put

Unless .... right away we'll go without you.

4 We only eat there because the prices are so low.

charge

If they .... low prices we wouldn't eat there.

5 I won't eat any more cake because I'm full.

full

If I .... eat some more cake.

6 If that noise doesn't stop soon I won't feel like eating.

put

That noise will .... it stops soon.

7 I'll only leave the waiter some money if he's quick.

tip

I won't .... he's quick.

8 Take my advice and don't drink so much whisky!

if

I'd drink .... you!

> ◀ **HELP**
>
> All the sentences you have to complete are
> conditionals.
> In questions 3, 4, 6, 7 and 8 you need to
> make a second change.

LISTENING 🔊

1 Look at these parts of a main meal and answer questions 1–4 about the customs in your country.

starter   fish (or shellfish)   soup   salad   vegetables   main course
dessert (sweet)   fruit   cheese

1   Which of them do you not normally have?
2   Which of them are usually separate courses?
3   Do you often have any other courses?
4   What is the most common order of courses?

2 What are your favourites for each of the courses above, and what do you drink with them?

Example: *Starter – prawn cocktail, egg mayonnaise or artichokes, with mineral water.*

3 Read the Listening Part 4 instructions below. The important point in this *Yes / No* exercise is whether the idea is stated or not.

Example: *0 Kathy would have a starter made with eggs.*   **Y   0**

On the recording, Kathy says she would have a Spanish omelette as a starter. An omelette is made with eggs, so the answer is 'Yes'. Now follow the exam instructions.

You will hear two people talking about their ideal meal. For Questions **1–7**, decide whether the idea was stated or not and mark Y for **Yes**, or N for **No**.

1   Kathy and Phil would eat the same kind of shellfish.   **1**

2   She would have red wine.   **2**

3   Phil dislikes French cheese rolls.   **3**

4   Kathy would have an Indian curry.   **4**

5   Phil would drink beer.   **5**

6   Kathy would have coffee after her dessert.   **6**

7   She would have a very sweet dessert.   **7**

4 Which of the foods mentioned do you particularly like or dislike?

SPEAKING

1 In Speaking Parts 3 and 4, and of course in conversations generally, you will feel more confident both as the speaker or as the listener if you know how to avoid breakdowns in communication. Here are some of the strategies you can use.

1   Describing approximately: *... or that kind of thing.*
2   Hesitating, playing for time: *... um, well, let me think ...*
3   Correcting yourself: *What I meant to say is ...*
4   Using other words: *It's the thing you use for ...*
5   Checking the listener understands: *Are you with me?*
6   Asking the speaker to repeat: *Could you say that again?*
7   Making it clearer or simpler: *In other words ...*

2 Look at these extracts from the Listening text above and match each of them with one of strategies 1–7.

Example: *A – 5 (checking understanding)*

A   *Do you know what I mean?*
B   *And er – let me see, a slice of tortilla*
C   *Sorry, what was that?*
D   *bacon or ham or something like that*
E   *the main dish, I mean the main course*
F   *the Italian one, you know, with lots of fresh veg*
G   *that's to say a really spicy one*

3 Think about your own 'perfect meal'.

1 Note down a plan for your ideas, with details of each of the courses.

2 Work in pairs. Discuss your meal and your partner's meal. As you do so:

- use mainly the *would* + infinitive form of the verb, or contracted forms like *I'd have*.
- try to use *unless*, *as long as* and *provided*, as in the Listening: *Some freshly-picked strawberries, as long as they were just ripe, would be perfect.*
- when you need to, use communication strategies from activity 1.

STUDY CHECK

1 Write a complete sentence using *if*, *unless*, *as long as* or *provided* about something you would:

1 like to eat or drink every day.
2 sometimes like to eat or drink.
3 only eat or drink in special circumstances.
4 never eat or drink.

2 Imagine that you are going camping in a remote area for three days with your partner. Decide together what you will take, following these instructions:

- You have to carry everything, so the maximum weight of food and drinks that you can take is six kilos between you, including water.
- Choose from the items in the picture.
- Say what you will take in possible or probable circumstances (for example, if you want to eat hot food) and discuss alternatives, (e.g. 'If we took X we could take Y but we couldn't take Z'). Say how much or how many of the items you could carry.

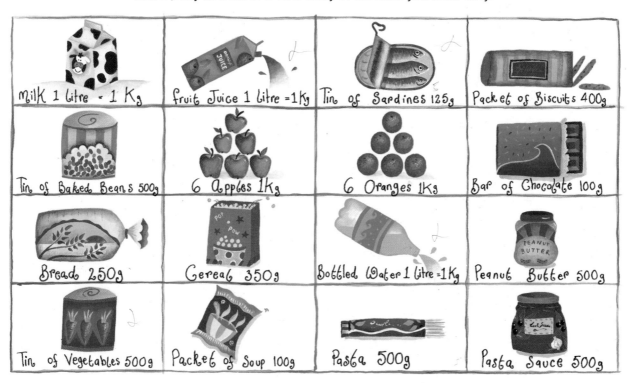

Milk 1 litre = 1 Kg Fruit Juice 1 litre =1Kg Tin of Sardines 125g Packet of Biscuits 400g

Tin of Baked Beans 500g 6 Apples 1Kg 6 Oranges 1Kg Bar of Chocolate 100g

Bread 250g Cereal 350g Bottled Water 1 litre =1Kg Peanut Butter 500g

Tin of Vegetables 500g Packet of Soup 100g Pasta 500g Pasta Sauce 500g

3 Imagine the ideal place for a meal or drink on a special occasion such as a birthday, a celebration or an engagement and write a description of what it would be like. Mention some or all of the following:

- where you would go: the country, town and place
- what the surroundings, temperature and atmosphere would be like
- whether there would be music and if so what kind
- what you would wear
- what time you would arrive and when you would leave
- what you would eat and / or drink
- how you would be feeling
- something that would make the occasion even better

When you have finished writing, check your work against your list of six most common mistakes.

7 This sporting life

READING: multiple matching

1 What is this sport called? Which country do you think it started in? What do you know about it?

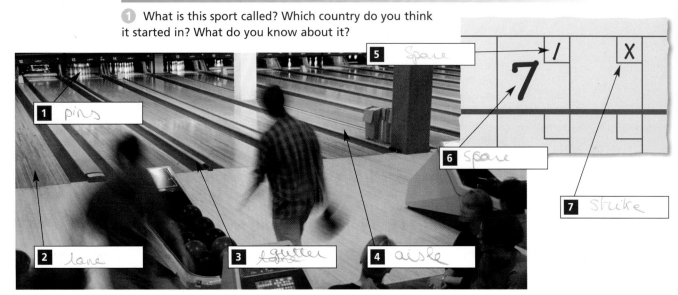

2 Read the rules below and fill in labels 1–4 on the diagram. Now look at the score card. How many pins were knocked down each time? Fill in answers 5–7.

LANE	Wooden playing surface, with gutters along either side, separated from the next lane by an aisle.
PINS	Ten wooden pins, one foot apart.
GAME	Ten frames. A player delivers two balls in each frame unless he or she scores a strike.
SCORE	Put the number of pins knocked down by the player's first delivery in the main square and the number knocked down by the second delivery in the small square in the upper right hand corner, unless it is a strike.
STRIKE	When all ten pins are knocked down at once. Put an 'x' in the small square.
SPARE	When any remaining pins are knocked down with the second delivery. Put a '/' in the small square.

3 Read this text about Reading Part 4 and fill in gaps 1–4 with clauses A–D.

Part 4 consists of a text in up to nine sections with between 13 and 15 questions. The length of the text and the number of questions might make it look difficult, but you don't have to understand everything in it and the answers are usually easier to find than in other parts of FCE Reading.

First, study the instructions, the title of the text and any headings. Next, read the whole text quickly for gist. Then study the questions and identify the key words, (1) ....
Go through the text, thinking about the words (2) .... as you look for the answers. Look at the example and think of reasons why it is right. Note down answers as soon as you find them, but be prepared to change your mind.

Remember that each section may provide more than one answer and that there may be questions (3) .... Never, though, get stuck on individual questions. If you don't know an answer, move on quickly. You can always come back to it later and if all else fails, you can guess. Don't forget that in Part 4 there is only one mark for each correct answer, (4) ....

A   that have answers in more than one section
B   which is half what you get in Parts 1, 2 and 3
C   that you have underlined
D   which you should underline

④ Follow the advice in 3 and these exam instructions:

You are going to read an article about ten-pin bowling. For Questions **1–15**, choose from the bowling centres **A–D**. The centres may be chosen more than once. When more than one answer is required, these may be given in any order. There is an example at the beginning (**0**).

Which bowling centre:

serves a good potato snack?	**0**	B
gives out written information?	**1**	
lets beginners try the equipment on the way in?	**2**	
does not give beginners enough information?	**3**	
lets you see the action while you have a drink?	**4**	
is particularly good for children?	**5**	
is particularly good for older people?	**6**	
has lots of different video games?	**7**	

has dancing at weekends?	**8**	
is especially clean?	**9**	
has unattractively-dressed staff?	**10**	
has good seating?	**11**	
hasn't enough seats?	**12**	
has plenty of room in the playing areas?	**13**	
hasn't enough room in the playing areas?	**14**	
	15	

> ◀ **HELP**
>
> Here is the number of times each section contains the correct answer:
>
> Section A: 3   Section C: 4
> Section B: 3   Section D: 5

BOWLED OVER

A lthough its origins go back as far as ancient Egypt, and nine-pin bowling was played in England in the 12th century, it was the Americans who first organized professional bowling in 1959. So how do British bowling alleys compare to their American counterparts? Some Americans in England decided to try them out by visiting four centres, each from a different chain.

A	MEGABOWL £3.76–£4.35 per game

This bowling centre is not called 'mega' for nothing. Not only is it a huge complex, it also boasts 36 lanes, a Pizza Hut, bar, pool tables and a video-game area. Michael, whose bowling roots are in Ohio, loved the place: 'I was smiling from the time I walked in the door until the time I walked out.' MegaBowl seemed to be very child-friendly and its hilarious dog mascot, which walked around talking to the kids, made us laugh. 'It's truly a great place for the entire family to go!' exclaimed Massachusetts-born Jaime, enthusiastically. The only problem we found was that the automatic scoring system did not have instructions, which made it difficult for new bowlers. The look of the place was plasticky and the staff's uniforms were a bit too brightly coloured for our liking.

B	AMF BOWLING CENTRE £2.70–£4.50

Although not the flashiest of the bowling centres, the AMF which we visited is equipped with 25 lanes, a snack bar and video games. The staff were, on the whole, very helpful and the snack bar did a great plate of chips. There was a good video-game selection. We were disappointed, however, by the lack of space. 'The seating was inadequate,' said Jaime. And Kate, who is from Texas, thought that 'the aisles between the lanes were too small.' Even given its spatial disadvantages, AMF was fine for an evening hanging out with friends and improving bowling skills. Michael thought AMF 'was as good as any bowling alley I've ever been to in the States.'

C	WESSEX SUPER BOWL £2.60–£3.55

The Wessex Super Bowl has a games area and a snack bar. It was also the only one of the centres we tried out with seats and tables overlooking the 24 lanes. We loved being able to watch the other bowlers while waiting in the bar. The bar area also had a small dance floor for Friday and Saturday nights, (when the Super Bowl puts on a disco). The decor was more tasteful here and the music funkier, which made for a much better atmosphere. A handy leaflet 'Easy Steps to Bowling' was provided, although the place itself didn't seem to be very well designed, becoming crowded and sometimes lacking space for the players. 'It was a little cramped for my style,' Michael concluded.

D	HOLLYWOOD BOWL £2.50–£3.50

Like MegaBowl, the Hollywood Bowl was large and spacious. Jaime and Kate walked in and both said: 'The best.' There were wonderful amounts of space around the lanes and Kate commented on the comfortable, large seats provided. At the reception desk there was a model bowling ball with different size finger-holes, so that new bowlers could find out which size was best suited for their hands. And everything from the lanes to the snack bars was spotless and shiny. Appealing to a more mature crowd and not overrun with packs of noisy children, Kate summed it up as 'a colourful atmosphere for serious bowlers.' Most definitely a winner.

⑤ What do you, or (if you have never tried it) would you like and dislike about bowling?

GRAMMAR: *can, could, may* and *might*

We use *can* when somebody has an ability, or senses something:

She can play well.
They can see the difference.

We also use *can* (or *could*) when a certain effect is possible:

Bowling can be quite tiring.
That surface could be slippery.

To say there is a chance that something will happen, however, we do not use *can*. Instead, we use the modals *may*, *might* or *could*:

They may (or might, or could) open more centres next year.

These three modals are also used for something that is possibly true now:

This could be the right place.
They may be closed by now.

The continuous is also possible:

We might be doing this all wrong.
They may be waiting there already.

The negative of *might* and *may* is used for something that is possibly not the case:

It might not (mightn't) be as easy as you think.
They may not be there at all.

If it is impossible that something is the case, we use *could not* (*couldn't*) or *cannot* (*can't*):

They couldn't (can't) be the same couple we saw at the other centre, they're too young.

1 Six of these sentences contain an error. Underline and correct each one.

1 We'd better go early because it might be very popular.
2 We can't find it easy at first so let's watch the others.
3 Don't run or you can fall over.
4 He couldn't be the instructor but there's a chance he is.
5 She can be the person I spoke to on the phone.
6 You may be quite fit but you'll still get tired.
7 That boy over there can be trying that new game.
8 That mightn't possibly be the time!

2 Follow these Use of English Part 3 instructions:

Complete the second sentence so that it has a similar meaning to the first sentence, using the word given. **Do not change the word given.** You must use between two and five words, including the word given.

1 They might not be here tomorrow.
   will
   It's .... here tomorrow.
2 Usually, the human body is capable of repairing itself.
   can
   The human body .... itself.

3 Maybe it won't be so easy the next time.
   may
   The .... be so easy.
4 Perhaps they aren't actually doing it the same way as us.
   might
   They .... it the same way as us.
5 There's no chance of us winning the prize.
   possibly
   We .... the prize.

GRAMMAR: relative clauses

A relative clause comes immediately after the person or thing you are referring to and often begins with a relative pronoun like *who* or *that*. A defining relative clause says who or what you are talking about:

1 *There may be questions **that have answers in more than one section**.*
2 *Words **which you spell incorrectly** in Paper 3 will be considered wrong.*

When the relative pronoun is the object of the defining relative clause, you can leave it out. In 1 above, *that* is the subject of the relative clause so you must include it. In 2, however, the subject is *you* and the object is *which*, so you could put:

*Words **you spell incorrectly** in Paper 3 will be considered wrong.*

A non-defining relative clause adds extra information which is not essential to identify who or what you are talking about:

*First Certificate, **which is an upper-intermediate exam**, can be taken twice a year.*

The relative clause is separated from the main clause by commas and you must not leave out the relative pronoun (which is never *that*) even when it is an object:

*First Certificate, **which people can take twice a year**, is an upper-intermediate exam.*

You can also begin defining or non-defining relative clauses with *why*, *where* or *when*, to refer back to reasons, places and times respectively, as well as the possessive *whose*:

*Look at the example and think of reasons **why it is right**.*
*Candidates **whose answers are not clear** will lose marks.*

1 In pairs, look at extracts 1–10 from the Reading text. In each case:

a   underline the relative clause, as in the examples on page 70.

b   write D for defining or ND for non-defining after it.

c   if there isn't a relative pronoun, write one in.

d   if the relative pronoun isn't necessary, cross it out.

1   It was the Americans who first organized professional bowling.

2   Michael, whose bowling roots are in Ohio, loved the place.

3   Its hilarious dog mascot, which walked around talking to the kids, made us laugh.

4   The only problem we found was that the automatic scoring system did not have instructions.

5   The automatic scoring system did not have instructions, which made it difficult for new bowlers.

6   The AMF which we visited is equipped with 25 lanes, a snack bar and video games.

7   Kate, who is from Texas, thought that 'the aisles between the lanes were too small.'

8   AMF 'was as good as any bowling alley I've ever been to in the States.'

9   The bar area also had a small dance floor for Friday and Saturday nights, (when the Super Bowl puts on a disco).

10   The decor was more tasteful here and the music funkier, which made for a much better atmosphere.

2 Three of these sentences are correct but seven are not. Find the mistakes, say what is wrong and correct them. When you have looked at all the sentences, say what sport they are about.

1   That's the player who he won the singles last year.

2   The match the crowd enjoyed most was the final.

3   The shot what he likes best is the volley.

4   That's the kind of racket that she prefers it.

5   His serve, which is the fastest in the world, won the game.

6   Her mother who was also a player is now her coach.

7   The semi-final, that was very exciting, went to five sets.

8   The court where they played on last week is closed.

9   I don't know which player the umpire was speaking to.

10   The champion, first shot ended up in the net, tried again.

3 Work in pairs, Student A and Student B. Join the sentences in 1–6 using the words given plus a defining or a non-defining relative clause.

Student A: Form one sentence using part of the first sentence as a relative clause.

Example: *Some referees are unfair. They help one team win.*
Some referees, ... who are unfair, help one team win.

Student B: Form one sentence using part of the second sentence as a relative clause.

Example: *Some referees are unfair. They help one team win.*
Some referees, ... who help one team win, are unfair.

When you have finished all six questions, compare your answers. Are there any differences in meaning? What sport does this activity describe?

1   The court is 26 metres long. It is 14 metres wide.
    The court ....

2   Jones was the best player. He scored 12 points.
    Jones ....

3   A spectator ran onto the court during the time-out. He was shouting.
    The spectator ....

4   Some players are extremely tall. They find it easiest to score.
    The players ....

5   Pushing an opponent is not allowed. It is called a personal foul.
    Pushing ....

6   A free throw was given in the last minute. It decided the match.
    The free throw ....

4 Complete these sentences using a defining or a non-defining relative clause.

1   Baseball, ... , is a team sport.

2   The sport .... is football.

3   People .... are sometimes injured.

4   Boxing, ... , is still very popular in some countries.

5   Cricket is a game .... understand.

6   The Tour de France, ... , is famous all over the world.

7   Gymnasts .... must train hard every day.

8   The Olympic Games, ... , are held every four years.

5 Ask your partner:

a   what kinds of sports he or she doesn't enjoy watching and doesn't like playing.

b   what kinds of players and teams he or she doesn't like.

c   when he or she doesn't like sport on TV.

LISTENING

It is a good idea to think about the topic before you do a Listening exercise or test, but until you have heard the whole recording you should always keep an open mind about the facts. You may not hear what you expect.

1 Before doing the Listening Part 2 below, look at the picture and ask your partner questions using some or all of these prompts:

- what she's been doing
- how she felt during the race
- what the dangers were
- how she avoided them
- how she's feeling
- how she prepared for the marathon

2 Now do the activity.

You will hear the director of a sports research centre talking about running the marathon. For Questions **1–10**, complete the notes.

During a marathon, many runners lose a centimetre in	**1**
One way to protect the body is to use good	**2**
Runners must breathe more deeply and with greater	**3**
The slowest runners reach the finishing line in a time of	**4**
Runners feel they have no energy left after a distance of	**5**
Some try to build up their energy reserves by eating lots of	**6**
The amount of energy used by fast and slow runners is	**7**
The amount of sweat produced by a runner may reach	**8**
The temperature of a runner who couldn't sweat would reach	**9**
Compared to other people, marathon runners will live	**10**

3 Did any of the information surprise you?

VOCABULARY: compound words

1 Look at these expressions from the Listening and their meanings on the right:

lunchtime = the time when people normally have lunch
running shoes = shoes that are worn for running
a *70-kilo* runner = a runner who weighs 70 kilos
long-distance running = running that takes place over a long distance
a *sports research centre* = a centre which does research into sport

Which of the underlined words are compound adjectives and which are compound nouns?

How are they formed? Why is *70-kilo* singular, but *sports* plural?

2 Complete the compound words from the Listening that mean the following:

1   The line that shows where a race finishes: f.........   l.........

2   Known by a lot of people: w...... - k.........

3   The point at which a liquid boils: b.........   p.........

4   A sudden, serious illness of the heart: h.........   a.........

5   Threatening to one's existence: l......... - t.........

3 Say what these compound words mean by using a relative clause.

Examples:

ice-skater = a person who skates on ice   notebook = a book which is used for taking notes

volleyball player homework racing car hockey stick bookshelves weightlifter car park sports teacher teacup surfboard fair-haired First Division footballer left-handed hairdrier 20-kilometre walk e-mail			

④ Form at least one compound word from each of the words below. For each one, ask your partner to write its meaning using a relative clause.

Example: *record*
You write: *record-breaker, record-holder.*
Your partner writes: *record-breaker: a person who breaks a record, record-holder: a person who holds a record.*

bus	player	class	good	ball	skates	tooth	school	golf	medal	first

⑤ With your partner, take turns choosing from this list of Olympic sports. In each case, describe the sport without mentioning its name. Your partner must guess which you are describing. Try to use relative clauses where you can.

Example:
It's an athletics event which takes place inside the stadium, but not on the running track. One at a time, people run up to a raised bar and try to get over it. Answer: high jump

long jump   table tennis   water polo   windsurfing   triple jump   ice-hockey   canoeing
javelin   rifle shooting   diving   tennis   100 metres sprint   volleyball   ski-jumping
pole vault   badminton   200 metres backstroke

GRAMMAR: punctuation

① Match the punctuation marks in the first column with their names in the second column and their use in English in the third column.

-	brackets	to enclose information
?	hyphen	to show surprise, anger, etc.
'	question mark	to give alternatives
( )	apostrophe	to indicate direct speech
/	inverted commas	to join words
!	exclamation mark	at the end of a question
" "	slash (informal)	possessive / missing letter(s)

Are any of these punctuation marks used differently in your first language? If so list them with their uses here:

....

....

....

An example of the slash is *possessive / missing letter(s)* above. Find examples of the other six kinds of punctuation in the Reading text on page 69.

② Now think about the kinds of words that begin with a capital letter, and those that do not. For each of categories 1–10, write an example English word, underlining the first letter. Then do the same with the same (or a similar) word in your first language. There is an example of the first one.

		English	Your first language
1	Nationalities	*Spanish*	*español*
2	Countries		
3	Languages		
4	People's names		
5	Months		
6	Days of the week		
7	Cities and towns		
8	Street names		
9	Book / film titles		
10	Nouns in general		

WRITING: a report

Follow these Writing Part 2 instructions and the advice in 1–5 below:

You work at a leisure centre and your boss wants to add another activity to those already available to the public. You must write a report for your boss in **120–180** words. Write your **report**, describing a sport, saying why you believe it will be popular and mentioning its good and bad points.

1   Think about all the sports that you know. Choose one that you like and also know enough about, in terms of both facts and vocabulary.

2   Read the instructions again and write down four headings you are going to use.

3   Look back at the advice on report writing on page 56 and Question 3 on page 161 and make a plan. Ask yourself some or all of these questions about your chosen sport:

- Is it an indoor or outdoor sport?
- What equipment do you need?
- What costs would be involved?
- Who enjoys this type of activity?
- Would it appeal to both sexes?
- What health benefits are there?

4   Write your description. As you do so, think about the following:

- the style: remember that you are writing for your boss, so avoid informal language, but you are writing about your choice, so be enthusiastic, too!
- the content: include as many facts as you can, including some disadvantages.
- the correct use of relative clauses.
- the correct use of punctuation, especially commas for relative clauses, and capital letters.

5   When you have finished, check your work for mistakes as suggested on page 63.

VOCABULARY: prepositional phrases with *in*

They fill up with pasta, bread and bananas <u>in an effort</u> to increase their carbohydrate stores.

A prepositional phrase consists of a preposition and its object: *in control, in my opinion, in the first place.*

1   Fill in each of the gaps with one of these phrases. There is one you do not need to use.

| in fact   in particular   in trouble   in private   in love   in danger   in common |
| in the end   in other words   in half   in public |

1   'Sport is .... of losing all its ideals about fair play.'
2   'Olympic athletes say they are amateurs but most of them are .... professionals.'
3   'They should say .... how much they earn and let people know the truth.'
4   'There are too many Olympic sports so I think they should cut the number .... now.'
5   'Some Olympic events have more .... with war than with the spirit of sport.'
6   'Many competitors will admit, ... , that they regularly take drugs.'
7   'Spectators in general, and soccer fans .... , should remember it is only a game.'
8   'Violent players should find themselves .... with the law.'
9   'He used his hand to score a goal; .... he cheated and should have been sent off.'
10 'People who fall .... with sports stars who they've only seen on TV must be mad.'

2   Look again at completed comments 1–10. Tell your partner whether you agree with what each person says, and why. Then write a controversial comment of your own using the phrase that you did not use in activity 1. Remember to use inverted commas. See if your partner agrees with what you say.

COMMON ERRORS

The winners celebrated in the end of the match.

What is wrong with this sentence? Why? See the Grammar Reference on page 177.

USE OF ENGLISH: error correction

Follow these Use of English Part 4 instructions:

For Questions **1–15**, read the text below and look carefully at each line. Some of the lines are correct, and some have a word which should not be there. If a line is correct, put a tick (✓) **at the end of the line**. If a line has a word which should **not** be there, write the word **at the end of the line**. There are two examples at the beginning (**0** and **00**).

A bad start

0	It was one of those days when you wished what you hadn't bothered	*what*
00	to wake up. Nothing at all went right from the moment the alarm	(✓)
1	clock was went off twenty minutes late and I had to rush to get	
2	dressed and have my breakfast in time to catch the bus. Then of	
3	course I couldn't find my trainers. I looked in for them everywhere	
4	but they had been disappeared. I'd searched most of the house and	
5	was about to give up when suddenly I spotted them lying in my	
6	brother's room. He wouldn't admit taking them but I was sure that	
7	they hadn't got there by on their own! Grabbing my sports bag I	
8	rushed out of and looked at my watch. It was nearly twenty past	
9	eight. That had meant my bus might have gone and sure enough	
10	when I turned the corner there was nobody at the stop. You could	
11	always rely on the bus for to come on time when you were late.	
12	So I did the only thing I could possibly do it: I tried to thumb	
13	a lift. Hundreds of cars streamed past. I was being cold, fed up	
14	and wishing I had stayed in the bed. Just then a truck stopped,	
15	a door flew open and a voice who I'd heard a thousand times	
	on TV said 'Where're you going?'.	

> **HELP**

All the mistakes in this text are either pronouns (*it*, *her*, etc.), auxiliary verbs (*do*, *was*, etc.), prepositions (*in*, *from*, etc.), determiners (*a*, *some*, etc.) or relative pronouns (*who*, *that*, etc.).

PHRASAL VERBS: *give*

I'd searched most of the house and was about to <u>give up</u> when suddenly I spotted them.

1 For each of questions 1–7, match the phrasal verb in italics with one of meanings A–G. Notice that some have more than one common meaning.

1	When are you going to *give back* that racket you borrowed?	A	surrender
2	Is it true that she plans to *give away* her prize money to charity?	B	reveal
3	Do you think he'll *give in* or will he fight until the end?	C	return to the owner
4	Will you *give out* the certificates to the winners or shall I?	D	hand to
5	Did you *give in* all your exam papers after you finished?	E	stop doing (habits)
6	Who *gave away* the secret?	F	give as a present
7	Didn't you say you would *give up* watching sport on TV?	G	distribute

2 Now match answers a–g with questions 1–7.

a Yes, one of the supervisors took them.
b Perhaps everyone could help themselves.
c Somebody told everyone at the party.
d Yes, she's always been generous like that.
e When I've played with it just one more time.
f I think the other player will be too strong for him.
g No, I said 'cut down', which isn't quite the same!

COMMON ERRORS

Give it back the ball you borrowed.
What is wrong with this sentence? Why?
See the Grammar Reference on page 175.

3 Ask your partner questions using each of the phrasal verbs in activity 1.

Example: *Have you given in your homework?*

EXAM STUDY GUIDE

Whenever you do a Listening activity, get into the habit of thinking about how sure you feel about your answers by marking each one SURE or UNSURE as you write it. Then, when you have done the activity, keep a note of which answers were correct. Do this with several exercises, decide which of the four patterns below best describes your work and follow the advice given.

HIGH SCORE, MOSTLY SURE: Carry on with the good work!

HIGH SCORE, MOSTLY UNSURE: You may lack confidence, in which case you should do more listening
                          practice, or you may be guessing *too* much.

LOW SCORE, MOSTLY SURE: You may be answering too quickly and not concentrating enough.

LOW SCORE, MOSTLY UNSURE: You probably need a lot more listening practice. Look back at the
                          Exam Study Guide on page 17. Should you change your priorities?

Here are some ways that students have suggested for practising listening in English:

'A lot of books are now recorded on cassette. I've just listened to a Ruth Rendell mystery – it was great!' Maria

'There's a really good programme for young people on the BBC World Service every Tuesday evening. I never miss it.' Elisabeth

'I record radio and TV programmes so that I can listen to them a couple of times, as in First Certificate.' Kostas.

'I've got a "cassette friend" in Ireland. She's like a pen friend, but instead of letters we send each other spoken messages.' Ana

Work in groups. Could you put some of these ideas into practice? Can you think of any other ways of practising listening outside the classroom?

LISTENING

1 Work in pairs, Student A and Student B.

Student A: Look at these points about Listening Part 4 True / False questions. Seven are true. Which one is false?

1 There are always seven questions.
2 The text is usually a single conversation that lasts about three minutes.
3 The written instructions always say something about the speakers and / or the situation.
4 The questions can often tell you how the conversation develops.
5 The questions always follow the order of the information in the recording.
6 It is essential to carry on listening while you write your answers.
7 If you think a statement is neither true nor false, you should leave a blank.
8 You should only write the initial letter T or F on your answer sheet.

Now check your answers by asking Student B.

Student B: Read the information about Listening Part 4 on page 166 and then answer Student A's questions about it. Help him or her to correct any mistakes.

2 In groups, look at the picture. What sport do you think she is involved in? Quickly make a list of words connected with this sport. What does she have to do? How old do you think she is? How do you think the players react to her decisions?

3 Read these Listening Part 4 instructions. Put SURE or UNSURE next to all your answers.

You will hear part of an interview with Abigail McGahan, who is a referee in junior league football. Answer Questions 1–7, by writing **T** for True, or **F** for False in the boxes provided.

1	Her father taught her how to referee matches.	1
2	She was scared before her first match as referee.	2
3	The manager of the other team complained about her.	3
4	In one match, she gave a lot of yellow cards.	4
5	She occasionally watches professional matches.	5
6	She admits that referees sometimes make mistakes.	6
7	Her ambition is to referee an important match.	7

◀ HELP

Speakers sometimes seem to be saying one thing but then go on to say something quite different. Because of this, take care not to answer Question 3 too quickly or you may get it wrong.

1 Work in pairs. Decide who will discuss the two pictures above (Student A), and who will talk about the two below (Student B). Prepare to talk about them as follows:

Student A: Think about the similarities and differences in: the places, the playing surfaces, the number of players, their physique.

Student B: Think about the similarities and differences in: the atmosphere, what they are wearing, why they are playing and how they are probably feeling.

2 **Student A:** Compare and contrast your pictures saying what you think about these two sports. As you do so, try to include relative clauses such as *It's a sport that …* or *There's a player who …* .

Student B: When Student A has finished, say which of the sports in Student A's pictures you would prefer to play and / or watch.

3 **Student B:** Compare and contrast your own pictures, saying what you think about these two kinds of match as in 2 above.

Student A: When Student B has finished, say which of the two kinds of sport you prefer: highly competitive or relaxed and friendly.

STUDY CHECK

1 Work in groups. Discuss and vote on the following:
1 The best sportsman and sportswoman at present
   a in your country   b in the world
2 The best sportsman and sportswoman ever
   a in your country   b in the world
3 The sport which is
   a the most exciting in the world
   b the most boring in the world

2 You have been invited by an international magazine to write an article saying why your country should host a major international sporting event. Decide on an occasion such as the Olympics or the soccer World Cup and give reasons why it would be the best place. Think of advantages like climate and geography (for water sports, etc.), benefits to the country and outstanding local athletes. Also mention any big disadvantages in order to give your article some balance.

8 In the spotlight

SPEAKING

Look at the pictures on these two pages and for each one discuss these questions:

- Who are these TV characters? What are they famous for?
- What age group particularly likes them?
- Do you think they are funny? Why? Why not?
- Do they think or behave like real people? In what way?

READING: gapped text

1. In Reading Part 3, sentences can be missing from the beginning, the middle or the end of different paragraphs. When the gap is at the end of the paragraph, the clues may be immediately before it or in different parts of the paragraph. Look at the example (0): the first paragraph is mainly about how seriously the programme has been taken, particularly in the USA. This links the meaning to sentence H. In addition, H begins *All of which*, referring back to the main points in the first paragraph (*debate, warning*).

There may be clues at the beginning of the next paragraph after a gap: for gap 3, the use of *couch potatoes* in the first sentence of the following paragraph matches the content of the missing sentence. Follow the exam instructions below.

 HELP

Some of the missing sentences are in inverted commas. Use this as a clue to make connections with other things that the speaker in the text says.

You are going to read a magazine article about two cartoon characters. Seven sentences have been removed from the article. Choose from the sentences **A–H** the one which fits each gap (**1–6**). There is one extra sentence which you do not need to use. There is an example at the beginning (**0**).

A   Once you see a real person make those sly facial expressions, and hear that unmistakeable laugh, you can't help smiling.
B   After all, sitting on the sofa and watching music videos is what a lot of real people spend their time doing.
C   'My aim is to make it as funny as possible, and sometimes things that happen to be funny also happen to offend some people.'
D   'That's like saying it's a movie about Einstein, so it's a clever movie.'
E   'Then they came up to me and said they were huge fans of *Beavis and Butthead*.'
F   Part of the fun of the film involved trying to work out who was in it.
G   MTV saw the recording in early 1992 and handed the animation over to teams in New York and South Korea, who created the first series of *Beavis and Butthead*.
H   All of which goes to show that it's not just Europeans who take American pop culture too seriously.

The man behind
Beavis and Butthead

Mike Judge is responsible for the only cartoon with a health warning.

Mike Judge, the balding 35-year-old creator of the most famous duo since Batman and Robin, must wonder what he has done to western civilization. Since Beavis and Butthead first appeared on MTV in 1993, the show has been a subject of debate in the United States Congress and it's probably the only cartoon in history that has had to go out with a warning not to imitate the duo's moronic behaviour. `0` `H`

10 Unfortunately for critics of the show, Judge has some heavyweight supporters. Bernardo Bertolucci and Stephen King are big fans, and when it came to casting the voices for *Beavis and Butthead do America* — the characters' first full-length movie — Judge had no problem getting the sort of big stars normally associated with major Disney animations. They may not have been in the credits but, yes, those were the voices of Demi Moore and Bruce Willis. `1`

It's Judge, though, who provides the sound of Beavis and Butthead themselves, as well as co-writing the scripts. Sitting opposite him in a Beverly Hills hotel, it soon becomes clear that despite Judge's normal appearance, Butthead lurks just below the surface. `2`

But fans of the programme have long known that they could go into any town anywhere and find people who have startling similarities to the undynamic duo. Despite being animated, the pair seem more convincing than most characters in US sitcoms.

`3`

Apart from the brilliantly idiotic running commentary by the two couch potatoes, the show is also about their endless search for women who will speak to them for longer than ten seconds, jokes about US institutions like the Senate or the FBI and of course super-violent humour. 'I'm not trying just to shock people,' says Judge. `4`

Judge denies that he has helped to lower the general level of America's intelligence. 'I actually think the opposite. To me, it's so simple-minded just to look at something and say it's about stupid characters, so it's a stupid show.' He pauses for a second. `5`

Judge was never trained as an animator (he studied physics at university), but, inspired by Terry Gilliam of Monty Python fame, he saw it as a way to break into comedy. 'Terry did those amusing little animations and wrote some, so I thought that is what I would do: I would make a tape of those things,' says Judge. `6`

Judge now has spin-offs from the show (*King of the Hill* and *Daria*) and is thinking about more films. Only one thing is certain: the duo will never get those girlfriends. If they did, it would be as if they had grown up.

2 Match these compound words from the text with their meanings on the right.

full-length (line 13)   unintelligent

sitcoms (line 26)   series derived from a similar, successful one

couch potatoes (line 28)   TV comedy series

simple-minded (line 35)   art forms for ordinary people

spin-off (line 44)   not shortened

pop culture (sentence H)   lazy people

What examples of pop culture and sitcoms can you think of?

3 Use the context to work out the meanings of these words:

> critics (line 10)   casting (line 12)   animations (line 15)   credits (line 16)
> scripts (line 19)   commentary (line 27)

4 Work in pairs. Student A is a big fan of *Beavis and Butthead*. Student B thinks it is a bad influence on young people. Use your own ideas and ideas from the text to argue your point.

GRAMMAR: the present perfect

1 *Since Beavis and Butthead first appeared on MTV in 1993, the show has been a subject of debate in the United States Congress.*

1 Discuss these questions in pairs:

- What verb tenses are used here? When did these two events happen?
- What tenses would you use in your first language to say the same thing?

2 Why does English use *has been* in the example? Choose from the uses of the present perfect (A, B, C and D) below.

A For something that started in the past and continues in the present

B For a completed action in the past but in a time period that still continues

C When you can see the results now of a recent event in the past

D For something that happened in the past but we don't know when

3 Now match each of the following examples with one of the remaining uses above.

a Look! I've found the remote control!

b I've had an awful nightmare.

c They've already been on the telly once this week.

2 To save space, newspaper headlines often use the present simple instead of the present perfect:
Plane makes emergency landing.

In a TV news bulletin, though, (where the results of the event are shown) the present perfect is normally used:
A plane has made an emergency landing.

Imagine you are a newsreader. How would you report the following? Add articles and other words where necessary.

1 TEENAGER SAVES CHILD FROM RIVER

2 LOCAL HERO WINS WORLD CHAMPIONSHIP

3 VOTERS ELECT NEW GOVERNMENT FOR NEXT 5 YEARS

4 STORM HITS ATLANTIC COAST – HOMES DAMAGED

5 BOMB EXPLODES IN CITY CENTRE – NOBODY HURT

6 Student passes exam with highest-ever score

3 The present perfect is often used with expressions like *today* that refer to a time period that is still continuing, while the past simple tends to be used with those like *yesterday*, that refer to a past period. Which of the following would we use with sentence 1, and which with 2?

last year recently this month since January
last Friday so far this year while I was listening
already a few days ago when it happened

1 They've mentioned her in the news at least once
....

2 They mentioned her in the news at least once
....

4 We often use *since* (plus the time when something started) or *for* (plus the period of time it has lasted) with an action or situation that started in the past and continues in the present.

Examples:
We've had a satellite dish since October.
I've used teletext for many years.

COMMON ERRORS

I've known her during five years.
What is wrong with this sentence? Why?
See the Grammar Reference on page 177.

Think about the TV in your country and complete 1–5. If you are not sure about any of the dates, ask other students questions beginning *How long have / has ...?* For the second gap in each sentence, use the present perfect form of one of these verbs:

enjoy hate watch be ~~broadcast~~
avoid follow

Example:
The oldest channel is TV1, which has broadcast for about 50 years.

1 My favourite music programme is .... , which I .... for ....

2 The most successful quiz show is .... , which .... on since ....

3 The most popular soap is .... , which many people .... since ....

4 The best comedy is .... , which I .... for ....

5 The worst show on TV is .... , which I .... since .... !

5 Think about changes in television since you were a child and write a sentence choosing from prompts 1–8. In each case use the present perfect of one of these verbs, but without saying when the change happened.

get worse   rise   change   improve   ~~get better~~
drop   increase   stay the same   fall

Example: *sound quality – The sound quality has got better.*

1   programmes in general
2   amount of advertising
3   number of channels
4   picture quality
5   number of video recorders
6   price of TV sets
7   programmes for young people
8   number of programmes in English

6 Work in pairs, Student A and Student B.
Student A:
1   Quickly make a list of your all-time favourite TV and / or radio programmes. Then, for each one, ask your partner 'Have you ever seen … ?', 'Have you ever listened to … ?' or 'Have you ever watched … ?' When the answer is 'No', try to persuade him or her to do so.
2   Now ask about newer programmes like this: 'Have you seen … yet?'

Student B:
1   Answer your partner's questions beginning 'Have you ever …?' by saying 'Yes, I have.' or 'No, I haven't'. When your answer is 'Yes', give your opinion of the programme. When your answer is 'No', say why not and listen to what your partner says about the programme.
2   Answer questions ending '… yet?' like this: 'Yes, I've already seen it.', 'No, I haven't seen it yet.' or 'No, I still haven't seen it.'

7 Complete the second sentence so that it has a similar meaning to the first sentence, using the word given. **Do not change the word given.** You must use between two and five words, including the word given. All the answers require the present perfect.

1   It's a long time since he was last on TV.
    not
    He .... for a long time.

2   I've never seen a documentary as good as this before.
    best
    This is the .... seen.

3   The last time I watched it was two weeks ago.
    have
    I .... two weeks.

4   They've never shown such a bad series on TV before.
    ever
    It's the .... shown on TV.

5   I am afraid there is no time left.
    run
    I am afraid we .... time.

6   The introduction of satellite TV made it possible for people to see many more channels.
    able
    Since the introduction of satellite TV, people .... many more channels.

8 Work in pairs to do the activity below.

1   **Student A:**

Think about what is in the news this week. Tell Student B what has happened:

a in your town.
b in your country.
c in the world.

Use the present perfect, without time expressions. When you answer B's questions, use the past simple, with or without time expressions.

   Student B:

Listen to what Student A says, then ask for more information by asking questions in the past simple beginning 'Who … ?', 'Where … ?' and 'What … ?'

2   **Student A:**

Tell B what you have done in English outside the classroom since the course began. Talk about what you have listened to, what you have read, what you have written and who you have spoken to. Don't say which day or at what time: it's the action that is important, not when it happened. Then answer B's questions, using the past simple.

   Student B:

Ask A for more details, as in 1 above.

VOCABULARY: the arts

① Which of these do you associate with
1 art?
2 music and dance and theatre?
3 the arts in general?

> exhibition opera house masterpiece portrait abstract sculpture concert hall
> ballet shade watercolours sketch canvas art gallery ballerina tenor drawing
> frame stage applause oil painting soprano carving landscape creative audience

② Describe each of pictures a–e, using words from activity 1. Which do you like most, and which least?

LISTENING

① Follow these Listening Part 4 exam instructions:

You will hear a conversation which takes place at a school between an art teacher, a parent – Mrs Ray – and her daughter, Kate. Answer Questions 1–7 by writing **T** for teacher, **R** for Mrs Ray or **K** for Kate in the boxes provided.

1 Who mentions finding something? **1**
2 Who explains what another person means? **2**
3 Who does not believe what someone else says? **3**
4 Who gives a warning? **4**
5 Who says that other people behave in the same way? **5**
6 Who needs to leave the house early in the morning? **6**
7 Who tells someone not to be concerned? **7**

HELP

At the beginning, you will hear the speakers in this order:
1 the teacher
2 the girl
3 her mother

FIRST CERTIFICATE FACTS

To help you understand the context, there are sometimes background sounds on the FCE Listening recording, but they always end before anyone starts speaking.

② Do you think Kate should take more notice of what her mother says or what the teacher says? Why?

82 In the spotlight UNIT 8

GRAMMAR: present perfect continuous

She's been doing drawings like that since she was six.

1 Use these three words to fill in the four gaps in the sentence below: *perfect participle present*

We form the present perfect continuous by using the .... of the verb *be* plus the .... of the main verb.

2 We use the present perfect continuous:

1 to talk about actions or situations that began in the past and which are still continuing.
2 to emphasize how long something has been happening.
3 when you can still see the results of an action or situation.

Match each of examples **a**, **b** and **c** below with the most likely use of 1–3 above:

a We've been looking forward to this moment for months.
b They've obviously been making careful preparations for this performance.
c He's been writing a play but he won't finish it until next year.

3 In some cases we cannot use the present perfect continuous. Decide which of these sentences are wrong and correct them.

1 Nobody's been recognizing her yet.
2 I've always been wanting to study drama.
3 We've all been feeling a bit tired lately.
4 I think I've been losing my ticket for tonight.
5 I've been hoping to meet you for a long time.
6 This town has been having a theatre for centuries.
7 Shakespeare isn't easy, but I've been understanding so far.
8 They've been stopping putting good plays on TV recently.
9 I've been having a rest before the next act begins.
10 I've been liking his acting since I was a child.

4 Fill in gaps 1–11 with the past simple, the present perfect or the present perfect continuous form of the verb in brackets.

Last night I (1) .... (go) to Stratford-upon-Avon to see *Macbeth*, a play which I (2) .... (admire) since I was a child. In the queue outside, I (3) .... (speak) to some of the young people there. Marisa, from Tarragona, said 'I (4) .... (wait) here since six o'clock, but I think it'll be worth it. We (5) .... (study) *Macbeth* for a while so I really want to see it.' Yiorgos, from Thessaloniki, (6) .... (tell) me 'I (7) .... (see) it once already; I (8) .... (be) here last Friday with the school. But they arranged another visit to Stratford today so ever since they (9) .... (say) I could come along I (10) .... (look) forward to seeing it again. I (11) .... (think) about the Witches scene all week.'

USE OF ENGLISH: word formation

1 In Use of English Part 5 you will sometimes need to use present or past participles, often as participle adjectives (see page 26).

What are the answers to 1 and 2 in this extract?

We found the script (1) .... and particularly enjoyed the dialogue between the main characters, who, I was (2) .... to learn, had never	**FASCINATE** **AMAZE**

2 Follow the exam instructions.

For Questions **1–10**, read the text below. Use the word given in capitals at the end of each line to form a word that fits in the space in the same line. There is an example at the beginning (**0**).

THE PEOPLE'S THEATRE

The nearest thing to the theatre that many people (**0**) ..*actually*..	**ACTUAL**
manage to see is their (**1**) .... TV soap. For true fans it is an essential	**FAVOUR**
part of life, bringing emotional topics for (**2**) .... into the home and	**DISCUSS**
(**3**) [p] .... issues that will be talked about in workplaces and school	**RAISE**
playgrounds up and down the country the (**4**) .... day. Far from	**FOLLOW**
(**5**) [p] .... Hollywood-style escapism, the storylines in today's soaps	**PROVIDE**
aim right at the heart of current moral dilemmas (**6**) [p] .... by	**FACE**
ordinary people. The (**7**) .... is often of the highest standard, with	**ACT**
the leading actors managing to give top-class (**8**) .... three	**PERFORM**
times a week, week after week, (**9**) [p] .... what many	**PRODUCE**
consider to be some of the most (**10**) .... drama in recent years.	**POWER**

> **◀ HELP**
>
> The spaces where you need to put a present or past participle form are marked [p].

WRITING: a transactional letter

1 This table shows some of the possible variations in Writing Part 1. Study the exam question below and choose the correct answer for each category a–f. The first one is underlined as an example.

a Number of texts: one   <u>two</u>   three
b Notes: linked to text   separate from text   none
c Text type(s):   advert   letter   postcard   diary   note   timetable   notice   article   other
d Text by: company   stranger   friend   relative   other
e Your writing style: formal   semi-formal   informal
f Your writing aim: inform   request information   complain   suggest   other

You replied to this newspaper advertisement and paid a year's subscription. Now you have watched the channel for a week but you have been very disappointed.
Read the advertisement carefully, on which you have made some notes. Then, using the information, complain to the Customer Relations Officer. You may add other relevant points of your own.
Write a **letter** of **120–180** words in an appropriate style. Do not write any addresses.

2 Read this sample answer to the question above. As you do so, match each of the handwritten notes with the relevant part of the letter, as in the example.

Dear Mr Tait,

I am writing to complain about Channel Extra. I recently took out a year's subscription but I am afraid the programmes have not been up to the standard I expected.

Usually means 'old'! ——— In the first place, your advertisement mentions 'classic movies' but in fact this is just another way of saying old films in black and white. To make matters worse, these and other programmes are translated into our own language so we do not have the chance to practise listening to English, or any other foreign languages.

As well as this, the comedies are spoilt by all the commercial breaks, which people in the USA may be used to but we are not. Also, in this country we do not think of baseball or American football as top sports. The news programmes, too, have been a disappointment, with the same stories repeated hour after hour, rather than the regular updates I had hoped for.

I would therefore like you to cancel my subscription and return my money immediately.

Yours sincerely,

Paula Marin

❸ Here is some advice about writing transactional letters. Check the letter opposite to see if Paula has followed points 1–9.

1   In the first paragraph, say why you are writing.
2   Organize your letter into suitable paragraphs.
3   Use a style that is right for the reader, the reason for writing and the content.
4   Write in full sentences, even if the texts use note form in places.
5   Try to use your own words, although you can build on key words in the text.
6   Deal with all the main points in the text, plus any notes.
7   Tick (✓) each of the points and notes as you mention them in your letter.
8   You can add relevant information, requests or suggestions of your own.
9   If you are writing to complain, end by saying what you want the reader to do.

❹ Read the instructions and follow the advice below.

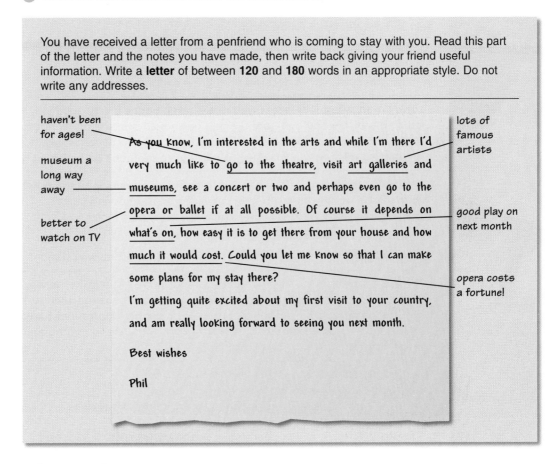

You have received a letter from a penfriend who is coming to stay with you. Read this part of the letter and the notes you have made, then write back giving your friend useful information. Write a **letter** of between **120** and **180** words in an appropriate style. Do not write any addresses.

haven't been for ages!

museum a long way away

better to watch on TV

As you know, I'm interested in the arts and while I'm there I'd very much like to go to the theatre, visit art galleries and museums, see a concert or two and perhaps even go to the opera or ballet if at all possible. Of course it depends on what's on, how easy it is to get there from your house and how much it would cost. Could you let me know so that I can make some plans for my stay there?

I'm getting quite excited about my first visit to your country, and am really looking forward to seeing you next month.

Best wishes

Phil

lots of famous artists

good play on next month

opera costs a fortune!

Before you write:
• Analyse the task using categories d–f in activity 1 opposite.
• Use your analysis and the instructions to decide on the appropriate style and aim.
• Highlight the key words in the letter and the handwritten notes.
• Make a plan, with a purpose for each paragraph.
• Note down some useful expressions.

While you write:
• Check that you are following points 1–8 in activity 3 above.
• Show your ability to use a range of language, both structures and vocabulary.
• Try to include expressions from Vocabulary activity 1 on page 82.

After you write:
• Check that you have followed the instructions exactly, that there aren't any obvious grammar, spelling or punctuation mistakes and that your letter begins and ends suitably. Will it have a positive effect on the reader, do you think?
• Swap letters with your partner and check for mistakes, particularly those on his or her list of most common ones.

Look at the instructions for Listening Part 1. When the question is *Who ... ?*, concentrate particularly on the register and on pronouns as clues (as in example 1 below). When it is *Where ... ?*, pay special attention to whether they say *this* or *that*, *here* or *there*, etc., and to any expressions of place (as in Example 2). In every case listen for relevant vocabulary, but don't jump to conclusions.

> You will hear people talking in eight different situations. For Questions **1–8**, choose the best answer, **A**, **B** or **C**.

This part of the exam sometimes includes questions about people's roles and relationships, or about where the speakers are. Answer Questions 1 and 2 by looking at the transcripts of the text and the clues that follow them.

1   When you arrive for an appointment at an office, the secretary is talking on the phone. Who is she talking to?

A   her boss   **B**   a decorator   **C**   a customer   ☐ 1

> Look, I'm sorry but let's face it, you really haven't done a very good job, have you? The walls are still wet and there are tins and brushes all over the place, not to mention paint splashed on the chairs. Where is she supposed to sit, for heaven's sake? Or do you think she shouldn't come in to work today just because you couldn't be bothered tidying up?

Think about the register: does it sound like a secretary talking to the boss?
Which person would you associate most with tins, brushes and paint?
Who does the secretary mean when she refers to 'she'?

2   You hear a reporter talking on the radio. Where is he?

A   an art gallery   **B**   the radio studio   **C**   a railway station   ☐ 2

> This huge building used to be a station, and it still has its massive railway clock, but since 1986 it's housed much of the nation's finest art from the period 1848 to 1914, so I'm surrounded by superb pictures by Impressionist and pre-Impressionist artists. There are also, to my left, sections devoted to masterpieces of sculpture and photography, as well as magnificent examples of the decorative arts.

What does the use of *This* at the beginning indicate?
Don't let individual words on the recording mislead you.
Use expressions of place like *surrounded by* and *to my left* as clues.

Now listen and answer Questions 3–8.

3   This man is telephoning someone about his car. Who is he talking to?
   A   a friend   **B**   a mechanic   **C**   the man who sold   ☐ 3
                                                                   it to him

4   You hear this couple talking. Where are they?
   A   in a theatre   **B**   in a bar   **C**   in the street   ☐ 4

5   You hear this girl telephoning someone. Who is she talking to?
   A   her mother   **B**   her friend   **C**   her teacher   ☐ 5

6   You hear this reporter talking about what he can see. Where is he?
   A   in an aeroplane   **B**   in a very tall building   **C**   on top of a   ☐ 6
                                                                   mountain

7   Listen to this woman speaking on the phone. Who is she talking to?
   A   a customer   **B**   the manager   **C**   a colleague   ☐ 7

8   You hear two people talking about a painting. Where are they?
   A   in a shop   **B**   in a house   **C**   at an exhibition   ☐ 8

1 Look at these notes on Speaking Part 1 and write the advice and information in complete sentences. The first one has been done as an example.

- Mark sheet: give to examiner.
  Give your mark sheet to the examiner.
- Examiners: one talks, the other assesses.
- Examiner's questions: listen carefully.
- Repetition: ask if you don't understand.

- Your answers: the longer the better.
- Speaking: not too quiet.
- Not allowed: speeches learnt before exam.
- Main aim: get used to partner/examiners.
- Max. time: about 2 mins each candidate.

2 In Part 1 the examiner will ask questions about yourself. Write down as many questions as you can think of under each of these headings:

1 Your home town
2 Your family
3 Your work or studies
4 Your leisure activities
5 Your future plans

EXAM STUDY GUIDE

When you practise speaking for Paper 5 of the exam, how well do you do the following? In each case, give yourself a mark out of five by circling a number.

1 Use a variety of grammatical structures accurately.	1 2 3 4 5
2 Use appropriate vocabulary.	1 2 3 4 5
3 Organize what you say in a logical way and link it together well.	1 2 3 4 5
4 Speak clearly, at a natural speed and with good stress and intonation.	1 2 3 4 5
5 Communicate well in English with other students.	1 2 3 4 5
6 Successfully carry out tasks like comparing photos and solving problems.	1 2 3 4 5

Remember, though, that the examiners do not expect you to sound like a native English speaker. Of course, you should try to avoid mistakes – but don't worry so much about accuracy that you lose fluency. The aim of the exam is to let you show what you can do with the language. Here are some suggestions for practising speaking:

- Record yourself on cassette and check your fluency, pronunciation, vocabulary and grammar.
- Read aloud.
- If you don't know how to pronounce a word, check its pronunciation in the dictionary.
- Get a 'cassette friend' (see page 76).
- Roleplay 'Examiners / Candidates' with friends and relatives. They don't need to be at FCE level.
- Find places where you can talk English to people. They don't have to be native speakers.

3 Work with two other students.

Student A: You are an FCE examiner. Interview the candidate by asking at least one question from each of categories 1–5 in activity 2.
Student B: You are an FCE candidate. Answer all the examiner's questions as fully as you can.
Student C: You are an FCE assessor. Give the candidate marks out of five for each of scales 1–4 in the Exam Study Guide above.

STUDY CHECK

1 Note down the names of your three closest friends or relatives. Then, for each one, write sentences using the present perfect about what they have done (or not done) recently.

Example:
Simon. He's bought a new PC. He's had a row with his girlfriend. He's felt a bit lonely since then. He hasn't been out a lot lately. He hasn't phoned me for a while.

Now write about what they've been doing (or not doing), feeling, reading, etc.

2 Think back to as many positive experiences in your life as possible. In each case, write a short sentence.

Examples:
I've been to lots of interesting places. I've met some wonderful people.

3 In class you have been discussing the subject of entertainment. Your teacher has asked you to write a composition giving your opinions on the topic *The best I have ever seen.*

Write your **composition**. You can write about a television programme, a film or a play. Give reasons for your choice.

9 What happened next?

VOCABULARY: crime

1 In groups, look at the following newspaper extracts. Which crime does each describe? Choose from this list:

| shoplifting   terrorism   vandalism   theft   murder   kidnapping |
| burglary   smuggling   blackmail   ~~bank robbery~~ |

What do we call the person who commits each of these crimes?

Example: *1 – bank robbery, bank robber.*

1 The two men and two women who held up a branch of Barclay's and escaped with £1.4 million in new banknotes were today sentenced to long terms of imprisonment.
2 Three local youths were accused of damaging public telephone boxes and breaking several shop windows in the High Street.
3 The court was told that Ms Wright had threatened Mr Neville that unless he paid her £100,000 she would send the photographs to his wife.
4 67-year-old Mrs Collins, a widow, was seen leaving the supermarket without paying for two items of food. In her defence she said that as a pensioner she could not afford to eat properly.
5 A man has been arrested in connection with the disappearance of a Porsche 911 Turbo from its owner's garage. Police sources say he attempted to sell the stolen car abroad via the Internet.
6 Customs officers who searched the boat found heroin with an estimated street value of over £5 million. The captain denied all knowledge of the presence of the drug but was found guilty.
7 A policewoman told the court that on the night in question she had seen Mr Keane climbing out of an upstairs window carrying property belonging to the owner of the house.
8 She was charged with being in possession of explosives with intent to endanger life, of belonging to an illegal organization and of planting a bomb outside Parliament two years ago.
9 The prosecution claimed that the gang had seized the businessman, held him captive and said they would kill him unless a ransom of one million dollars was paid.
10 The assault took place at night outside a club, where a man, aged 35, attacked the victim. He died instantly.

2 Complete each of 1–6 with one of these punishments:

| jail sentence   fine   suspended sentence   community service   life imprisonment   death |

1 As it was her first offence, she only had to pay a .... of £100.
2 In those days, the penalty for murder was .... , usually by hanging.
3 The judge gave the violent attacker a .... of ten years, to begin immediately.
4 He received a six-month .... , which he will serve if he commits any further offence.
5 The vandal was ordered to do 200 hours of .... working in the local parks.
6 Some people believe that .... should mean what it says: no release from jail, ever.

① Narrative texts do not always follow a chronological order of events, so do not expect Reading Part 1 headings to do so. If you look at headings A–I, you might expect I to be the last one, but stories can change the order of events and may include flashbacks to things that happened earlier.

Be careful with this as you follow the exam instructions.

You are going to read a short story about a bank robbery. Choose the most suitable heading from the list **A–I** for each part (**1–7**) of the article. There is one extra heading which you do not need to use. There is an example at the beginning (**0**).

A	Showing the police the way	**F**	Nearly home
B	Getting the cash	**G**	Careful preparations
C	What he had forgotten	**H**	Changing to public transport
D	Firing warning shots	**I**	In prison
E	Into the arms of the law		

A POLICEMAN'S bestfriend

0   I

He was not a happy thief. Sitting alone in his cell he thought once more about how the police had caught him and he decided that he was probably one of the most unfortunate convicts in the history of crime. He
5 also knew that he would not have much else to think about for several years to come.

1

His feelings had been very different, he remembered, as he walked confidently along the road towards his house, the heavy sack over his shoulder almost
10 overflowing with cash. The police, he was sure, would be miles away, looking for a clown in a car on the other side of town.

2

He'd planned the robbery down to the finest detail, observing the staff and their routine over several
15 weeks and making sure that his raid would coincide with the busiest payout of the week. He'd even gone to another town to steal the car he would use, changing the numberplates and keeping it locked up in the garage until the big day arrived. With so many
20 young car thieves around these days, he reflected sadly, nobody's car was safe.

3

The hold-up itself had run like clockwork. His imitation pistol and large, scary-looking dog quickly made everyone co-operate, and a rather sinister
25 clown mask meant there was no chance of him being recognized from the closed-circuit television security video. The bag he had brought was soon filled up and,

pausing only to give the camera a final ironic wave, he made a quick exit.

4

30 Leaving nothing to chance, he'd taken off his disguise in the getaway car. He then left the stolen vehicle deep in an underground car park before catching the bus home dressed as a busy postman carrying a mountainous mailbag. So far so good.

5

35 It was only when he got indoors with the brimming sackful of cash that he realized he'd left something behind: his faithful hound. Still, with all the money he now had, he could easily afford to buy a new dog, and a pedigree one at that.

6

40 Then, suddenly, there was a loud knock at the door. Snatching up his sack, the startled robber made a dash for the back door, only to run straight into an extremely large police sergeant, who grabbed him by the scruff of the neck and unceremoniously marched
45 him back inside.

7

The crook couldn't believe it. 'How on earth did you find me so quickly?' he asked miserably. 'It was the Sergeant over there,' replied the Inspector. 'He's the one who noticed that you'd left your dog tied up
50 outside.' The thief looked astonished. 'But he hasn't got a name tag, or even a collar for that matter ...' 'It's simple really,' said the Inspector, 'the Sergeant just shouted "Home, boy!" and here we are.'

② Discuss this question in pairs: what sentence do you think the thief in this story deserved?

GRAMMAR: past perfect

The hold-up itself <u>had run</u> like clockwork.

1 How do we form the past perfect? What is the negative of *had run*?

2 We often use the past perfect to talk about an action that happened before another past action. Look at the underlined verbs in these examples from the Reading text.

In each case, say which action happened first and which happened later.

1 He <u>thought</u> once more about how the police <u>had caught</u> him.
2 His feelings <u>had been</u> very different, he <u>remembered</u>.
3 He <u>realized</u> he'<u>d left</u> something behind: his faithful hound.

3 To emphasize continuity, repetition or duration, we use the past perfect continuous:
The police <u>had been trying</u> to catch him for years and at last they succeeded.

However, as with other continuous forms (see the present perfect continuous on page 83) there are cases where we cannot use it. Look back at the examples in activity 1 and activity 2: in which of them is it grammatically possible to replace the past perfect with the past perfect continuous?

4 Some of these sentences contain mistakes. Correct them and in each case say why it is wrong, giving one of these reasons:

a the actions are in the wrong order   b the past perfect continuous is not possible

1 Crime had been rising until the new laws came into force.
2 By the time the guards had noticed the tunnel, several prisoners escaped.
3 His strange behaviour had been surprising me but then I saw the jewels.
4 They arrested a suspect on Monday but yesterday they had released her.
5 People had been worried about how much vandalism increased.
6 He told her he'd changed but she didn't believe him.

5 Fill in the gaps using the past simple, the past perfect or the past perfect continuous of the verb in brackets.

BIRD THIEF JAILED

A man caught with a stolen parrot was given away when the bird (1) .... (tell) police its real name. Clive McLeod insisted the bird, worth more than £1,000, was called Billy and that a friend (2) .... (give) it to him. But when suspicious officers introduced the bird to its real owner, Sacha Hinds, it (3) .... (say) 'Hello' and gave its name as Primrose.

McLeod, aged 40, was jailed for 15 months. At his trial he had insisted that he (4) .... (own) the parrot for nine months. Sentencing him at Harrow Crown Court, Judge Barrington Black said that Primrose (5) .... (be) a popular attraction at Miss Hinds' shop, 'Pets Are Us', in Ealing, west London. Local people had known the parrot and it (6) .... (perform) tricks on the morning of its disappearance.

The judge said that McLeod (7) .... (neglect) the bird during the time prior to its discovery in a small cage at his home. Judge Black (8) .... (add) that the sentence took into account the fact that McLeod (9) .... (deny) the crime, necessitating a three-and-a-half day trial with expert witnesses, which (10) .... (cost) an estimated £28,000.

6 Imagine the situation described in sentences 1–8 and fill in the gaps using the past perfect or past perfect continuous of a suitable verb.

1 I'd gone to bed early because I .... a very long and tiring day.
2 I got up later on in the night, though, because I thought I .... a noise.
3 I went into the living room and saw that someone .... a window.
4 I couldn't see anything else because I .... on the light.
5 There was a sound behind me as if somebody .... the door.
6 I turned around but it seemed that the burglar .... out of the room.
7 Then I heard somebody breathing very close to me: he .... in, not going out.
8 At that moment I woke up and realized it wasn't real, I .... all the time.

GRAMMAR: narrative time links

Crime had been rising <u>until</u> the new laws came into force.

1 Fill in gaps 1–4 with the following, using each once only:

just before   as soon as   by the time   once

COMMON ERRORS

When he made sure nobody was around he went in.
What is wrong with this sentence? Why? See the Grammar Reference on page 178.

Ferguson was a professional criminal and (1) .... the police caught him he had become quite rich. They had started watching his house (2) .... they realized who he was, as they suspected that (3) .... they began to take an interest in him he had broken into a jeweller's shop. Following another robbery they had detained him (4) .... he arrived home.

2 Continue the story by matching parts 1–9 on the left with parts a–i on the right. Note the use of time links, *until, after* and *when*.

1 After he had spent the night in the cells
2 As soon as his lawyer had spoken to the police
3 In court, his girlfriend told a story that
4 She said that the accused had been with her
5 It had seemed he would be found innocent
6 But just before the case ended
7 She now knew, she said angrily, that
8 Once the jury had heard this evidence
9 When they had given their verdict

a they quickly decided he was guilty.
b until the trial was nearly over.
c the ring he had given her was stolen.
d she had decided to help the prosecution.
e the judge jailed him for five years.
f he was woken up early and charged with theft.
g until after the crime took place.
h they released him on bail and he went home.
i she had prepared with him before the trial.

3 To say that one thing happened immediately after another we can also use these forms:

The offices had <u>hardly</u> closed <u>when</u> the robbery happened.
The staff had <u>no sooner</u> left <u>than</u> the gang struck.
The lights had <u>hardly</u> gone out <u>before</u> three of them broke in.

Which tenses are used, and in which order?

Rewrite the following sentences using each of these forms at least once.

1 Security cameras had started filming them as soon as they broke in.
2 The alarm went off just when they'd opened the safe.
3 They had to escape once they'd taken some of the money.
4 Just after their getaway car had gone round the corner the police arrived.

4 When we use time links we don't always have to use the past perfect, for example when the order of events is obvious, or one action is the immediate result of another:

After he opened the safe he took out the money.
When the security guard appeared, they ran away.

We also sometimes use *after that, then* or *afterwards* before the second action:

They stole a valuable painting. <u>After that</u> they left the country.
She identified the mugger. <u>Afterwards</u> he was arrested for robbery with violence.

Complete the following using the past simple.

1 After the driver lost control of the stolen car, it ....
2 The suspect's picture was shown on TV. Afterwards ....
3 When the hijackers started shooting, the police ....
4 Two youths on a motorbike stole her handbag. Then ....
5 There was very little crime here until drug dealers ....
6 A burglar was given ten years in prison. After that ....

5 Work in pairs. Imagine there was a bank robbery in your town yesterday. Think of as many things as you can that the robbers had done in preparation. Decide what you are going to say. Use the past perfect and past perfect continuous and time links. Tell your story to another pair. Begin like this:

'Before they robbed the bank they had been staying ...'

No litter Penalty £50

Anyone found defacing these walls will be prosecuted

Persons under the age of 18 will not be served alcohol

Passengers travelling without a valid ticket face a fine and possible imprisonment

Nobody under the age of 18 will be admitted to see this film

It is an offence to use a bicycle after dark without front and rear lights

1 Work in groups. These signs refer to things that are against the law in Britain. For each one explain the meaning and say whether there is a similar law in your country.

2 In Listening Part 3 you quickly have to form a picture of each situation in your mind, and sometimes the questions can help you do this. Look for a few moments at A–F below and decide where each incident probably took place.

3 Follow the exam instructions. Listen out for clues to the places where you think A–F happened.

You will hear five people talking about occasions when they broke the law. For Questions 1–5, choose which of A–F each speaker is talking about. Use the letters only once. There is one extra letter which you do not need to use.

A selling tickets for an adult film to people under 18

B travelling on public transport without a ticket   Speaker 1   [ ] 1

C cycling at night without lights   Speaker 2   [ ] 2

D dropping rubbish in a public place   Speaker 3   [ ] 3

E spraying graffiti on walls   Speaker 4   [ ] 4

F serving alcoholic drinks to people under 18   Speaker 5   [ ] 5

4 Can you defend the actions of the people interviewed? What do you think the police should do in each case?

SPEAKING

Look at the picture. She has been arrested for something she did not do. Think of a crime she might be accused of and imagine what might have happened. Then tell your partner a short story that includes some or all of the following:

- where and when it happened
- the events leading up to her arrest
- who and what sort of person she is
- the arrest itself and what happened then
- anyone else who was involved
- how she felt then and now
- her relationship with them
- what she can do about the situation

WRITING: a narrative

1 In Writing Part 2 there is sometimes a short story question (narrative). The instructions may make it clear whether you need to write in the first or the third person. There will also be a title, or some words that you have to use. These words might have to begin the story, or end it.

Look at Question 4 on page 162 for an example of how to answer this type of exam task. Then look at these notes on how to write a First Certificate narrative and use them to write one complete sentence for each set (1–10). You can add words and change the form of the words in the notes, but do not add any extra information. The first one has been done as an example.

1 Use words given or make sure content relevant title.
   Use the words given or make sure the content is relevant to the title.
2 Attract attention – make him / her want read on.
3 Say where when, give background info past continuous.
4 Describe main characters & relationships each other.
5 Paragraph each main part story – events logical sequence.
6 Some direct speech – bring characters life, create variety.
7 Perfect & past events – join time links.
8 Not too many events: max. no. words 180!
9 End explanation, mystery or surprise reader.
10 Check – esp. narrative tenses, one mistake → others.

2 Look at the exam instructions and note down your answers to these questions: Who are you writing for? Why? What do you have to write? Do you need to write in the 1st or the 3rd person? Where do the words given have to go? Do not write your story yet.

You have decided to enter a short story competition set by an international English-language magazine. The competition rules say that the story must begin like this: *There I was, alone in my cell – and it was all so unfair.* Write your **story** for the competition in **120–180** words.

---

3 Ask yourself these eight questions and make a note of your answers.

* Is your story going to be fact or fiction?
* Were you in your own country or abroad?
* Were you in a police cell awaiting trial, or in prison as a convict?
* What sentence had you received or did you expect to receive?
* Were you the victim of an unfair law or a false accusation?
* Did other people know where you were? Could they help you?
* How did you feel in your cell?
* Will your story have a happy or a sad ending? How will it finish?

4 Look back at the Reading text on page 89.

1 Put these stages of the story in the order the writer tells them:
a Plans
b Action part one
c Action part two
d Success
e Something goes wrong
f Caught
g Current situation
h Explanation

2 Decide on the stages your story will have. The Reading text is longer than an FCE composition, but you could use some similar stages.

3 Now decide in what order you will put the stages in your story. You may want to include a flashback. To give your story a happy ending, you could finish with a stage that has the idea of 'Success', 'Freedom' or 'Home', for example.

4 Write your story using your notes.

VOCABULARY: transport

1. In pairs, make a list of at least ten common ways of travelling, e.g. *bus*.

2. Which of these adjectives do you associate with each form of transport you mentioned?

> cheap   warm   healthy   convenient   safe   reliable   comfortable
> fast   relaxing   exciting   sociable   environment-friendly   flexible

What are the opposites of these adjectives? Which forms of transport would you apply them to?

3. Which forms of transport do you associate these words with?

> cabin staff   service station   gridlock   terminal   boarding card

4. Put these expressions into two groups: those which can be used as adjectives to mean 'cheap' and those that mean 'expensive'.

> cut-price   full-fare   economy   budget   full-price   dear   bargain

COMMON ERRORS

We left our bikes and continued by foot. What is wrong with this sentence? Why? See the Grammar Reference on page 178.

LISTENING

1. Sometimes when you want to fly somewhere you can choose between an ordinary (often expensive) ticket from one of the big national airlines and a much cheaper one from a smaller company. What differences would you expect in what you get for your money?

2. Follow these Listening Part 4 exam instructions.

You will hear part of a consumer programme about the prices different airlines charge. For Questions 1–7, choose the best answer, **A**, **B** or **C**.

1 When did he pay for his first flight?
   A Before he went to the airport.
   B In the airport.
   C On the plane. `[1]`

2 He wanted to sit by the emergency exit because
   A he is afraid of flying.
   B he is tall.
   C he had a lot of hand luggage. `[2]`

3 What does he say about the staff on the first flight?
   A They were very helpful.
   B They kept giving him things he did not want.
   C There were fewer of them than on other flights. `[3]`

4 The passengers arrived in the airport terminal
   A before their luggage.
   B at the same time as their luggage.
   C after their luggage. `[4]`

5 On the way back, he went on
   A the flight he had intended to catch.
   B a later flight on the same day.
   C a flight on the following Wednesday. `[5]`

6 He says that on this flight
   A there was more space.
   B the food was excellent.
   C the drinks were horrible. `[6]`

7 What happened after he left the airport?
   A He went for a cup of tea.
   B He drove his car to London.
   C He was held up by traffic. `[7]`

3. Listen again. How many examples of the past perfect are there?

SPEAKING

1 In Speaking Part 4, the examiner asks you questions about things connected with the topic of Part 3. For example, if the topic is 'Transport', he or she might ask:

a   Could you tell me how you got here?
b   Which way of travelling do you like best?
c   Is traffic pollution something that you are concerned about?
d   What's the most interesting journey you've ever made? What happened?

You will also be talking to the other candidate. One way to keep the conversation going is by asking questions that require full answers (not just *Yes / No*), but you must form them correctly.

Look at these four rules and find an example of each in sentences a–d above:

1   If *what*, *which* or *who* is the object of the sentence, use an auxiliary verb.
2   If *what*, *which* or *who* is the subject of the sentence, don't use *do*, *did*, etc.
3   An indirect (and therefore more polite) question, which begins with a phrase like *Can you explain to me …* , has the same word order as a statement.
4   When we are speaking, we usually put any preposition at the end of the question.

2 These questions can be used to encourage your partner to speak or ask for repetition, but some of them contain a mistake. Find the errors and correct them.

1   What you feel about this?
2   Do you think could you say that again?
3   On which of them are you keen?
4   What would you do in that situation?
5   Can you tell me what do you think?
6   Sorry, what did you said?

3 In pairs, discuss Questions a–d in activity 1 above, also using questions like those in activity 2.

4 Although you will not have to tell a complete story in the oral section of the exam, you may find it useful to be able to talk about past events in Speaking Part 1 or Part 4.

1   Work in pairs. Choose one of the four pictures and imagine that when you were travelling you were faced with this scene. Tell your partner what had happened before you got there and what you did afterwards.

2   Listen to your partner and ask questions.

3   Choose another picture each and repeat.

PHRASAL VERBS: *take*

1 *I was sitting on the plane, which was ready to take off.*
All the fussing about seems to take up so much time.

What do the underlined verbs mean in these extracts from the Listening text?

What do they mean in the two sentences below? Use the other verb in each sentence as a clue. In which do the two verbs mean the same and in which are they opposites?

After she had removed her wet coat, she took off her muddy boots.
He stopped playing football in his early thirties and took up golf instead.

2 Work out the meaning of each of the underlined verbs in 1–10 by using the clues *in italics*:

1   She *looked just like* her mother, and her daughter took after her, too.
2   *Nobody else wanted to do* the job but she took it on as soon as they suggested it.
3   The rail company, which had been *reducing its workforce*, started to take on new staff.
4   He'd *only just suggested* changing everything so I *needed some time* to take it all in.
5   I'd no sooner *bought it* than it *stopped working*, so I took it straight back to the shop.
6   She found her English classmates more *reserved*, but she soon started to take to them.
7   As soon as they had *bought the* road haulage *firm* they took over all its operations.
8   Once they had *added up* the income, they took away the total costs to *calculate* the profit.
9   It was such a good geography lesson that they took down nearly *every word the teacher said*.
10 When he was arrested for *fraud* it was clear that he had taken many honest people in.

3 Write sentences with as many of the phrasal verbs in 1 and 2 as you can. Use one verb in the past perfect and another in the simple past, as in these examples:

After the plane had taken off, we all relaxed.
Once she had taken on the job, she found it easy.

USE OF ENGLISH: open cloze

1 In Use of English Part 2, there may be more than one possible answer (although only one possible mark!) for some gaps. This happens when words mean the same (*anyone / anybody*) or are very similar (*get / become*), but it can also occur with quite different words because of the context.

1   Look at this extract from a Part 2 text. Which words could we put in the gap?
She remembered she had taken the train there (1) .... a girl.

2   Reference words like *this* and *it* are often tested, and there may be a choice between *this* and *that*, *these* and *those*, or between one of them and *the*, *it* or *they*. Which are possible here?
There was pollution, noise and ugliness. It had all (2) .... features of an industrial town.

When you realize there are alternative answers, the important thing is not to waste time trying to choose between them.

2 Look at the text below.

1   Read the title and write down six words you expect to see, for example: *sand*.

2   Follow these exam instructions:

For Questions **1–15**, read the text and think of the word which best fits each space. Use only **one** word in each space. There is an example at the beginning **(0)**.

◀ **HELP**

The questions where more than one answer is possible are marked with an asterisk (*).

Across the Western Desert of Egypt

The train took me to Mersa Matruh on the Mediterranean from where I began my journey to the Nile valley near Luxor. **(0)*** *This/It* is one of the most arid regions on earth – there are places that have not seen rain **(1)** .... 40 years – but the landscape is fantastic. Dunes **(2)** .... to heights of 500 feet and there are sands of **(3)** .... imaginable colour, amazing sunsets and grotesque rock formations. You get giant rocks on stalks that look **(4)** .... 60 foot-high mushrooms **(5)*** .... the bases have been worn away by sandstorms. It is like walking **(6)** .... the surface of Mars.

You might go for days **(7)** .... seeing anybody, then you will come to an oasis, such as Siwa, **(8)** .... there are 250,000 palm trees and a couple of villages. When you've been for **(9)*** .... long without seeing a tree or blade of grass everything seems so intense – the colour, the smell of water, the presence of people. I woke one morning **(10)** .... see the sky black with thousands of flamingos migrating north; it is at moments **(11)** .... as this that you feel an intense connection with nature.

After completing the first stage by jeep, I travelled with a Bedouin companion and five camels for the remainder of the journey. The **(12)*** .... difficult part of the trip was crossing the Great Sand Sea where you can sink up to your thighs **(13)** .... the soft sand. We lost two of the camels there. During the trip we lived **(14)** .... a diet of tinned sardines, onions and bread, **(15)*** .... we baked in the sand. By the end, all I wanted to do was relax on a slow boat back to Cairo.

In Unit 6 you thought about the kinds of mistake, such as verb forms and spelling, that you often make in your written work. Now you should also think about <u>why</u> you make them.

1   Look at these four reasons (A, B, C and D) and then match explanations 1–4 to each one.
    A slips of the pen   B carelessness   C trying out new language   D lack of knowledge

    1   These are errors you make because you don't know the correct grammar, word or spelling.
    2   These mistakes happen when you write quickly. You might make them in your first language, too.
    3   You know the rule but you still make these mistakes – as your teacher often reminds you.
    4   Experimenting is part of the learning process, so these mistakes can help you (but not in the exam!).

2   Here are eight typical mistakes. Correct them and in each case say what the reason would be (A, B, C or D) if <u>you</u> made this mistake.

    1   Look! It snows!   5   He went by plane for to get there faster.
    2   They hav taken a different route.   6   He no sooner got on the horse than he fell off.
    3   I enjoy to drive a truck for a living.   7   The ship is thought to had sunk last night.
    4   Phone me when you will arrive.   8   I saw the two woman on the ferry.

3   Look at your list of your six most common mistakes (from Unit 6). For each one, decide what the reason is and how you will avoid making that mistake again.

STUDY CHECK

1   Make brief notes and tell your partner a short story involving as many different forms of transport as possible. It can be real, made up or taken from a book, TV programme or film.

2   Think about your progress in English before you started preparing for First Certificate. Tell your partner what you'd learned by the time you began the FCE course. Mention which schools you'd attended, which books you'd used and what activities you'd enjoyed most.

3   Follow the exam instructions and the advice below.

You have been asked to write a story for an English-language student magazine beginning with these words:
It was the first time he had ever had to go to the police for help.
Write your **story** in **120–180** words.

- Answer the questions in activity 2 on page 93.
- Decide the stages your story will have, and their order.
- Write your story, making sure what you write follows the instructions exactly.
- When you have finished, check for your six most common errors.
- Give your story to your partner to read and check for mistakes.
- Correct them and decide which category above (A, B, C or D) each mistake is in.

UNIT

SPEAKING

1 Work in groups. Look at the photos. What do you think about their clothes, hairstyles, etc? Make a list of clothes, accessories and so on that are currently fashionable among young people in your country. Now think of things that are fashionable among people of your parents' generation.

2 Work in pairs.

1 Decide who will talk about the two women (Student A) and who will discuss the two men (Student B). Think about what you are going to say, especially the similarities and differences in appearance between the people in your picture. Concentrate not only on clothes but also on hairstyle, make-up (if any) and accessories. Remember to use the present continuous, for example:
The woman on the left is wearing … , while the other one is …

2 **Student A**: Compare and contrast your pictures.
3 **Student B**: Look at A's pictures. Say who looks more fashionable.
4 **Student B**: Compare and contrast your pictures.
5 **Student A**: Look at B's pictures. Say who looks more fashionable.

3 What happens if older people try to look and behave like younger people? Can you think of any examples in films or on TV?

READING: multiple choice

1 Look quickly through the text and note down all the items of clothing that are mentioned, together with their adjectives. Which do you associate with:
a young people?
b older people?

2 Sometimes one or more of the multiple-choice questions in Part 2 focus on the meaning of individual phrases or words. This is not a vocabulary test. It is a chance for you to show your ability to work out the meaning of the words by using their context. Study the exam instructions, read the text and then look at the first question, which has been done as an example.

You are going to read a magazine article about parents who try to look like teenagers. For Questions **1–7**, choose the answer (**A**, **B**, **C** or **D**) which you think fits best according to the text.

PARENTS BEHAVING BADLY

They are every young person's nightmare, and they're on the increase. They wear expensive trainers and tiny shorts, knee-length black boots with pink mini-skirts, or tight jeans with T-shirts that are a couple of sizes too small. They never stop talking about 5 MTV, youth TV and all the latest films for the under-20s. They own huge collections of pop CDs, listen to boy bands on their Walkman and have tattoos of their favourite groups. Nothing very strange, then, but there is something a bit odd about these people: nearly all of them are over 40. They're part of that growing social 10 phenomenon – parents who behave like teenagers.

Many teenagers find their parents embarrassing enough when they are just acting normally, without having to put up with them wearing hair extensions, nose rings and tongue studs, squeezing into clothes designed for 16-year-olds and collecting them from 15 school with last month's hits blasting out from the car stereo. Worse still, whenever there is talk of an earlier decade coming back into fashion, out come the high-heeled shoes, the patterned tights and the narrow skirts; or the faded denim, the slim-fit shirts and the striped jackets. It doesn't matter that the clothes no longer 20 fit, the perfume is too young and make-up too heavy. It's time to head down to the disco and remind the world what style really is.

The most important thing, of course, is to ensure that newly-teenage parents are kept well away from the young person's friends and – even more importantly – enemies. There are few 30 sources of gossip as rich as badly-behaved mothers or fathers, so all risk of contact between the generations must be avoided. Especially at parties. Don't ever let parents set foot in a house where a teenage party's being held. They are quite likely to say enough embarrassing things to keep the whole place laughing for 35 hours, and the slightest possibility of them staying to have 'just one dance' is too awful even to imagine.

The best thing with parents like these is to take them to one side for a quiet word, explaining that if they behave exactly like teenagers it is impossible for their children to rebel against grown-40 ups. Reasonable mothers and fathers should understand that this just isn't fair. Unreasonable ones may need more convincing, and might need to be advised a little more forcefully that they would look and feel a whole lot better in a nice woollen suit or cotton blouse rather than the leather and the fur, the nylon and the plastic. 45 And that nothing sounds worse than out-of-date slang.

If all else fails, and if they really do insist on being born-again teens of whatever generation, the only solution may be to tell them you accept the situation, and hope that they too will accept your decision if you decide to change your name and disown your 50 family. And move to another country a very long way away.

1 What does the writer mean by the phrase 'Nothing very strange, then' in line 7?
- **A** Young people who do these things are very unusual.
- **B** Lots of young people do these things.
- **C** Young people never do these things.
- **D** Many young people dream about doing these things.

Answer: B. Clues: *Nothing very strange* refers back to all the things listed before, so the whole phrase means 'It is not unusual to do these things'. The next part of the sentence – *but there is something a bit odd* – is clearly a contrast, and as *odd* means 'strange' it confirms the meaning of the phrase in the question.

Look quickly at Questions 2–7. Which of them are lexical reference questions?

2 It is becoming more common to see
- **A** young people wearing both modern and old styles.
- **B** young people wearing old styles.
- **C** parents wearing only modern styles.
- **D** parents wearing both modern and old styles.

3 Who minds if parents have outgrown their clothes?
- **A** Their children.
- **B** The parents themselves.
- **C** The parents' friends.
- **D** Nobody.

4 According to the writer, the main aim should be to prevent parents from
- **A** making enemies.
- **B** meeting teenagers' friends.
- **C** meeting other parents.
- **D** going to discotheques.

5 What does 'take them to one side for a quiet word' mean in line 37?
- **A** give them some advice in private
- **B** teach them some up-to-date slang
- **C** tell them not to speak to other teenagers
- **D** argue about it with them in public

6 Teenagers may have to tell their parents to dress in different
- **A** sizes.
- **B** colours.
- **C** materials.
- **D** patterns.

7 What is meant by the expression 'If all else fails' in line 46?
- **A** If no one wants to help you
- **B** If you've tried every other possibility
- **C** If you don't want to say anything
- **D** If other people have tried unsuccessfully

GRAMMAR: the passive

1 Look at this example from the Reading text:
... newly-teenage parents <u>are kept</u> well away from the young person's friends ...

How is the underlined verb formed here? Why is there no 'agent' such as *the young person*?

Which of **a**, **b**, **c** or **d** is the most likely reason why *keep* is in the passive?

a Because the sentence is rather formal.
b Because we don't know (or don't care), who or what does something, or it is obvious from the context.
c Because we don't want to say who or what is responsible for something.
d Because we want to put particular information at either the beginning or the end of the sentence.

Underline the passive form in these sentences and say which of a–d above is the reason why it is used.

1 I'm sorry, Jane, but I think that old dress of yours has been thrown out.
2 Customers are politely requested to refrain from handling the garments.
3 That beautiful dress was designed by Versace.
4 Colours that clash shouldn't be worn together.

2 Fill in the passive forms of the sentences below, using an agent if necessary. In each case, decide with your partner why the passive has been used: is it reason **a**, **b**, **c** or **d**?

1 Present simple:
People everywhere wear blue jeans.
Blue jeans are worn everywhere   Reason: b

2 Present continuous:
They're planning a new look for next season.

....

3 Present perfect:
We have received your application for employment with this firm.

....

4 Past simple:
I'm afraid I took the wrong measurements.

....

5 Past (*used to*):
They used to make clothes in places like Manchester.

....

6 Future simple:
The fast-growing fashion industry will create many new jobs.

....

7 Future (*going to*):
Nobody's going to notice that tiny little mark.

....

8 Past continuous:
They were considering the matter when the incident occurred.

....

9 Past perfect:
People had known about the health risks for years.

....

10 Modal verbs:
A top model might wear McQueen's new creations.

....

Now check your sentences in the Grammar Reference on page 178.

3 Use the passive form of the verb in brackets to complete these sentences. Use each of the forms from activity 2 once only, underlining the time expression that indicates which tense to use. The first one has been done as an example.

1 A new design ....*is being discussed*........ at the <u>moment</u>. (discuss)

2 The press were at <u>yesterday's</u> fashion show, but no photos .... (take)

3 We are determined that safer materials .... in <u>future</u>. (use)

4 It's still not certain, but your dress .... <u>later today</u>. (might finish)

5 Visitors .... not to touch anything <u>at any time</u>. (ask)

6 We've known <u>for ages</u> that the shop .... <u>next year</u>. (close down)

7 Three more shops .... since they started selling designer goods in 1997. (open)

8 The theft happened <u>while</u> the necklace .... to the public. (show)

9 It was a brilliant idea, but <u>by then</u> all the money .... (spend)

10 In those days, clothes used .... by women working at home. (make)

4 Complete the second sentence so that it has a similar meaning to the first sentence, using the word given. **Do not change the word given.** You must use between two and five words, including the word given. In this activity all the answers require the use of the passive.

COMMON ERRORS

People should be let do what they want.
What is wrong with this sentence? Why?
See the Grammar Reference on page 179.

1 You can buy swimwear over there.
bought
Swimwear .... over there.

2 Nobody told us anything about the incident.
were
We .... about the incident.

3 They are building an even longer catwalk there.
   is
   An even longer catwalk .... there.

4 We will not refund money on sales items.
   refunded
   Money .... on sales items.

5 The manufacturers had promised better material.
   been
   Better material .... by the manufacturers.

6 The new trend is going to excite people.
   excited
   People .... by the new trend.

7 Poor quality has caused most of the complaints.
   by
   Most of the complaints .... poor quality.

8 It happened while they were showing off their collection.
   was
   It happened while .... off.

5 Look at the diagram showing how an item of high fashion is created. Describe the process using passive forms of verbs such as these:

| measure draw cut sew stitch fit shorten |
| lengthen widen adjust try on |

Use linking words like *first, next, then, before, for example, after, once* and *finally*.

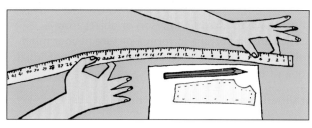

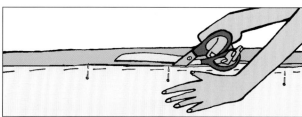

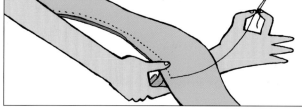

1 Look at these passive questions and answer them using the active form of *bring* plus the adverb particle in capitals, as in the example. The best way to do this activity is to:

a look at the passive verb for the meaning of the phrasal verb.

b note what tense is used in the passive sentence and use the same in the active.

c make any other changes that are needed.

FIRST CERTIFICATE FACTS

Questions that test your knowledge of phrasal verbs are common in FCE Use of English, particularly in Parts 1, 2 and 3.

1 How was he revived after he fainted?   ROUND
   A sip of brandy *brought him round.*

2 Do you know how that situation was caused?   ABOUT
   Yes, a mistake ....

3 Is the subject of pay going to be mentioned?   UP
   Yes, we .... later on.

4 Can the time for the photo shoot be changed?   FORWARD
   Yes, we .... to the early afternoon.

5 Is it likely that such a failure will be turned into a success?   OFF
   Yes, I think they .... somehow.

6 Is it true that as a child she was looked after by an aunt?   UP
   No, her grandmother ....

7 Are you sure the suit will be returned tomorrow?   BACK
   Yes, my husband .... first thing in the morning.

8 Wasn't a new system introduced here last year?   IN
   Yes, they .... after the report came out.

9 When is her biography being published?   OUT
   They .... in the New Year.

10 Weren't you reminded of some good times by that photo?   BACK
   Yes, it .... a lot of memories.

2 Now rewrite your answers to 1–10 using the phrasal verb in the passive.
Example: *He was brought round by a sip of brandy.*

VOCABULARY: describing appearance

These expressions all describe aspects of people's appearance. Which do you like and which don't you like? Put *yes* or *no* next to each. In some cases you may want to put different answers for men and women, or boys and girls.

slim   well-built   overweight   skinny   pale   dark   dark-haired
fair-haired   blonde   plain   smartly-dressed   casually-dressed

Now compare your answers with your partner.

Look at this group of people. Choose one of them and, without saying who it is, describe this person to your partner. He or she must guess who you are talking about. When you use opinion adjectives like *good-looking*, say why you think so. You can also make the adjectives a lot stronger by using words like *really*, *very* and *extremely*, or a little stronger by using expressions such as *rather*, *quite* or *fairly*.

Examples:
'He's quite slim' – this means he is slimmer than average but not *very* slim.
'She's rather pale' – this means paler than average (which you don't think is good).

LISTENING

In some questions in Listening Part 1 you have to identify a person or object from a description. With this kind of task it is particularly important to form a picture in your mind of the situation and the speaker(s). You should also be careful not to be misled by individual words on the recording that are also in one of the options.

Follow the exam instructions. In all eight situations you will hear descriptions.

You will hear people talking in eight different situations. For Questions **1–8**, choose the best answer, **A**, **B** or **C**.

1   You hear this description on the radio. Who is speaking?
   A a newsreader   **B** a policeman   **C** a witness   [1]

2   You hear a girl talking to a friend about clothes. What is she describing?
   A a pair of trousers   **B** a skirt   **C** a pair of shorts   [2]

3   You hear a commercial on the radio. What is it advertising?
   A an umbrella   **B** a handbag   **C** a raincoat   [3]

4   You hear this woman talking to a friend. What is her job?
   A nurse   **B** policewoman   **C** soldier   [4]

5   You're in a shop when you hear these two men talking. What are they looking at?
   A a pair of jeans   **B** a pair of gloves   **C** a pair of shoes   [5]

6   You hear one girl speaking to another. What is she talking about?
   A clothes   **B** hair   **C** make-up   [6]

7   You hear this woman talking to a group of people. What is her job?
   A She is a photographer. **B** She is a painter.   **C** She is a make-up artist.   [7]

8   You hear a woman talking on the phone to a man. Who is she?
   A someone he has never met   **B** someone he has met once   **C** someone he knows well   [8]

2 Write a brief description of yourself on a piece of paper without your name on it. Include the same details as the speaker in Question 8: height, build, hair, eyes, complexion, what you are wearing and anything you often carry. Give the piece of paper to your teacher, who will give you another in return. Try to identify the person in the classroom from the description.

WRITING: describing a person

1 In Writing Part 2 you might need to describe somebody's appearance as part of a story, a report, an application or an article. Look at the instructions for this exam question and decide what two things you have to do:

> Your teacher has asked you to write about how somebody's appearance affected you in some way. Describe this person and explain briefly what happened. Write your **story** in **120–180** words in an appropriate style.

2 With your partner, look at this student's answer.
1 Find ten mistakes and correct them.
2 Decide which parts of the text match the two parts of the question.

He was an attractive young man, six feet high and well built. He had a dark complexion and a lovely thick black hair. His features were regular, his nose was straight and his tooth were white, and when he gave that warm friendly smile there was a twinkle in his eye. His clothes were casual but smart, and they always seemed to match him well. His favourite dresses were a white short-sleeved shirt with a light blue trousers and he usually carried expensive white trainers.

We had been going out together for a while and everything seemed fine between us. I knew that he was so good-looking that some people was jealous, but I didn't care about because I was mad about him and I was sure he wouldn't even look at anyone else. Or so I thought. One day I found out that he was also dating my best friend. I was very, very upset and I also lost two very special people from my life.

Ever since then I am more interested in people's personalities than their appearance.

3 Here are some suggestions for the descriptive part of writing tasks. Which of them has the writer of this text followed?
- Describe the main details and the impression they create.
- Mention anything unusual or significant about the person or the person's clothing.
- Show how aspects of the person's appearance reflect his or her character.
- Vary the adjectives so that you do not use *nice* and *good* (or *bad*!) all the time.
- Where you can, use more than one adjective, for example: *warm brown eyes*.
- Decide whether you need to use past or present tenses to describe the person, and be consistent.
- Choose an appropriate writing style – informal, neutral or whatever – and stick to it.

4 Plan and write your composition. Here is some advice:
- Consider various ways of doing this task. Alternatives include writing about someone famous whose style has influenced you, or describing a friend or relative whose appearance you admire.
- Make notes under two headings, one for each part of the task.
- Use expressions from Vocabulary.
- In the narrative part of the task, use a variety of verb tenses – as in the sample answer above.
- Be careful not to make any of the mistakes you corrected in activity 2.
- When you have finished, check for errors – especially your most common ones – and think about why you made them.

1 Look at these words and phrases and decide whether you associate each one with:

a a small shop   b a supermarket   c a department store

shop assistant 4th floor trolley till counter checkout try on basket guarantee
shopkeeper   receipt   special offer   own-brand   5p off bargain   January sales aisle

2 Statements 1–6 are about shopping in Britain. In pairs, compare each one with shopping in your country by writing *the same* or *different* plus a short description of any differences.

Britain	Your country
1 Most small shops open at 9 am and close at 5.30 pm.	....
2 Most supermarkets stay open until later, or even all night.	....
3 A lot of people drive to big out-of-town supermarkets.	....
4 Many of them do all their weekly shopping there.	....
5 Most young people choose their own clothes.	....
6 Shopping centres are often meeting places for teenagers.	....

EXAM STUDY GUIDE

1 To pass FCE, you need a certain level of vocabulary. Except in Papers 1 and 4, where sometimes you use clues to work out the meaning of difficult words, you do not need to understand words above that level to answer questions. In pairs, look at these groups of words. Which word is:

a   elementary?   b   about FCE level?   c   above FCE level?

1 expenditure, payment, cost
2 buy, acquire, purchase
3 earnings, money, remuneration
4 impoverished, poor, bankrupt
5 affluent, wealthy, rich
6 expensive, uneconomical, extortionate

Remember, though, that you can use words of any level you like when you speak or write.

2 Which of these ways of learning words have you found useful? Which would you like to try?

1 listening to and repeating new words
2 writing lists of words as they come up
3 noting words and their translations
4 writing the words in example sentences
5 writing each new word several times
6 learning words by topic, e.g. types of shops
7 word building, e.g. *assist, assistant, unassisted*
8 recording the words in sentences on cassette

LISTENING

1 While some Part 2 question papers ask you to fill in gaps or complete statements, others ask you direct questions. In these, *What*, *Who* or another question word at the beginning tells you the kind of information you need to listen out for. Follow these exam instructions:

You will hear part of a radio programme about shopping. For Questions **1–10**, answer the questions.

1	What was Dr Walsh buying when he first became angry?	*customer service (meat counter)* **1**
2	When will there be more cakes on sale?	*next morning* **2**
3	Who is afraid of him?	*Manager → staff* **3**
4	Who laughed at him?	*Check out girl* **4**
5	Where did he force some shops to close?	*US* **5**
6	How does he feel about the people who lost their jobs?	*He doesn't care* **6**
7	What does he like at his local supermarket?	*Cherries pies* **7**
8	How often does he go shopping abroad?	*twice a month* **8**
9	Who, according to Dr Walsh, never complain?	*British* **9**
10	What angers him most about some of the products on sale?	*Over priced products* **10**

2 Have you ever complained about the service in a shop, or taken something back? What happened? Is there anything you wish you had returned, or complained about?

SPEAKING

1. Read what the manager of the supermarket said about Dr Walsh.

'Perhaps his is not simply a vendetta against our store. Perhaps it's a vendetta against all supermarkets – perhaps it's a vendetta against the whole world. I just feel sorry for the staff, though. We have had a couple of girls leave because of Dr Walsh. OK, maybe we get things wrong sometimes, but we are the first to admit a mistake and put things right. However, when someone is complaining for the sake of complaining, it's dreadful for the staff, whose life is stressful enough anyway.'

In groups, decide who you sympathize with more: the manager or the 'Consumer Crusader'.

2. Follow these instructions for Speaking Part 3 and the advice which follows:

Imagine that you are going to spend Saturday morning shopping in this town centre. Look at the shopping list and talk to each other about where you will buy everything and in what order you will go to the shops. Decide how you will avoid both too much walking and too much carrying.

5 kilos potatoes	floppy disks
brown loaf	2 tins beans
newspaper	dictionary
3 kilos oranges	packet aspirin
new CD single	bunch roses

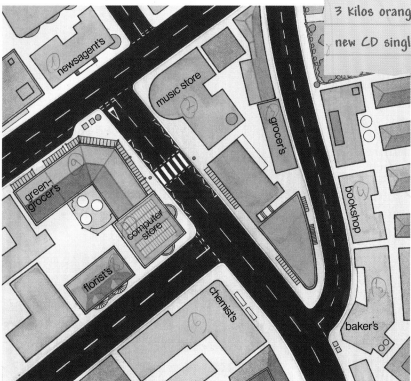

- Make sure you know exactly what you have to do. If in doubt, ask your teacher.
- Think about the items and shops. In your mind, match them. Which shop will sell two of the items?
- You may decide to leave buying the biggest or heaviest items until last.
- To begin, ask your partner a question such as 'Where shall we start?'
- Use linking expressions from activity 5 on page 101.
- Make suggestions like 'Why don't we ...?', 'Let's ...' and 'How about ...-ing ...?'
- Remember the shopping list is in note form, so add articles and prepositions: *a bunch of roses*.
- Work together with your partner – don't argue. Take turns: possibly one shop each at a time.

3. You have now arrived home and are looking at the things you have bought. Unfortunately, you will have to take four of the items back to the shops: for example the CD is damaged. Decide with your partner what is wrong with each item, what you will say to each of the shopkeepers or managers, what they might reply and what you will threaten to do if you do not get what you want.

VOCABULARY:
facilities and services

1 Decide where you would go if you needed:

1   a stamp for a letter
2   emergency treatment for an injury
3   to have your car repaired
4   a map of the city centre
5   to find work
6   to report a robbery
7   to cash a cheque
8   a room for the night
9   to borrow a book

Which of the following would you associate with each of 1–9?

routine maintenance	the reference section
packages and parcels	a sightseeing guide
a witness statement	receptionist and porters
an application form	a current account
the health service	

2 Work in pairs. Ask where your partner would go if he or she felt like:

1   having a quick snack
    Example: *fast-food restaurant*
2   going for a drink
3   seeing the latest film
4   trying a variety of sports
5   dancing
6   getting a new hairstyle
7   looking at some paintings
8   going for a swim in winter

GRAMMAR:
the gerund/-ing form of the verb

1 *Where would you go if you felt like having a quick snack?*

The -ing form of the verb is used here because it follows a preposition, in this case *like*.

Study uses 1–5 of -ing and fill in the gaps in the examples with a suitable word.

1   As part of a continuous form of a verb: The bank clerk was .... a dark suit.
2   As an adjective: It was an .... experience to spend the day with the firefighters.
3   As a noun and subject: .... is my favourite way of spending Saturday mornings.
4   As a noun and object: One of the council's responsibilities is .... the grass in the park.
5   After certain verbs: After I had finished .... my homework, I watched TV.

2 Fill in the gaps in sentences 1–10 by using the -ing form of these verbs once only. There is an extra verb that you do not need to use.

skate	bore	lie	contact	dial	drink
hire	collect	advise	spend	go	

1   By the time the care workers found him, he had been .... on the floor for days.
2   You really can't put off .... to see the dentist any longer.
3   How about .... a couple of mountain bikes for the weekend?
4   Sometimes I really enjoy .... an hour sitting in the gardens next to the ponds.
5   .... is only one of the activities catered for by the local leisure services department.
6   A solicitor's job consists of .... people about the law and representing them in court.
7   Among the essential services is .... rubbish and disposing of it.
8   Some say accountancy is .... , but many accountants enjoy their work.
9   It's not worth .... the water company over a tiny leak like that: fix it yourself.
10 Before .... the number, check that you have inserted your phone card.

3 Finish these sentences using a gerund and other words.

1   Working as a postman or postwoman involves ....
2   When I get on a bus I usually try to avoid ....
3   He was sent to prison, even though he denied ....
4   A specialist in hypnosis helped her give up ....
5   Although my ring was insured, I didn't want to risk ....
6   To improve my fluency in English I need to practise ....
7   It was a lovely sunny spring day, so I suggested ....
8   I know it's very fattening, but I'm afraid I just can't help ....
9   When the police found the money, the security guard admitted ....
10 Visiting New York for a few days is great, but I can't imagine ....

COMMON ERRORS

I'm looking forward to see you soon.
What is wrong with this sentence? Why?
See the Grammar Reference on page 179.

4 Think about the meanings of these verbs: what do they have in common? Which of them usually refer to the future? Which is normally used about the past?

like	love	enjoy	hate	can't stand	mind
dislike	detest	regret	can't bear	fancy	
adore	dread	look forward to			

Write down three things you like or love doing, and three things you hate or can't stand doing. Add three things you wouldn't mind doing, one thing you dread doing and something you regret doing. When you have finished, discuss your list with your partner.

USE OF ENGLISH: error correction

1 Look back at the Use of English activity on page 75 in Unit 7. Now read these suggestions for doing Use of English Part 4. In each case, put DO or DON'T at the beginning of the sentence.

1   ..DO.. read the whole text first in order to understand the overall meaning.

2   .... read the example lines (0 and 00), as these often introduce the topic.

3   .... look for more than one mistake per line.

4   .... study the lines above and below each line to check the context.

5   .... expect at least three of the lines to be correct.

6   .... expect more than five of the lines to be correct.

7   .... replace or alter any words that seem to be wrong.

8   .... read through the text when you've finished to check that it all makes sense.

9   .... forget, in the exam, to put your answers on the separate answer sheet!

2 Now do the activity below. Be careful with the use of passives and gerunds.

For Questions **1–10**, read the text below and look carefully at each line. Some of the lines are correct, and some have a word which should not be there. If a line is correct, put a tick (✓) by the number. If a line has a word which should **not** be there, write the word **at the end of the line**. There are two examples at the beginning (**0** and **00**).

Financial services for students

0	Most students start with a current account, which you can to do	*to*
00	by paying in just a few pounds. With some banks you will probably	✓
1	have to pay too account fees plus, in a few cases, extra charges	
2	for certain services. In return you will be being given a cheque-book,	
3	which is a much more convenient and most safer way of paying bills	
4	than carrying cash around, or posting it. Once a cheque has been	
5	made out to somebody, even though if it is stolen there will be	
6	little risk as a thief would have the great difficulty in cashing it. Doubts	
7	about whether a cheque can be cashed, however, might have affect	
8	you in more negative ways, for example if somebody refuses to	
9	accept one because they are not convinced you have enough of money	
10	in your account. You can avoid to having this happen by asking your	
11	bank for a cheque card, which guarantees payment of your cheques	
12	up to an agreed maximum amount. Something else what you will find	
13	useful is a cash card, which enables the holder for to withdraw money	
14	at any cashpoint, often is called a 'hole-in-the-wall'. All you do	
15	is insert your card, give your personal number and take out your cash.	

STUDY CHECK

1 Ask your partner what clothes he or she would consider wearing in these places and situations: a wedding, a first date, a prize-giving or degree ceremony, at the beach, a disco or nightclub.

Then ask what clothes he or she could never imagine wearing anywhere.

2 Think about the services in Vocabulary on page 106, plus others mentioned on these pages, e.g. dentist, sports centre, hairdresser. Choose six and briefly describe, using passives, the service you were given the last time you used each one. Then write what you feel about going there.

Example:
At the post office, I was kept waiting for twenty minutes and then I was told they were closed. I hate going there!

3 Follow these Writing Part 2 instructions.

You bought an item of clothing from a store but it was faulty. When you took it back, the shop assistant was unhelpful. Write to the manager, saying what happened and what you think should be done. Write your **letter** in **120–180** words in an appropriate style. Do not write any addresses.

11 The place to go

VOCABULARY

1 In the sentences below, three of the four possible answers are correct and one is wrong. Complete each sentence, choosing from the expressions below it. Then write an example sentence using the expression that is wrong.

Example:

It is becoming more and more popular to choose a ...camping / package / self-catering... *holiday.*

camping   package   voyage   self-catering

At the end of the voyage we left the ship and continued by train.

1 For some destinations you do not have to .... your flight in advance.
  book   pay   pay for   reserve

2 If you are going to a hot country, check that your room has ....
  air conditioning   a balcony   a fan   refrigeration

3 In summer, ... fill the ferries between the most popular islands.
  riders   holiday-makers   tourists   travellers

4 When you arrive by ship, you see very few buildings on the ....
  beach   coast   resort   shore

5 Many visitors go on a .... through the mountains by train.
  journey   ride   travel   trip

6 Others prefer to go to the seaside and spend a pleasant day ....
  getting sunstroke   getting sun-tanned   in the sun   sunbathing

7 It is best not to buy .... for family and friends in tourist areas.
  gifts   memories   presents   souvenirs

8 In some hotels, ... are asked not to make noise after midnight.
  guests   occupants   residents   visitors

9 If anything goes wrong with your holiday plans, tell the ....
  director   manager   tour operator's rep   travel agent

2 What can go wrong during a holiday? Imagine as many things as possible that can spoil it.

READING: gapped text

1 Quickly read the text and missing paragraphs opposite, to get a general impression. Then write your answers to these questions:

1 Where, when and at what time of day did this happen?
2 What went wrong?
3 What was the reaction of   a   the manager?   b   the porter?   c   the rep?

2 Now follow the Reading Part 3 instructions. As you read, underline the main events in both the text and the missing paragraphs. This will give you an outline of the story and make it easier to match the paragraphs to the gaps. The events linking gap 0 and paragraph I have been underlined as an example.

You are going to read a true story from the travel section of a newspaper. Seven paragraphs have been removed from the article. Choose from the paragraphs **A–H** the one which fits each gap (**1–7**). There is one extra paragraph which you do not need to use. There is an example at the beginning (**0**).

HOLIDAY NIGHTMARE

FOR ME, holidaying alone in sun-drenched Majorca, it was a kind of nightmare. Temperatures were zooming in Palma that July when I stepped out onto my balcony at the Pallas Atanea hotel. <u>I closed the balcony door behind me</u> and after 10 minutes was so hot that it was time to retreat to my air-conditioned room.

0	I

Nobody was about, all the other balconies on that side of the hotel were empty. No sounds came from any of the rooms. My room was at the back of the building, far away from the main entrance. And it was siesta time.

1	

I thought of dropping something over the balcony to the street below. An ashtray perhaps, or, if things got really desperate, a chair. But what if I hit a passer-by? Would my holiday insurance cover it?

2	

I kept shouting for help, waving my arms and leaning as far over the balcony as seemed safe. I told myself not to panic. If the worst came to the worst the chambermaid would find me next morning.

3	

Hours seemed to pass and the balcony was like an oven. But eventually my cries reached a girl on the footpath far below. She stopped and stared at this strange woman with arms waving.

4	

My hopes rose briefly again when a few minutes later she walked slowly back the same way. I shouted louder, but once more she passed by.

5	

So I used my fingers to count it out. It worked. The second girl nodded and disappeared round the block to the front of the hotel. A few minutes later a porter came to free me.

6	

The hotel manager was smoothly sympathetic and apologetic but he could not see how it had occurred. All balcony doors had been adjusted to prevent just such a thing happening, he claimed. He later sent a basket of fruit to my room.

7	

As for me, I swore I would never again close the door of a hotel balcony behind me. Particularly when it's 35° centigrade and rising.

A The tour operator's rep promised to warn other visitors of the danger but I felt this would not be her top priority. Foreign tourists in Spain, I gained the impression, are capable of much sillier things than getting stuck outside their rooms.

B Or had I left the 'Do not disturb' notice outside my door? What happens in a big hotel if a guest goes missing? How long does a 'Do not disturb' sign hang there … a day, a week perhaps? Would the room's next occupant arrive to find my fried remains?

C Meanwhile the balcony was becoming hotter and hotter, and I felt trapped and helpless. In desperation I began to call for help, but there was no one to hear me.

D Then, what seemed like an age later, she returned with another girl and I was able to signal that I was locked out of my room, but as I do not speak Spanish I could not tell them my room number.

E I couldn't ring the tour operator to find out, even though they had promised to be on the other end of the telephone. I couldn't ring anyone – the phone was on the other side of the double glazing.

F Fortunately, she understood English and shouted back that she was going to get help. Then she went quickly round the corner in the direction of the hotel reception.

G He thought it was rather funny and assured me that it had happened before. I never did get to thank the two girls who noticed my plight.

H She must have thought I was slightly mad, or a victim of sunstroke. She shrugged her shoulders and walked on. I was almost in tears.

I But I couldn't. <u>The door had locked by itself.</u> A latch on the room side of the door had dropped down. It was a few minutes before I realized I was trapped.

3 What would you have done in this situation? What wouldn't you have done?

4 Imagine that you are speaking to people at the hotel after you escaped. Write, in one sentence, what you would say to each of them. The first one has been done as an example.

1 the tour operator's rep. *I hope you'll make sure this doesn't happen to anyone else.*
2 the porter (who thought it was funny)
3 the manager (who thought it was your fault)
4 the people who helped you

GRAMMAR: reported speech

1 There are several examples of reported speech in the story on page 109. Here is what people might actually have said. Find the reported speech versions of 1–4 in the text and underline the verbs, as in the example. What differences are there?

1 'I <u>can't</u> see how it <u>occurred</u>.'
   simple present   simple past
   He <u>could not</u> see how it <u>had occurred</u>.
   simple past   past perfect
2 'I'<u>ll</u> never again <u>close</u> the door of a hotel balcony behind me.'
3 'I'<u>m going to get</u> help.'
4 'It'<u>s happened</u> before, of course.'

2 What do you think happens in reported speech to these tenses?

present continuous, present perfect continuous, past continuous, past perfect

What happens to these modals?

can, will, would, could, should, must, may

3 When we report a statement or somebody's thoughts we use a reporting verb, often (but not always) followed by *that*:

He thought it was rather funny and <u>assured</u> me <u>that</u> it had happened before.
Fortunately, she understood English and <u>shouted back</u> <u>that</u> she was going to get help.
As for me, I <u>swore</u> I would never again close the door of a hotel balcony behind me.

The reporting verb can also follow the statement, after a comma and without *that*:

All balcony doors had been adjusted to prevent just such a thing happening, <u>he claimed</u>.

To report advice, orders or requests we use the infinitive after a verb such as *ask* or *tell*:

She <u>asked</u> them <u>to go</u> for help.
He <u>told</u> them <u>to break down</u> the door.

Reported questions often use a reporting verb plus words like *what, who* and *how* (*wh-* questions):

They <u>asked</u> her <u>which</u> room she was in. I <u>enquired why</u> it had occurred.

Questions that can be answered *yes* or *no* use *if* or *whether* after the reporting verb:

The girls <u>asked</u> her <u>if</u> she could speak Spanish. She <u>wondered whether</u> she would survive.

1 For a–g, change the sentence to reported speech or direct speech and match it with one of these functions, as in the example:

> statement   advice   order   request   intention
> *wh-* question   *yes / no* question

a 'Will I see you tomorrow?'   *He asked her if he would see her the next day*   (*yes / no* question)
b 'I'm fed up with this room.'
c She asked them to let her know the same day.
d 'It'd be a good idea to buy a flat here.'

e He asked me where I had gone the week before.
f 'Bring the cases down to reception.'
g She decided to leave right away.

2 What other differences are there between the direct speech and the reported speech forms in a–g?

Example: a *tomorrow / the next day*

4 You work for a tour operator and have been travelling with a group of tourists. Back at the office you wrote down some of the comments you heard. Report what people said, using each of these verbs once only:

Example: *'The weather's a lot better here.'*
He said the weather was a lot better there.

> admit   advise   ask   complain   enquire   promise   refuse   request   tell   threaten

1 'To be honest I don't think much of the food.'
2 'You should give out free local maps to the guests.'
3 'Do you have similar accommodation in Italy?'
4 'This is the worst flight I've ever been on.'
5 'We're not paying extra for deckchairs!'
6 'Could you arrange taxis from the airport?'
7 'I've thoroughly enjoyed this holiday.'
8 'Refund my money or I'll take you to court!'
9 'Yes, I'll <u>definitely</u> tell them to come next year!'
10 'Please tell your staff how wonderful they've been.'

COMMON ERRORS

I asked her where was she going.
What is wrong with this sentence? Why?
See the Grammar Reference on page 180.

5 Work in pairs.

Student A: Think back to your ideas in activity 2 of Vocabulary on page 108. You are a holiday-maker who has just returned home. Tell Student B about something that went badly wrong. Try to remember what you were thinking at the time, what you said and what other people said to you. Use verbs from the activities above, for example:

I told myself everything was going to be all right.
The owner even suggested it was my fault!

Student B: You are a journalist for *TravelWatch*, the television consumer programme. Interview Student A about what went wrong, making notes on what he or she thought at the time, what this person said to other people and what they said to him or her.
Ask '*wh*-questions' using verbs from the activities above, for example:

What had they told you about safety? Who warned you of the danger? What did they offer to do?

When you have finished the interview, write what he or she thought and said in reported speech as part of the script for the programme.

1 It is easy to see which questions in Use of English Part 3 test reported speech because there will usually be inverted commas somewhere in the first sentence but not in the second. In these cases look at the reporting verb, such as *told* or *admitted*, and identify its function, for example *order*, *statement* or *advice*. This will help you decide what structure to use (see activity 3 on page 110). Now follow the exam instructions. The first question has been done as an example.

Complete the second sentence so that it has a similar meaning to the first sentence, using the word given. **Do not change the word given**. You must use between two and five words, including the word given.

1 'What went wrong, Frankie?' said Paul.   Reporting verb: *asked*

   asked   Function: *wh*-question

   Paul ..*asked Frankie what had gone*.. wrong.   Structure: *what* + change to past perfect

2 'Can I stay here for a couple of days, Jude?' said Phil.

   there

   Phil asked Jude .... for a couple of days.

3 'Yes, I went there on my own,' Haskins said.

   gone

   Haskins admitted that he .... own.

4 'Don't mention this ever again, Chris,' said Brenda.

   to

   Brenda told Chris .... again.

5 'I think, Joe, that you should tell the council about it,' said Mr Green.

   advised

   Mr Green .... the council about it.

6 'What time does this pub close at weekends, Jack?' said Alexis.

   time

   Alexis asked Jack .... at weekends.

7 'You will ask for a receipt, won't you?' Anna said to Steve.

   reminded

   Anna .... a receipt.

8 'We're going tomorrow,' said Melanie.

   going

   Melanie said that .... day.

9 'Don't touch this cable,' the electrician said to us.

   touch

   The electrician warned .... cable.

10 'Show me what's in your hand, Smith,' said the policeman.

   show

   The policeman ordered Smith .... in his hand.

2 Look back at your answers. Which of them use a reporting verb + infinitive construction?

LISTENING

1 All these words are used in the recording you are going to listen to. Put them into two groups, those you associate with:

a the seaside
b the countryside.

> sand   stream   coastline   peaks   river-bank   tide   waves   valley
> inland   shore   waterfall   undergrowth   spray

2 Read the instructions for Listening Part 4 and quickly note down all the things you can think of which would make a holiday perfect. Now do the activity.

You will hear two people talking about the perfect holiday. Answer Questions **1–7** by writing **T** for True or **F** for False in the boxes provided.

1 Steve would like to see snow on the mountains in summer.   **1**

2 He would go into the mountains before going to the seaside.   **2**

3 He says he would swim in the sea.   **3**

4 He would spend a night in the mountains.   **4**

5 Jill disagrees with all his ideas for a good holiday.   **5**

6 She is an experienced surfer.   **6**

7 She would go to bed early.   **7**

3 Discuss these questions:

• Do you think Steve and Jill should go on holiday together? Why? Why not?
• Do you know a place that might suit one or both of them? What is it like?

SPEAKING

1 In Speaking Part 2, the examiner will show you two photos, tell you what the subject is and ask you to talk about them for about a minute. Then the other candidate will talk about them for around twenty seconds. The other candidate will be given two different pictures to discuss for a minute and then it will be your turn to talk about them briefly. Part 2 lasts about four minutes.

Look at this exam advice and fill in the gap in each sentence with SHOULD or SHOULDN'T. If the answer is SHOULDN'T, say why. The first one has been done as an example.

1 You ..SHOULDN'T. give a detailed description of the pictures. ..You're not asked to.
2 You .... look for links between the pictures. ....
3 You .... say what they show and then compare them. ....
4 You .... hide your pictures from the other candidate. ....
5 You .... give your own reaction to what they show. ....
6 You .... talk without stopping for about one minute. ....
7 You .... listen to what the other candidate says. ....
8 You .... have a good look at his or her photos. ....
9 You .... interrupt during his or her one-minute talk. ....

2 Work in pairs. This is what you must do:

Look at photographs 1 and 2, which show different kinds of holiday. **Student A** should compare and contrast these photographs, saying which are the advantages of both. **Student B** should listen to **Student A**, then say which of these places he or she would prefer for a holiday.

This is how you should do it:

Student A:

- Say what is in the pictures, pointing out the similarities between them, e.g. *They both show ...*
- Mention the differences: *While in the first ... , in the second ...*
- If you're not sure, say what you think you can see: *It looks as if ...*
- If you don't know a word, paraphrase: *It's what you use to ... , It's a sort of ...*
- Say what you could do in one kind of holiday but not in the other: *If you were ...*
- Finish by saying how you would feel if you were there now.

Student B:

- Say which you would prefer for your holiday: *I think I'd rather ...*

3 Now change roles. Do the same with these two photos (3 and 4) of city holidays. Work as above, but instead of talking about the seaside and countryside, think about these points:

Similarities: traffic, parking, pollution, noise, crowds, tourists, shopping and city centre prices.
Differences: weather, sights, things to do, food and drink, clothes, language, culture and people.

VOCABULARY:
British and American English

Most of the words used in Britain and the USA are the same, but there are some differences. Among these are words often used to talk about travelling. Match pairs of words in the box below, saying which is British and which is American – and what they both mean. For example, *railway* (UK) and *railroad* (US) both mean transport by train.

> ~~railway~~ holiday sidewalk line freeway
> underground vacation ~~railroad~~ lift aeroplane
> pavement subway queue lorry elevator
> truck motorway airplane

FIRST CERTIFICATE FACTS

American words, pronunciation and spelling are acceptable in the exam as long as they are used consistently.

READING: gapped text

1 Do people in your country generally queue in the following situations?

- Buying a train ticket
- Waiting for a bus
- Taking a taxi at a busy station
- Buying something in a small shop

What happens in your country if someone tries to jump the queue in these situations?

2 Follow the Reading Part 3 instructions opposite. As you do the activity, underline the words that link the sentences to the main text. Look at the example: for gap 0 the words *multi-server queues* are underlined, as are *In contrast* and *'snake' line* in sentence I.

3 There are many ways of linking parts of a text. For example, in gap 0 there is a contrast between two kinds of queue, in gap 5 there is a time comparison, while in gap 7 the same word is used in both. Very often, though, repetition is avoided by using reference words such as *this, that* and *it*, as in gap 1: *The difference is not efficiency. It's fairness.*

Look at the expressions that you used as clues to filling in the other gaps and answer the following. You may be asked questions like these in Reading Part 2.

1   Sentence H: What does *them* refer to in *all of them*?
2   line 32: What does *Those* refer to in *Those with luggage*?

4 Work in pairs. How would you react to, or feel about, the following situations?

1   You are in a 'multi-server' queue and the line next to you is moving much faster.
2   Somebody cuts in front of you in a queue, saying 'I'm in a hurry'.

You are going to read a newspaper article about queuing and waiting. Eight sentences have been removed from the article. Choose from the sentences **A–I** the one which fits each gap (**1–7**). There is one extra sentence which you do not need to use. There is an example at the beginning (**0**).

A   Such research can be used to mislead the public.
B   Arriving passengers, the airline discovered, had only a one-minute walk to get to either the exit or the luggage carousel.
C   It's fairness.
D   The complaints stopped.
E   To do so they would have to leave the queue, threatening the integrity of the line still further and therefore breaking another of the unwritten rules which govern it.
F   It is not how long you have to wait that bothers you, it is how long you think you had to wait.
G   A more modern example comes from Houston airport, where a major airline recently got a series of complaints from passengers arriving on morning flights about how long they had to wait to pick up their bags.
H   Then he asked all of them how long they thought they had waited.
I   <u>In contrast</u>, over the last decade US banks, railroads, airlines and some fast-food restaurants have switched over to what is known as the <u>'snake' line</u>, where all counters are served by one single-file line.

You are how you wait: Queue Psychology

By Malcolm Gladwell – Washington Post Service

People spend billions of hours a year waiting in lines. It all began in Britain during World Wars I and II and passed on to the United States, Canada and parts of Europe, developing rules that sociologists, psychologists and economists have recently been studying.

In Europe, the most common kinds of lines in railroad stations and banks are what are known as <u>multi-server queues</u>, where each serving counter has a separate waiting line. **0** **I**

The difference is not efficiency. **1** In the multi-server system, a customer lucky enough to pick a fast line can get served ahead of someone who has been waiting longer in a slower line.

2 This seemingly obvious principle was recently confirmed by researcher Jacob Hornik. He timed how long each of 640 people stood in grocery store checkout lines. **3** On average, the study showed that perceptions of the waiting period were about 30 percent longer than the real waiting time.

4 Some businesses have discovered that they can improve customer satisfaction by concentrating as much or more on reducing perceived waiting time than on reducing actual waiting time. Thus in the 1950s, when high-rise hotels and office buildings began to get persistent complaints about waiting times for elevators, they did not speed up the elevators. They simply put large mirrors next to the elevator doors so that people were too busy smartening up their appearance to notice how long they were waiting.

5 The airline discovered that the supposedly objectionable wait was about eight minutes – exactly the industry average.

Why the unhappiness? **6** Those with luggage then had to wait another seven minutes to get to their bags – which meant they had to watch as everyone who didn't check any baggage got an earlier start on the business day.

The airline didn't hire more baggage handlers. To deal with the complaints it simply began parking its airplanes at the other end of the terminal, so that everyone walked seven minutes, and those who checked bags only had to wait an additional minute to get them. **7**

Researchers at City University have also looked at the effects of queue-jumping by pushing into 129 lines around New York. What they found was that the person most likely to object was the one directly behind the intruder, and that even though people standing three or four places further back are inconvenienced just as much, they rarely protest.

GRAMMAR: the infinitive

The *to* infinitive is used to express purpose:

They simply put mirrors next to the elevator doors <u>to make</u> the wait appear to go faster.

Many verbs are usually followed directly by the *to* infinitive:

afford	agree	appear	arrange	attempt
decide	expect	forget	help	hope	learn
manage	mean	offer	prepare	pretend
promise	refuse	seem	swear	want

We couldn't <u>afford to buy</u> a detached house.
It <u>seemed to be</u> a real bargain.

The *to* infinitive follows the object of some verbs, particularly reporting verbs such as *ask, encourage, order, permit, persuade, request, remind, tell* and *warn* (see reported speech on page 110):

I <u>advised them to rent</u> a cottage.
She <u>invited us to stay</u> at her place.

We do not use *to* after modals and the objects of *hear, feel, let, make, notice, see* and *watch*:

You <u>must see</u> our new flat.
They <u>made him go</u> to the police station.
I didn't <u>hear the bell ring</u>.
We have <u>watched this village grow</u>.

1 Fill in the gaps in these sentences, using one of the above verbs and an object where necessary.

Example:
We didn't ..<u>encourage them</u>.. to build it right next to the school.

1   They generously .... to pay the whole cost of the repairs.
2   I'm going down to the phone box .... a couple of calls.
3   The pub manager wouldn't .... buy drinks because they were too young.
4   After a number of thefts, the police .... to keep valuables locked away.
5   I'm afraid I .... to tell her today but I'll try to remember to do so tomorrow.
6   Nobody .... break into the post office, steal the money and get clean away.
7   The garage .... to have the car ready for today but as usual it's going to take longer.
8   The lift wasn't working but we .... to climb the stairs to the twentieth floor.

The verbs *begin, continue* and *start* can be followed by either the *to* infinitive or the gerund, without any difference in meaning:

*   *Thus in the 1950s, when high-rise hotels and office buildings <u>began to get</u> persistent complaints about waiting times for elevators, they did not speed up the elevators.*
*   *To deal with the complaints it simply <u>began parking</u> its planes at the other end of the terminal.*

With *hate, love, prefer* and *can't stand* the difference is slight, but with *like* it is greater:

*   *I <u>like being</u> on holiday. (I enjoy it)*
*   *I <u>like to be</u> in bed by eleven. (I choose to do it)*

With other verbs, though, the meaning changes completely according to which form follows:

*   *In those days, going to town <u>meant taking</u> three buses. (meant = involved)*
*   *I <u>meant to take</u> the bus but I missed it and had to walk. (meant = intended)*

COMMON ERRORS

They don't usually make you to wait long.

What is wrong with this sentence? Why? See the Grammar Reference on page 181.

2 Study these pairs of sentences and in each case give the meaning of the second one.

1   She <u>stopped talking</u> to the neighbours after they were rude to her. = She hasn't talked to them since.
    She <u>stopped to talk</u> to the neighbours on her way home. = ...
2   Do you <u>remember going</u> to that castle when we were kids? = Can you recall?
    <u>Remember to go</u> to the chemist's after work. = ...
3   I <u>tried opening</u> the door, but I didn't feel any cooler. = To experiment: see what happens as a result.
    I <u>tried to open</u> the door, but without the key I couldn't. = ...
4   I <u>regret coming</u> to live in this awful block of flats. = Sorry about a past action.
    I <u>regret to tell</u> you this, but there has been an accident. = ...
5   I'll <u>never forget climbing</u> right to the top of that skyscraper. = Something remembered from the past.
    I hope you <u>won't forget to send</u> me a postcard when you're there. = ...
6   We <u>went on walking</u> until we reached the coast. = Continued the same activity.
    We <u>went on to take</u> a boat after we had walked to the coast. = ...

3 Tell your partner about the following, using one sentence in each case.

1   A place you hope to visit one day.
2   Something you meant to do at the weekend.
3   Something you stopped to do on the way here.
4   What you mustn't forget to do this evening.
5   The thing in your life that you most regret doing.
6   Something you have tried to do, but failed.
7   Something you have managed to do this week.

WRITING: describing a place

1 Quickly read the Use of English Part 4 text below and write a title for it. Then do the activity below.

For Questions **1–15**, read the text below and look carefully at each line. Some of the lines are correct, and some have a word which should not be there. If a line is correct, put a tick (✔) by the number. If a line has a word which should **not** be there, cross it out. There are two examples at the beginning (**0** and **00**).

Title: ....

0	✓	Birkenhead is a town of 140,000 inhabitants, situated on the Wirral Peninsula
00	*by*	across ~~by~~ the River Mersey from the port of Liverpool. To the north it is bordered
1		by Wallasey and the seaside resort of New Brighton, while to the west is lies the
2		River Dee and the mountains of North Wales. The M53 to the south links it to
3		the motorway network, and it is a well placed for rail, air and sea connections from
4		Liverpool. Its old docks and shipbuilding industries are now being replaced of by
5		lighter higher-technology industries, but unemployment remains at extremely high
6		and there are serious drug abuse problems both also in the newer estates on the
7		outskirts of the town and in the districts of small terraced houses near from the
8		town centre. In the suburbs, however, there are any affluent areas of detached and
9		semi-detached homes. Many people who live there use the underground, the two
10		Mersey Tunnels or the famous ferry for to commute daily to the offices of
11		Liverpool. As in its too bigger neighbour across the river, many of the population
12		have ancestors from Ireland and other parts of the world, and they speak
13		with the distinctive Scouse accent. This part of Merseyside has also been produced,
14		in recent times, the well-known musicians, actors and sports people, as well as
15		being home to rugby union club Birkenhead Park and football team Tranmere Rovers.

2 Now read the text again and note down which of the following it mentions. The number of answers for each question is given in brackets. The first two have been done as examples:

1   Statistics (1): *140,000 inhabitants*
2   Urban areas (3): *town, port, resort*
3   Geographical features (4)
4   Nearby places (4)
5   Transport links to other places (7)
6   Jobs now (2)
7   Jobs then (2)
8   Parts of the town (4)
9   Types of housing (4)
10 Social problems (2)
11 Kinds of famous people (3)
12 Well-known sports clubs (2)

3 Read these Writing Part 2 instructions and then follow steps 1–4.

A British magazine has asked you to write an **article** in **120–180** words describing your town or a town you know well, for readers who may be interested in moving there but know very little about it.

1   Underline the key words in the instructions.
2   Write a plan. Look at points 1–12 in activity 2 for things you might want to include.
3   Write your answer, using a similar style to that in the activity 1 text and mention a few bad points as well as good ones! Use some of the vocabulary you found in activity 2.
4   When you have finished, check your writing carefully for mistakes.

STUDY CHECK

1 Look back at the sentences you wrote in Reading activity 4 (page 109) and change them to reported speech.

Example: *I advised her to make sure that didn't happen to anyone else.*

2 Ask your partner what he or she:

1   has started to do recently.
2   can't stand doing in the morning.
3   should stop doing.
4   loves to do in English lessons.

In each case write down, in reported speech, what he or she said.

12 Getting on well

SPEAKING AND VOCABULARY

① Think about your best friend. When and how did you meet? What do you have in common? Why are you 'best' friends?

② Underline the adjectives you would use for the ideal friend. Can you think of any more words?

> sociable   reliable   intelligent   sensitive   bossy   bad-tempered   shy   generous
> patient   selfish   serious   moody   cheerful   fair   boring   loyal   jealous   sincere
> lively   easy-going   practical   nervous   self-confident   aggressive   warm   funny
> helpful   adventurous   well-behaved   gentle   sensible

③ Compare the words you and your partner underlined. Discuss any differences.

READING: gapped text and multiple choice

① Quickly read the text opposite without filling in any of the gaps. Where do you think it is taken from? What is its purpose?

② Look at the Reading Part 3 instructions below. To replace a missing sentence in a text you should study the content and the language both before and after the space. If it is the first sentence of a paragraph it often tells us what that paragraph is about and may also refer back to the previous paragraph. Look at the example sentence H:

There are all sorts of things that can bring about this special relationship.

Can you find the following in the first two paragraphs:

- another reference to *this special relationship*?
- examples of *all sorts of things*?
- an expression related to the meaning of *bring about*?

You are going to read a magazine article about friends. Seven sentences have been removed from the article. Choose from the sentences **A–H** the one which fits each gap (**1–6**). There is one extra sentence which you do not need to use. There is an example at the beginning (**0**).

A It's unwise to isolate yourself when you're in a boy / girl relationship.

B Suppose you're going through a bad patch with your boyfriend or girlfriend.

C It's stimulating to be surrounded by a mix of personalities with their different attitudes and behaviour.

D Even your best friend may get jealous if they feel pushed out by your girlfriend or boyfriend.

E There might well be some more reserved characters too.

F To the majority of us this is someone we trust completely and who understands us better than anyone else.

G Or they may be someone you meet by chance and instantly get on with.

H There are all sorts of things that can bring about this special relationship.

F R I E N D S

To many people, their friends are the most important thing in their life. Really good friends share the good times and the bad times, help you when you've got problems, never judge you and never turn their backs 5 on you. Your best friend may be someone you've known all your life, someone you've grown up with and been through lots of ups and downs with.

0 H **There are all sorts of things that can bring about this special relationship.** It may be the result of 10 enjoying the same activities, having the same outlook on life, or sharing similar experiences. Most of us have met someone that we've immediately felt relaxed with, as if we've known them for years. But usually it really does take years to get to know someone well enough to 15 consider them your 'best friend'.

1 It's the person you can turn to for impartial advice and a shoulder to cry on when life lets you down. You know that no matter what the problem or what time of day or night it is, your best friend will drop everything 20 and put you first. No relationship is more important than the one with your best friend.

2 It will probably be your best friend you go to for help. Perhaps your parents are being too heavy-handed; maybe you're not happy at work or at school. 25 Whatever the problem, you know you can rely on your best friend.

Of course, not all friendships stand the test of time. All sorts of things can come between friends. Sometimes people just drift apart over time. One of you may leave 30 the area and you simply lose touch. But sometimes other relationships can conflict with your friendship and cause powerful emotions.

3 If they do and you want to keep them, it's important to make them feel valued. Set aside some 35 time to go out with them on your own, or introduce them to your new boyfriend or girlfriend, and do things together.

4 If you do, you may find that one day you break up and you've lost touch with all your old friends. And 40 besides, it's fun to go out in groups, especially when you're young.

5 People who you might not expect to get on with each other can often make a good combination. Usually in a particular group of friends there'll be a 45 ringleader, someone the rest look to to make decisions. Often there's a bit of a comedian, always cracking jokes and entertaining the rest. **6** They all have something to contribute.

Remember, unlike your family, you can choose your 50 friends. If you choose them carefully and treat them well, they could turn out to be friends for life.

---

3 For Questions **1–4**, the correct answer (**A**, **B**, **C** or **D**) is underlined. You have to write in the missing words as in the example. Write either a question or an incomplete statement beginning with the words given. The first one has been done as an example.

1   A best friend ....*is someone*....................
   A   who tells your parents everything you say.
   <u>B   who you can rely on.</u>
   C   who is usually a lot older than you.
   D   who probably makes you feel miserable.

2   If you ask ....
   A   they let you down.
   <u>B   they help immediately.</u>
   C   you feel relaxed.
   D   it won't matter.

3   If you are spending ....
   A   you might spend more time with your best friend.
   B   your best friend might refuse to speak to you.
   C   you may be upset for a long time.
   <u>D   your best friend may be upset.</u>

4   Where ....?
   <u>A   A magazine for young teenagers.</u>
   B   A book of short stories.
   C   An academic study of relationships.
   D   The editorial of a newspaper.

4 Add to the ideas in the text and discuss them with your partner. Think of other ways:
1   you can make friends.
2   friends can help each other.
3   friendships can be harmed, and what you can do to avoid this.

GRAMMAR: conditionals (0)

1 Look at these examples:

1 *If your friends go somewhere, you go there too.
You feel more secure if you have friends.*

These are examples of the zero conditional, which we use for something that always happens or is always true, including scientific facts. What form of the verb is used in these sentences?

2 We can also use the conditional to tell somebody what to do if something else happens. Which verb forms are used in this example?

If you feel at all lonely, give me a call.

2 In questions 1–5, make sentences by joining clauses 1–5 on the left with a–e on the right.

In each case say whether the sentence is: *if + present simple + present simple* or *if + present simple + imperative*.

1	If you go to a youth club,	a	please tell her I'm sorry.
2	If the glass is broken,	b	you meet people of your own age.
3	If you see Maria,	c	the lake gets covered in ice.
4	If the weather is cold,	d	the alarm goes off.
5	If you lose all your money,	e	don't ask me for any more.

3 For questions 1–5, complete the second sentence so that it has a similar meaning to the first sentence. Use *if* and other words to complete each sentence. You must use between two and five words.

Example: *When you press this key the system re-starts.*
The system ....*re-starts if you press*.... this key.

1 Talking to a friend always makes me feel better.
I always .... to a friend.

2 Unless you go out you never meet people.
You never meet people .... out.

3 We can't continue without your help.
We can't .... have your help.

4 Phone this number and they give you information.
They .... phone this number.

5 In the event of fire, close all doors.
Close .... a fire.

4 Finish these sentences using the present simple, or the imperative.

1 If you stay at home all the time   ....

2 If the temperature goes above 40°C   ....

3 If you don't do all your homework   ....

4 If I don't get enough sleep ....

5 You can't expect her to help if   ....

6 If anyone asks you what you're doing ....

7 Ice starts to melt if   ....

8 Don't get upset if ....

Conditionals (3 and mixed)

1 Look at this sentence and answer the questions below:
If he had spoken to her she would have given him some advice.

1 Did he speak to her?
2 Did she give him some advice?
3 What is this structure called?
4 Why do we use it?
5 Which verb forms are used in the example?
6 Is this structure the same in your first language?

2 Which verb forms are used in these sentences?

1 We would not have gone to that club if we had known.
2 If she had seen him at the party she might have spoken to him.
3 I could have phoned her if it had not been so late.

What are the contracted forms of the verbs in these examples? How do we pronounce them?

3 In mixed conditional sentences, the two clauses refer to different times.

1 If we'd left an hour earlier we'd be there by now.
2 He wouldn't be saying that if he'd read the whole report.

Which verb forms are used here? Which of them refer to the past and which to the present?

Check your answers to activities 1, 2 and 3 with the Grammar Reference on page 181.

4 We often use these conditionals with a feeling of regret: when we are sorry we did / didn't do something or that something happened / didn't happen. Answer questions 1–6 below.

Complete the second sentence so that it has a similar meaning to the first sentence, using the word given. **Do not change the word given.** You must use between two and five words, including the word given.

1 I couldn't warn you because I didn't know about it myself.
   warned
   I could .... had known about it myself.

2 The reason she found out about it was that he told his sister.
   if
   She wouldn't have found out about it .... his sister.

3 Not realizing how unhappy she was, he spent very little time with her.
   would
   He .... with her if he had known how unhappy she was.

4 I lost her phone number so I never saw her again.
   have
   I would .... I hadn't lost her phone number.

5 We're not living together any more because she went away to university.
   still
   We .... if she hadn't gone away to university.

6 She didn't take the trouble to find out why so she doesn't understand.
   had
   She .... taken the trouble to find out why.

5 Look at the situations below and write at least one third conditional sentence for each one.

Example:
You didn't see someone so you were unable to tell them something.
If I'd seen her I would have told her.
or *I would have told him if I'd seen him.*

1 You forgot to do something for your parents and they got angry.
2 You didn't go to a party so you didn't meet somebody you like.
3 You missed the last bus and two hours later you are still walking home.
4 Someone close to you got very jealous when they saw you with somebody else.
5 You didn't tell someone the truth because you thought it would upset her or him.
6 You were too shy to ask someone to dance and he or she left the disco with somebody else.
7 You accused someone of something they hadn't done and now you aren't friends.
8 You forgot to post the letter and so you didn't get the job.

6 Look at each of the pictures and say:
1 how you would have felt if you had been in that situation.
2 what you would – or wouldn't – have said and done.
3 how you would be feeling now about what happened then.

WRITING: a formal letter

1   1   Read these Writing Part 1 instructions and the advice which follows:

A friend has applied for a job as an Assistant Youth Leader at a summer camp for children and you have just received a letter from the Co-ordinator asking you for a reference. Read his letter and the notes which you have made after talking to your friend. Write a **letter** of between **120** and **180** words in an appropriate style. Do not write any addresses.

e.g. sports and art

other duties – cooking, organizing evening entertainment

Dear Sir or Madam,

We have received a job application from the above person, who has given us permission to ask you for a reference. The work involves helping to run a multi-activity camp for children in a beautiful area of mountains, forests and lakes during the summer holidays.

age 12–16

We would be most grateful, therefore, if you would supply us with a brief description of the applicant's personality as known to you, together with an assessment of this person's suitability for the position.

We look forward to hearing from you.

Yours faithfully,

B. Hall

B. Hall (Co-ordinator)

2   In pairs, study the letter and answer these questions:

- Is it written in a formal or informal style? What examples can you find?
- Who are you writing to? Why?
- What information do you have to give? Why?

2   1   Now think about your letter and make a plan. Use these prompts:

name / thanks / reason for writing / personality / suitability / final comment / ending

2   With your partner, make a list of all the qualities needed for the job.

3   Decide which of those qualities your friend has.

4   Note down some short sentences on his or her suitability, giving examples. Try to include:

- zero conditionals: *If there is an emergency, he / she stays very calm.*
- frequency adverbs + present simple: *When he / she does a job, he / she always likes to do it properly.*
- cause and effect links: *As he / she was in the Scouts, he / she has plenty of experience of camping.*
- adjectival phrases: *He / She is good at (tennis). He / She is an excellent (swimmer).*

3   When you have both finished, check each other's work for mistakes.

1 What does *IQ* measure? What do you think *emotional intelligence* might mean?

Now read example paragraph 0. How would you answer the question on line 6? Why?

2 Follow the exam instructions for Reading Part 1. Notice the use of zero conditionals in the text.

You are going to read an article about emotional intelligence. Choose from the list **A–I** the sentence which best summarizes each part (**1–7**) of the article. There is one extra summary which you do not need to use. There is an example at the beginning (**0**).

Emotional Intelligence

0 **I**

Imagine three children. The first is top of the class at maths but has few social graces and even fewer friends. The second is artistic and does well enough in her other lessons but easily loses interest and is rather lazy. The third child puts in twice as much work to get the same
5 results, but has a sunny personality and works brilliantly in groups. Which child do you think has the best chance of succeeding in life?

1

Most of us would automatically choose the third child. We know that to do well in the adult world you must work hard – but you must also be a pleasure to work hard with. Academic intelligence alone is not
10 going to get you very far. Character matters, too. But until recently most experts studying intelligence believed that it was impossible to measure, and so ignored it.

2

Now, however, psychologists have identified several types of emotional intelligence. One is 'emotional management', or being in
15 charge of your own emotions. This includes the ability to cheer yourself up after a big setback, pull yourself out of a depression, or even to stop, relax and go out for a walk when you've lost your temper. Although we like to think of anger as a way of getting rid of strong emotions, psychologists have found that expressing anger increases
20 it. If, by contrast, you have a cooling-off period, that's exactly what happens.

3

Another kind of emotional intelligence is how good you are at delaying rewards. A remarkable experiment to show the links between this skill and life success was carried out by a psychologist at Stanford
25 University in California. In stage one he put a series of four-year-olds in a room with a researcher. The researcher would say he was leaving the room and tell the children that they could have two sweets if they

could wait until he came back, but only one if they couldn't wait the required 20 minutes. Some couldn't, while others could.

4

30 Twelve to fourteen years later, the team tracked the children down. It found that the ones who had been able to wait were far more socially skilled and independent than the ones who had settled for an instant reward: as adolescents, the latter still had trouble postponing pleasures. They tended to be more argumentative, had low opinions of
35 themselves and dealt badly with stress.

5

The last two kinds of emotional intelligence involve other people. The first of these 'people skills' is empathy – the ability to imagine and share another person's feelings as if they were your own. If you are good at reading your own feelings, then you are likely to be good at
40 reading other people's.

6

If you can't, your chances of success in life are limited. You won't do well in politics or business if you're not sensitive to other people's emotions. You won't get very far as a parent if you can't imagine what children might be feeling. You can best appreciate the importance of
45 empathy if you consider the types of people who lack it. These include violent criminals and murderers.

7

The last type of emotional intelligence builds on self-management skills as well as empathy. It's about handling relationships without being taken over by them. People who are highly intelligent
50 emotionally make personal connections easily and are good at taking the heat out of explosive situations. These are hard skills to measure, but if you have ever talked your way out of a difficult situation, you'll know how important they are.

A They studied them again in their teens.	**E** It is not enough just to get good marks.
B You can understand other people's emotions.	**F** You can change the way you are feeling if you want to.
C They know how to calm other people down.	**G** They tested them at a very early age.
D You are likely to fail at work and at home if you do not have this ability.	**H** People without emotional intelligence have no feelings.
	I Different people have different characters.

3 Which of these are you good at?

• Changing your own emotions
• Sharing other people's feelings
• Dealing with difficult situations

LISTENING

1 Read this summary of Listening Part 1 and follow these instructions:

For Questions **1–10**, use the word given in capitals at the end of each line to form a word that fits in the space in the same line. There is an example at the beginning **(0)**.

Study the questions **(0)** *carefully* , possibly marking each one according to   **CARE**

the type of **(1)** .... required. For example, if you need to listen out for facts   **INFORM**

(see page 32) you could underline 'what' in that question. Another kind

might ask you to identify the roles of the speakers and the **(2)** .... between   **RELATION**

them (see page 86), so you would underline 'who' there. A third kind focuses

on their mood, attitude or **(3)** .... , so you could underline or write 'how'.   **FEEL**

    For this kind of information, you should listen for the tone of voice and any

words or phrases spoken **(4)** .... Ask yourself how the speakers feel while   **EMPHASIS**

they are talking, how they feel about each other and whether their feelings

have changed during the conversation. Pay special **(5)** .... to any   **ATTEND**

(6) .... of speakers developing ideas or changing their minds during the   **INDICATE**

conversation.

    The extracts you will hear are completely **(7)** .... and last about thirty   **RELATE**

seconds each. The first time you listen, you may find it **(8)** .... just to form   **USE**

a general **(9)** .... It is probably best with this kind of question to wait until   **IMPRESS**

you have heard the whole extract before you choose the answer. You can

make an initial **(10)** .... , then use the second listening to check.   **CHOOSE**

2 Now do the activity.

You will hear people talking in six different situations. For Questions **1–6**, choose the best answer, **A**, **B** or **C**.

---

1 You are listening to a radio discussion about magazine problem pages. The man sounds

    A disgusted   **B** sad   **C** patient   **| 1 |**

2 You are visiting a divorced friend when you hear this conversation. The man sounds

    A unfriendly   **B** miserable   **C** sociable   **| 2 |**

3 You hear someone trying to persuade an older relative to move in. The woman sounds

    A warm   **B** impatient   **C** disapproving   **| 3 |**

4 You hear a man talking about how he felt after a relationship ended. The man sounds

    A lazy   **B** hurt   **C** angry   **| 4 |**

5 You hear a young woman talking about the first time she fell in love. The woman sounds

    A cheerful   **B** insincere   **C** bored   **| 5 |**

6 You overhear a conversation at a party between two teenagers. The girl sounds

    A lively   **B** bad-tempered   **C** shy   **| 6 |**

GRAMMAR: short replies

Perhaps you laugh at something and so does he or she.

One way of showing you feel the same way as someone else is to answer using *so* or *neither* with an auxiliary verb:

Speaker A: 'I love chatting on the phone.'
Speaker B: 'Mm, *so do I.*'
Speaker A: 'I'll never speak to him again.'
Speaker B: '*Neither will I.*'

If we disagree we could say '*Do you? I'm afraid I don't.*' or '*Won't you? I think I will*'.

1 Match these statements and replies.

Example: *1 – c*

1	She hasn't met them.	a	So do I.
2	I'd really love to go.	b	Neither had they.
3	I hate going to discos alone.	c	Neither has he.
4	He won't make that mistake again.	d	So must I.
5	We hadn't been there before.	e	Neither will she.
6	She must get herself a new boyfriend.	f	So would I.

2 Reply to these statements; either agree or disagree.

Example: *'I'm a little bit shy sometimes.'* ...*'So am I.'* / ...*'I'm not.'*

1 'I need to have good friends.' ....

2 'I'd like to live in another country.' ....

3 'I don't like noisy people.' ....

4 'I thought the last lesson was easy.' ....

5 'I haven't got enough money.' ....

6 'I enjoy meeting new people.' ....

7 'I can't sing very well.' ....

8 'I'm going to pass the exam.' ....

3 In pairs, discuss some of your relatives. Use some of these adjectives, as in the first example.

single   engaged   married   separated   divorced   widowed

elder sister   nephew   cousin   elder brother   niece   grandfather   sister-in-law great-grandmother   brother-in-law   twin sister   stepmother

A: *'My elder sister is married.'*

B: *'So is mine.'* (or *'Mine isn't.'* or *'I don't have an older sister.'*)

A: *'I haven't got any nephews.'*

B: *'Neither have I.'* (or *'I've got one, two,'* etc.)

COMMON ERRORS

I think so that I've met him before.

What is wrong with this sentence? Why? See the Grammar Reference on page 182.

SPEAKING

1 Read these Speaking Part 3 instructions.

Imagine that you and your partner want to have a party like the one in picture A, avoiding a party like the one in picture B. Talk to each other about how you will organize it and make sure it is a success.

Consider these points: time, day, place, who to invite, music, noise, food and drink, tidying up, parents.

2 Follow the exam instructions in activity 1, concentrating on the points at the end of the activity. Make suggestions using some of these: *'Why don't we … ?'; 'How about … ?'; 'If we can … , let's …'; 'I suppose so, but …'; 'What about … ?'; 'I see what you mean, but I'd rather … '* .

USE OF ENGLISH: key word transformations

1 Use of English Part 3 (key word transformations) may test your ability to use conditionals in the second sentence. If so, the first sentence usually expresses two ideas, with one idea the reason for the other. These are often linked by cause or result words like *so* or participles (see questions 1 and 2 in activity 2 below). Fill in gaps 1–5 with these words:

mixed   opposite   zero   negative   third

In (1) .... conditionals the time reference is normally to a permanent truth, in (2) .... conditionals it is to something in the past, while in (3) .... conditionals there may be one reference to something in the past and another to something in the present. In third or mixed conditionals you often have to change verbs from the positive to the (4) .... (or the other way round). Be careful, though, with verbs that have (5) .... meanings (see question 1 below).

2 Follow the exam instructions, but before you answer each question:
- underline the linking expression in the first sentence.
- underline any references to the past in the first sentence.
- note the kind of conditional that is required (zero, third or mixed).

Then, when you have written your answer, underline any verbs that have changed from positive to negative, or vice versa. The first question has been done as an example.

Complete the second sentence so that it has a similar meaning to the first sentence, using the word given. **Do not change the word given**. You must use between two and five words, including the word given.

1   I <u>forgot</u> her number <u>so</u> I <u>couldn't</u> ring her. (third conditional)
    remembered
    If ..*I had remembered her number,*.. I <u>could</u> have rung her.

2   By pressing the button you lock all the doors.
    press
    All the doors .... the button.

3   I didn't wake up on time because I didn't hear the alarm clock.
    woken
    If I'd heard the alarm clock .... on time.

4   The reason the dog bit him was that he was in our garden.
    bitten
    The dog .... if he hadn't been in our garden.

5   She wrote very fast and as a result made a lot of mistakes.
    slowly
    If she .... she wouldn't have made so many mistakes.

6   Owing to technical difficulties the plane was not able to take off.
    able
    If there hadn't been technical difficulties, the plane .... take off.

7   He hasn't got any money now because he didn't save when he was working.
    would
    If he had saved when he was .... money now.

8   It's just as well you told me or I might have married him.
    you
    I might have married him .... me.

9   Eating too much makes you fat.
    eat
    If you .... you fat.

10 We couldn't play tennis yesterday because of the rain.
    rained
    If .... would've been able to play tennis yesterday.

1. Think of some important events in your life.

1   Note down the events and their consequences like this:

Events	Consequences
Joined youth club.	*Learned how to dance. Now have lots of friends.*

2   Now write third and mixed conditional sentences using your notes, for example:

If I hadn't joined the youth club, I wouldn't have learned how to dance.
If I hadn't joined the youth club, I wouldn't have lots of friends now.

2. Write down six true statements about yourself. They could be about things that you have or haven't got; like or don't like; can or can't do; did, have done, would like to do or are going to do. When you have finished say them to your partner, who should answer using *so* or *neither*.

3. Follow these stages:

1   Look back to the Writing activity on page 122. Imagine that you also worked at the summer camp. Look at this question.

The Co-ordinator has asked you to write reports on the children. Describe one of them, concentrating on his or her personality and ability to get on with others. Write your **report** in **120–180** words in an appropriate style.

2   Read this answer and decide if it follows the instructions. Think about:
1   the length
2   the style
3   the content

Alan is a lively and adventurous boy with a good sense of humour and a ready smile. He loves sports and is always keen to try new ones. He is also happy to spend time on his own: reading, playing computer games and listening to music. It is not always easy, however, to tell what he is thinking or feeling.

He makes friends easily and adapts well to what others want to do. He is a good team player and always like to see fair play, even if sometimes he can become a little too enthusiastic and noisy when playing football.

In conversation he has a quick and enquiring mind. Although he tends to lose interest if he thinks that people do not know their facts, he usually listens carefully to what people say and asks intelligent questions. Above all, he is very good company.

4. Study the answer again and answer these questions:
1   Which paragraphs describe his *personality*?
2   Which describe his *ability to get on with others*?
3   Which do you think are positive points and which are negative? Make two lists.
4   What expressions does the writer use to make contrasts?

5. Now write your answer to the question. Here is some advice:
- Make a plan, dividing the report into paragraphs and noting down your ideas for each.
- You could choose descriptive adjectives from the list in Speaking activity 2 on page 118.
- Remember to use mainly the present simple: *He loves sports …*
- Try to use conditionals: *He tends to … if he thinks …*
- Give examples: *He is also happy to spend time on his own: reading …*
- Avoid informal language to give an impression more of fact than of opinion.
- When you have finished, ask your partner to check your work – particularly for grammar and spelling.

13 Come rain or shine

SPEAKING

1 What are these kinds of weather called?

What kinds of problems can they cause?

Which of them have you experienced? What happened?

Do you think the world's weather is changing? How can this be explained?

2 Discuss these questions:

- Which of these places would you <u>least</u> like to be in during a thunderstorm? Why?

  in an aeroplane   next to an isolated tree   on an empty beach   on top of a mountain

- If you are out of doors, what can you do to avoid being struck by lightning?

READING: multiple choice

1 Put these steps for doing Reading Part 2 in the right order and give a reason for each one.

Example: *1 – b First you want to get the general idea, and not every part of the text is tested.*

a	Watch out especially for answers that contradict the text or suggest ideas that are not in it.
b	Quickly read the whole text, without worrying too much about difficult words or sections.
c	Look at alternative answers A / B / C / D and decide which is nearest to what you have understood.
d	Move on quickly to the next question and repeat all these steps except the first one.
e	Mark the part of the text which relates to the first question.
f	Look for evidence that the answer you have chosen is right and the others are wrong.
g	Study this part of the text to understand what it says about the topic.
h	If you still can't decide which one is right, eliminate the impossible answers and guess.
i	Look at the first question or unfinished statement, but not answers A / B / C / D.

Which of suggestions a–i have you never thought of before? Underline them.

Compare the ideas you have underlined with your partner's. Which do you think are the most useful?

2 Sometimes there is a global question. Read the text opposite quickly and answer this one:

What is the purpose of this text?

A To tell the story of two British climbers in the Alps.

B To describe everyday life in the village of Chamonix.

C To show how new technology can make climbing safer.

D To look at ways climbers can survive in thunderstorms.

3 Look at the first line of each question, read the text again and decide which paragraphs relate to which questions. Draw a vertical line alongside and write the number of the question, for example: 'Q1' next to the first paragraph. Now follow the other steps in activity 1, noting down why each of the alternatives is right or wrong. The first one has been done as an example.

You are going to read an article about the dangers of lightning to mountain climbers. For Questions **1–7**, choose the answer (**A,B,C** or **D**) which you think fits best according to the text.

LIGHTNING IN THE MOUNTAINS

Q1

ON JULY 24 two young British climbers were struck by lightning, though not fatally, on the summit of Petits Charmoz in the French Alps. It occurred just as they were preparing their equipment for the descent of the rock face. One of them suffered skin burns and he was hit with such force that his climbing boots exploded.

Although lightning is greatly feared by climbers and the inhabitants of mountainous areas, it claims relatively few lives in the Alps. But mountain guides have many stories about their nightmarish experiences when climbing in the Mont Blanc area.

'Being caught by an electric storm in the mountains is a terrifying thing,' wrote the guide and writer Lionel Terray. 'The bangs that deafen you, and the lightning strikes that shake and sometimes even lift you off the ground make danger so real that even the bravest are afraid.'

Guides and mountaineers who have miraculously survived such experiences describe very precisely the natural phenomena which precede the first lightning strikes, and which positively indicate the presence above their heads of an intense electric field. They talk of flashes that come from the tips of their ice-axes, of their hair standing straight up on end, of a sound like bees flying around. At that point, conditions are ideal for the first lightning to strike.

A slope covered in snow or small stones should protect people from direct strikes. A small lump of rock, used as a seat, is a good place in an emergency as it can prevent ground currents reaching the body, as long as the spot chosen is at least one metre away from any vertical rock.

But Chamonix mountain rescue teams note that all too often, under the combined effects of panic and haste, climbers faced with the sudden appearance of a thunderstorm forget even the most elementary rules of mountaineering. According to a surgeon at a local hospital, panic turns out to be responsible for over half of all accidents caused by lightning in the mountains.

Lightning experts disagree on whether or not it is a good idea for mountaineers to get rid of any metal objects they may be carrying as soon as a thunderstorm starts. Mountaineering professionals advise climbers to keep well away from equipment such as ice-axes, which should never be left with their tips pointing skywards: in that position they tend to attract lightning.

Some scientists, however, argue that metal instruments, attached to the lower part of the body, can encourage the electricity to jump and therefore reduce the charge passing through the body. They also advise mountaineers to hold on to their ice-axe and to point its tip towards the ground. That, they say, keeps the current away from those parts of the body that are most vulnerable to powerful electric shocks, such as the heart or the brain.

The energy lightning gives off may burn the person's clothes, tear their boots apart and even melt jewellery and necklaces. But there won't be any internal injuries as the electric current will not have penetrated the body. In such circumstances, someone struck by lightning runs a much smaller risk of being killed.

---

1   On July 24, lightning on Petits Charmoz caused
   A   deaths.   ✗ 'not fatally'
   B   panic.   ✗ There is no suggestion of this.
   C   injuries and damage to clothing.   ✓ 'skin burns', 'boots exploded'
   D   damage to climbing equipment.   ✗ There is no evidence for this.

2   Thunderstorms in the Alps
   A   do not frighten mountain guides.
   B   are so violent that many people are frightened of them.
   C   have killed many people there.
   D   are not so dangerous as in other mountains.

3   What may happen before lightning actually strikes?
   A   Ice-axes make a strange sound.
   B   People's hair is flattened.
   C   There is a buzzing noise.
   D   Insects become very active.

4   In thunderstorms, climbers should avoid
   A   parts of the mountain that are in the clouds.
   B   standing in snow on the mountain side.
   C   using individual rocks as seats.
   D   sitting too near to vertical rock.

5   Local people say that in sudden thunderstorms
   A   even mountain rescue teams sometimes panic.
   B   every mountaineer breaks the simplest rules.
   C   panicking climbers can make mistakes.
   D   most mountaineers who panic are killed.

6   Who suggests using metal objects for protection?
   A   lightning experts
   B   mountaineering professionals
   C   amateur climbers
   D   some scientists

7   Scientists say mountaineers are more likely to survive if they
   A   point their ice-axe up.
   B   point their ice-axe down.
   C   take off their boots.
   D   do not wear jewellery.

---

④   Use the context to work out the meanings of these words:

   summit (line 3)   *nightmarish* (line 11)   *slope* (line 28)   *haste* (line 34)

⑤   Imagine you are in the following situations. In each case, what would you do?

   1   You are lost in thick fog in the hills.
   2   Your plane has crashed into deep snow in a big mountain range.
   3   You are in an earthquake.

VOCABULARY: the weather

1 Work in pairs. Mark the January and July average daytime temperature in your country on the thermometer.

2 Think of words to describe each of the temperatures marked, e.g. *10° – mild*.

Then compare your choice of words with your partner's, for example: *When it's 10° you have to wear a coat, so I don't think that's 'mild'.*

3 Put a–f next to the words in the box to show which words you associate with each other.

In some cases more than one answer is possible, as in the example.

a cold b heat c rain d snow e wind f sun

shower ..c, d..	wet	shine ....
cloud	breeze	fog ....
humid	blow	hail ....
pour	chilly	damp ....
storm	bright	frost ....
drizzle	ice	clear ....
mist	sleet	

Which of these words are: nouns? verbs? adjectives? more than one of these?

COMMON ERRORS

Open the window please, I have hot.
What is wrong with this sentence? Why?
See the Grammar Reference on page 182.

GRAMMAR: *so/such ... that*

1 These two examples both express the results of something extreme:
They make danger <u>so</u> real <u>that</u> even the bravest are afraid.
He was hit with <u>such</u> force <u>that</u> his climbing boots exploded.

Which part of speech follows *so* in this structure, and which follows *such*?

2 Complete these sentences, using one of the adjectives or adverbs in List A and one of the nouns in List B. In some cases there is more than one possibility. The first has been done as an example.

List A	List B
low heavy hard	temperatures sky
~~loud~~ thick clear	wind rain ~~thunder~~
deep thin	ice fog snow

1 The *thunder* was so *loud* that it sounded like bombs exploding right next to us.
2 There was such a .... that you could see the mountains fifty miles away.
3 The .... on the roads is so .... that some people are using skis to get to the college.
4 There were such ...., sometimes reaching –25°C, that the sea froze.
5 The .... on the motorway was so .... that we could only see about 25 metres ahead.
6 The .... blew so .... that houses lost their chimneys and caravans were overturned.
7 The .... on the lake is so .... that even the ducks break it when they land!
8 There has been such .... that the reservoirs are full and the rivers in flood.

3 Now use weather adjectives ending in *-y* to make your own sentences.

Example:
The climate here is so <u>showery</u> that you have to take an umbrella whenever you go out.
1 The mountains can be so <u>misty</u> ...
2 It was such a <u>sunny</u> day ...
3 In the North they have such <u>stormy</u> weather ...
4 It's often so <u>foggy</u> in the morning ...
5 British summers are sometimes so <u>cloudy</u> ...
6 There can be such <u>snowy</u> conditions in winter ...
7 It is so <u>windy</u> out at sea ...

GRAMMAR: adjective order

1 When a number of adjectives come before a noun, they are usually in this order:
1 opinion (*beautiful, horrible*)
2 qualities (size, then age, then shape / temperature)
3 colour (*green, black and white*)
4 origin (*Greek, Roman*)
5 material (*ice, stone*)
6 purpose (*sports, camping*)

Now write the kind of adjective by putting a number 1–6 in the space that follows each one.

a magnificent (.........) tall (.........) mountains
b pointed (.........) metal (.........) objects
c small (.........) modern (.........) tent
d 25-year-old (.........) Swiss (.........) climber
e black (.........) leather (.........) driving (.........) gloves
f lovely (.........) thick (.........) woollen (.........) sweater

2 Decide whether the adjectives in 1–6 are in the right order and correct them if they are not.
1 hot Mediterranean nights
2 black nasty clouds
3 Aegean dramatic red sunset
4 cold school freezing bus
5 blue clear beautiful sky
6 grey unpleasant thick fog

PHRASAL VERBS: *turn*

Panic <u>turns out</u> to be responsible for over half of all accidents caused by lightning.

① This means that panic is discovered, or found, to be responsible for over half of all accidents caused by lightning.

Fill in the blanks in 1–8 with a form of *turn* plus one of these words:

up   out   back   over   off   into   on   down

Then match the phrasal verbs you have written with their meanings below.

1   The weather was so dreadful that the Antarctic explorers ....

2   It started as a light shower but soon .... a raging snowstorm.

3   After a week lost in the hills, they suddenly .... ninety miles away.

4   He was .... for the Everest expedition because of his age.

5   Some electrical equipment should be .... during thunderstorms.

6   When she reached the summit, it .... she had set a new record.

7   We kept the heating .... so that we wouldn't freeze.

8   The car went out of control on the ice and ....

a	was discovered	e	rolled upside down
b	operating	f	arrived after delay
c	reversed direction	g	became
d	disconnected	h	rejected, refused

② Imagine you were caught in a storm out at sea in a small boat. Describe what happened and what you did, using some of these phrasal verbs.

USE OF ENGLISH: open cloze

① Where do you think the wettest, the driest, the sunniest, the hottest and the coldest places on Earth are?

② Without filling in any of the gaps, quickly read the text and find out whether you were right.

③ Now follow the Use of English Part 2 exam instructions.

For Questions **1–15**, read the text below and think of the word which best fits each space. Use only **one** word in each space. There is an example at the beginning (**0**).

Extremes IN THE EARTH'S CLIMATE

The Earth is hottest near the Equator, (**0**) ...*as*... this is always roughly the same distance (**1**) .... the Sun and receives its strongest rays. The highest shade temperature (**2**) .... recorded was 58° in the Sahara Desert, in September 1922. In fact, the Sahara is (**3**) .... much hotter than anywhere else that the three countries with the highest average temperatures (**4**) .... the world are all in North Africa. The eastern Sahara is also the world's sunniest place (**5**) .... over 4,000 hours of sunshine a year, which is nearly 11 hours each day. To the south the Sahara is actually getting bigger, with many square miles of previously cultivable land turning (**6**) .... desert every year.

The world's driest place, (**7**) .... , is the Atacama Desert in northern Chile. It is (**8**) .... an arid area that until 1971 it had not rained there for 400 years. The wettest country, on the other (**9**) .... , is Colombia, which has an average of more than 11,000 mm of rain (**10**) .... year, while the place with the record for the most rain in a month is Cherrapunji in India, (**11**) .... once had 9,300 mm in a month. In parts of the Hawaiian mountains it rains so often (**12**) .... there are unlikely to be more than 15 dry days a year. The coldest places are of (**13**) .... near the Poles, where the sun never (**14**) .... very high in the sky and its rays are relatively weak. The lowest temperature ever is −89.2°, recorded in July 1983 at Vostok in Antarctica, (**15**) .... the Russians have a scientific base.

LISTENING

1 In Listening Part 1 and Part 4 you may have to choose the best of three possible answers: A, B or C. Some of the advice on page 128 for doing Reading multiple choice is also useful for Listening multiple choice – but there are some important differences. Complete each of sentences 1–8 using one of the suggestions in A–H below. The first one has been done as an example.

1 *D Look at one part of the test at a time*. because there is no connection between the four parts.
2 .... because these can tell you what the text will be about.
3 .... because this will help you understand the text better.
4 .... because you don't have to understand every word.
5 .... because you might miss something important.
6 .... because misunderstanding them can lead to mistakes.
7 .... because it is difficult to remember after the tape stops.
8 .... because you have one chance in three of being right!

A The second time you listen, write or check all your answers
B Don't worry if the text is sometimes difficult
C Think about the topic before the tape is played
D ~~Look at one part of the test at a time~~
E If you really don't know an answer, guess,
F Don't stop listening while you write your answers
G Be careful with linking words like *so* and *although*
H Read the introduction, questions and answers before you listen

FIRST CERTIFICATE FACTS

Not all the accents in FCE Listening will be standard British English, but none of them will be very strong.

2 Read the first sentence of the Listening Part 4 instructions below and discuss these questions:

- How do weather forecasters get their information?
- How accurate are their predictions?

Now follow the rest of the instructions.

You will hear part of a radio programme about weather forecasting. For Questions **1–7**, choose the best answer, **A**, **B** or **C**.

1 Colin feels that the weather is
   A a boring topic of conversation.
   B a British obsession.   [1]
   C much less boring than he thought.

2 Information about rainfall
   A is sold by the Meteorological Office.
   B is provided free by the Met Office.   [2]
   C is given by the National Rivers Authority.

3 What kind of information does the power industry get from the Met Office?
   A Details on the current weather in France.
   B Whether it is going to be hot or cold. [3]
   C How much electricity will be used.

4 Weather stations send information to the Met Office from
   A the Arctic.
   B Africa.   [4]
   C the ocean.

5 Forecasts for the roads frequently predict
   A frost followed by ice.
   B frost and ice at the same time.   [5]
   C ice followed by frost.

6 The weather in Britain
   A influences North American weather.
   B is influenced by North American   [6]
      weather.
   C is a separate system from North
      American weather.

7 Why are British forecasts less accurate than American ones?
   A The American weather does not
      change so often.
   B The American information comes   [7]
      from more places.
   C The Americans have much more
      advanced technology.

3 Where does the weather in your country usually originate from?

Who needs accurate weather forecasts to do their job properly in your country?

In what ways do changes in the weather affect your everyday life?

1 In Speaking Part 4 you will spend about four minutes discussing ideas with the examiner and another candidate. Sometimes, as in everyday life, you may not be able to think of the right word or phrase and it might be necessary to paraphrase, or to ask the other person for help. In pairs, look at sentences 1–12 and decide which of the following words the speaker is looking for in each case:

> shiver   melt   umbrella   hurricane   heatwave   soaked   shelter
> tornado   damp   drought   rise   avalanche

1   *It's the thing you use to* keep you dry in the rain.
2   *What's the name for* a very long time without rain?
3   *It's where you go* when there's very bad weather.
4   *It's when you're* completely wet.
5   *What's one word for* 'a bit wet'?
6   *What's the word for* when ice turns into water?
7   *What's the opposite of* a 'fall' in temperature?
8   *It's what you do when* you're so cold that you start to shake.
9   *What do you call* a really violent storm, like the ones they get in the Caribbean?
10 *It's a kind of* violent circular storm.
11 *It's what you call* a lot of snow and ice falling down the side of a mountain.
12 *What's another way of saying* 'a period of time when the weather is much hotter than usual'?

2 Choose six expressions from this list without telling your partner which they are. Then ask questions or make statements about them using the phrases in italics above. In each case, he or she must say which word you are talking about.

Examples:
What's the name for the water you find on the ground during the night?
dew
It's when water reaches 100°, or when you think the weather is very hot.
boiling

> raindrops   darkness   global warming   visibility   waves   ~~dew~~
> climate change   ozone layer   frostbite   sea level   greenhouse effect
> gust   high winds   calm   snowflakes   gale   hailstones   seasons
> evaporation   ~~boiling~~

Now think of six words of your own and do the same with each one.

3 Discuss these questions, paraphrasing or asking your partner for help where necessary:

• What do you like most and what do you like least about the weather in your country?
• Are the weather forecasts usually accurate? Why? Why not?
• What will happen if world temperatures rise? How will it affect your country?
• Is there anything we can do to stop this happening?
• Do you think people in hot countries are different from those in cold countries? Why?
• What differences does the climate cause in the way people eat, drink and dress?
• How does it affect their daily timetable and the kinds of places they live and work in?
• Which jobs are more difficult to do, or dangerous, in bad weather? Why?

VOCABULARY: jobs

In pairs, look at the list of jobs below and for each one decide:

a   what the person's job consists of.

b   which of the qualities or skills below are needed.

doctor   schoolteacher   bricklayer   secretary   engineer   musician   accountant journalist   farm labourer   shop assistant   computer programmer   factory worker ski instructor   disc jockey   charity worker   office worker   sales representative   nurse au pair   scientist   social worker   barman / barmaid   nursery assistant

patience   academic ability   organizational skills   friendliness   keyboard skills self-confidence   financial skills   physical strength   cheerfulness   artistic skills   politeness language skills   strength of character   telephone skills   concern for others

READING: multiple matching

1   Would you like to work abroad? Why? Why not?

2   In Reading Part 4 you have to find specific details quickly. The questions tell you what you are looking for and often this means you have to find the same information in the text, but in different words. Underline this part of the text, as has been done for example question 0.

You are going to read some advertisements for books about working abroad. For Questions **1–14**, choose from the books **A–E**. The books may be chosen more than once. When more than one answer is required, these may be given in any order. There is an example at the beginning **(0)**.

Which book or books:

tells you what to do to get a job serving drinks?	**0** **D**	
discusses the problems you might face?	**1**	
refers to entertainment in the places where work is available?	**2**	
includes reports by people who have practical experience?	**3**	
tells you how much money you will earn?	**4**	
suggests where you can learn a language?	**5**	
talks about places where there are more and more jobs?	**6**	
advises you on finding somewhere to stay?	**7**	
gives advice on training for a profession?	**8**	
talk about a job selling things to the public?	**9**	**10**
are bigger than the first edition of the book?	**11**	**12**
mention farm work?	**13**	**14**

A   The Directory of Jobs and Careers Abroad   408 pages

This new and enlarged edition of the definitive guide to all kinds of work abroad gives essential information on long-term career opportunities around the world for people from all walks of life, from school leavers to fully qualified professionals.

It lists the professions and trades in demand and gives all the facts on careers in Europe, Australia, New Zealand, the USA, Canada, etc., for teachers, doctors, nurses, bricklayers, secretaries, engineers, accountants, computer programmers, journalists, etc. It includes new chapters on the rapidly expanding possibilities in Eastern Europe and the Baltic States.

'Strong on how to get jobs and permits almost anywhere in the world.' Time Out

All you need to know to get a job abroad £9.95   **ISBN 1 85458 025 6**

B The Teenager's Vacation Guide to Work, Study & Adventure   224 pages

The first book to cover the wide range of jobs, study courses and adventure holidays that are available for teenagers in Britain and abroad during the school vacations.

It lists hundreds of employers: summer schools and other educational establishments; adventure holiday companies, multi-activity groups and non-profit youth organizations arranging courses, expeditions, homestays, exchanges and termstays in Britain, Europe and worldwide. Work picking grapes in France or rehabilitating ponds in Scotland; study Spanish in England, Spain or Mexico, music in the South of France, art in Florence or Dublin; adventure on land, sea or air.
'Plenty of good ideas.' Ideal Home

Bursting with ideas for the holidays £6.95   **ISBN 1 85458 044 2**

C Working in Ski Resorts – Europe   216 pages

The second edition of the book that contains all the information necessary in order to find seasonal work as a ski instructor, chalet girl / boy, teacher, au pair, shop assistant, disc jockey, snow cleaner, ski technician, courier, office worker or representative in a ski resort.

The first part of the book, 'A Job Before You Go', describes how to pre-arrange work with over 90 ski tour operators, school ski party organizers and other organizations. The second part, 'Finding a Job on the Spot', gives reports on over 40 resorts, explaining where the jobs are and how to get them, including information on the skiing, accommodation and nightlife.
'Thoroughly recommended.' I.S.C.O. Careers Bulletin

Work and play in the snow £5.95   **ISBN 0 907638 87 2**

D Work Your Way Around the World   480 pages

This new edition of the classic guide for the working traveller incorporates hundreds of first-hand accounts and offers authoritative advice on how to find work around the world, either in advance or on the spot. It includes new and expanded sections on working opportunities in Hong Kong and Eastern Europe, arranging a contract on a cruise ship, childcare jobs worldwide including in Australia, fruit picking from France to New Zealand, new voluntary projects in Latin America and much more.

Plus updated information on how to work a passage, dates and details of harvests, how to become a barmaid or barman, door-to-door salesperson, pineapple picker, ski tow operator, etc., etc.
'The budget globetrotter's bible.' The Independent
The working traveller's Bible £9.95   **ISBN 1 85458 074 4**

E Teaching English Abroad   320 pages

The definitive guide to short- and long-term opportunities for teachers in the challenging field of Teaching English as a Foreign Language. The book contains substantial chapters on over twenty countries where EFL is a major profession including Greece, Spain, Eastern Europe, Turkey, Japan and Taiwan, plus surveys of the range of possibilities in Latin America and Africa.

Each country chapter discusses the ways in which speakers of English can find work, the red tape involved, contracts and salaries, plus a list of language schools which hire English teachers. Plus: how to become qualified in EFL, the role of recruitment agencies, and the possible risks and how to avoid them.
'A must read for the would-be TEFLER.' Overseas Jobs Express

Talk your way around the world £8.95   **ISBN 1 85458 0485**

3 Which of these books would you find most interesting? Why?

Is there any work they mention which specially interests you?

WRITING: a letter of application

1 In Writing Part 2 you might be asked to write a job application letter, which will need to be in a formal style. Read this advertisement and choose a job that you would like to do.

MAJOR INTERNATIONAL ORGANIZATION...

regularly needs Administrators, Nursing Staff, Scientists, Technicians and Secretarial Assistants. Also Translators, Interpreters, Childcare Assistants, Shop and Sales Staff, Receptionists, Visitor Guides and Telephone Staff for temporary and / or part-time work. Interviews held frequently.

Apart from their mother tongue, candidates must be fluent in at least one other language and be willing to travel. Write in English, stating field of work interest and level of your qualifications, to:

▶ **RECRUITMENT SPECIALISTS, PO BOX 341, LONDON EC4 5YK, UK.**

2 Read this example letter. Fill in gaps 1–10 with a suitable form of the verb in brackets.

Dear Sir or Madam,

I (1) .... (write) to apply for the position of Secretarial Assistant, as advertised in the October issue of 'International Jobs'.

I am aged 19 and I (2) .... (be born) in Italy, but for the last three years I (3) .... (live) in London. Last June I (4) .... (pass) Cambridge First Certificate with a Grade A. In addition to English I speak Spanish and Catalan quite fluently, owing to the fact that I (5) .... (live) in Barcelona for several years before we (6) .... (move) to Britain.

As you will see from my enclosed curriculum vitae, I (7) .... (have) four temporary positions as a secretary and I can provide you with excellent references from each one. I like to work hard and I would particularly enjoy (8) .... (work) with staff from different countries.

I (9) .... (be) available for the position from next January as my contract with my current employers ends in December, and I could attend an interview this month on any Tuesday or Thursday. I look forward to (10) .... (hear) from you.

Yours faithfully,
Annabella Tarantino

3 Find more formal equivalents in the letter for these expressions, as in the example.

1 job   *position*
2 as well as ....
3 because ....
4 give ....
5 really good ....
6 very much ....
7 free ....
8 go to ....
9 please write soon ....

4 How would Annabella answer these questions when planning her job application?

1 Who are you writing to? Do you know the person's name?
2 Why are you writing? Which job?
3 Where and when did you hear about the job?
4 How old are you? What experience relevant to the job do you have?
5 Why do you want the job? Why would you do it well?
6 Are you enclosing / sending anything with the letter?
7 How will you end the letter?
8 In what style should you write?

5 Look at these instructions and then follow steps 1–3.

You have just read the advertisement above. Choose a job and write a letter of application in English to Recruitment Specialists. Write your **letter** in **120–180** words in an appropriate style. Do not include any addresses.

1 Answer questions 1–8 above and use this as a plan for your letter.
2 Group the answers into at least three paragraphs.
3 Write the application.

USE OF ENGLISH: error correction

1 There are many reasons why the extra words in Use of English Part 4 are wrong, but some of the most common errors involve auxiliary verb forms, articles, pronouns and prepositions. Other types include mistakes such as double negatives, incorrect positioning and incorrect forms of conjunctions, phrasal verbs and reflexive pronouns. As you follow the exam instructions, also note down the part of speech of each of the answers.

For Questions **1–15**, read the text below and look carefully at each line. Some of the lines are correct, and some have a word which should not be there. If a line is correct, put a tick (✓) by the number. If a line has a word which should **not** be there, write the word **at the end of the line**. There are two examples at the beginning (**0** and **00**)

TIPS FOR JOB APPLICATIONS

0	Before you put pen to paper, analyse the ad carefully so by you can show	*by*
00	how your skills and experience match the requirements of the job. Write down	✓
1	how you fulfil the key requirements, backing up what you say with a proof;	
2	but if only you don't exactly match the requirements, don't be put off.	
3	Follow instructions carefully, for instance if it says phone for an application	
4	form, don't send your CV instead of. Write your application in black, saying	
5	why you are being applying. Be positive about your achievements and don't mention	
6	work you've been turned down for or also ways in which you don't meet	
7	the job criteria. When you have finished, check it through in such case you	
8	have made any grammar or spelling mistakes, then photocopy it for to ensure	
9	that you keep a permanent record of what you have ever written.	
10	Your CV should to include your name, address and telephone number; education,	
11	training and qualifications; achievements; career history and work experience, plus any	
12	skills you have such as foreign languages. Work experience, incidentally, should be in	
13	reverse chronological order so as that the most recent job comes first. Adapt the	
14	CV to each job you apply for, but remember yourself that there's no need	
15	to mention salary details, referees, dependent children, marital status or the religion	
	unless for reasons of your own you want to do so.	

2 How do people in your country usually find jobs? What would you add to the advice given in the text above? What would you leave out? Why?

STUDY CHECK

1 Look at the advertisement on page 136. Imagine the perfect job for your partner and write an advertisement for it. You should write between 40 and 60 words in short simple sentences, but without any informal expressions. Include as many of these points as you can:

- the name or kind of employers
- minimum and / or maximum age
- qualifications required
- where the work will be

- the type of job
- languages needed, with level
- kind of person wanted
- how to apply

2 When you have finished your advertisement, think again about your partner and write some or all of these notes next to the main points:

← he / she would enjoy this job a lot
← exactly the right age!
← would be good at this kind of work
← that's his / her first language!
← will pass First Certificate soon, we hope!
← he / she has the right qualifications
← would like to work there, I'm sure
← is that sort of person, definitely!

3 1 Swap advertisements with your partner. Read the advert and the notes with it (as in Writing Part 1).

2 Write a plan for your letter of application using the questions in activity 4 on page 136.

3 Write your letter, making sure that you include all the information that is asked for.

4 When you have finished, check your work carefully. If you find any mistakes, decide why you made them and how you will avoid making them in future.

14 Making a better world

SPEAKING

① Look at the people in the pictures on these two pages. In each case, decide which two of these are their main aims:

to reduce waste   to avoid using fuel   to eat chemical-free food
to protect the countryside   to recycle used material
to avoid polluting the air   to stop the construction of roads
to discourage the use of artificial fertilizers

② Which of these are common ways of protecting the environment in your country?

Which of them do you think are the most effective?
Which are the least effective? Why?

③ What other ways of preventing damage to the environment do you know of?

READING: multiple matching

① Look at these Reading Part 4 instructions and then underline the key words in Questions 1–15. The key words in Question 0 have already been underlined as an example. Then do the exam task.

You are going to read a magazine article in which people are interviewed about the environment. For Questions **1–15**, choose from the people **A–D**. The people may be chosen more than once. When more than one answer is required, these may be given in any order. There is an example at the beginning (**0**).

Which of the people A–D:

was in <u>danger</u> of having an <u>accident</u>?	0 D
no longer drives a car?	1
thinks about the effect of tourism on other countries?	2
has tried to prevent new roads being constructed?	3
is sure the environmentalists are going to win?	4
throw out as little waste as possible?	5 6
had to eat cold food?	7
has stopped using a bicycle for some journeys?	8
says we need to change but we can still enjoy ourselves?	9
talks about media interest in protests?	10
has gone to live somewhere else in order to travel less?	11
believes that by the time people react it will be too late?	12
feel that politicians are out of touch with public opinion?	13 14
wants nothing to do with companies that make weapons?	15

Change your world

A John Humphreys, radio and TV presenter

'I bought a small dairy farm in Wales about 16 years ago but I became unhappy using artificial fertilizers and pesticides and so decided to change to organic farming. 5 I'm now looking for another farm which does not need any chemical input, where I can use plants and vegetables to make the soil richer. In my everyday life I am a typically urban person. I need the car for my job, but use it as little as possible outside that. I think the most 10 important thing about green living is to create minimum waste. I live on my own and I only fill one, possibly two, supermarket bags with rubbish each week. I recycle tins and bottles, and use energy-efficient light bulbs. I am very pessimistic about the future. I don't understand why 15 no one seems to care. Our rivers are drying up but people won't do anything until the water stops coming through their taps.'

B Melanie Palmer, marketing executive

'The first thing I did was change my shopping habits. I 20 started buying organic food and products with the Fairtrade label, which shows they're made from sustainable resources and the workers and farmers get a fair deal. Then I moved my bank account to the Co-operative to ensure my money was being invested 25 ethically, not in businesses like arms manufacturers or polluting oil companies. And nowadays I always book my foreign holidays through a tour operator that has good environmental and social policies. I realize that those of us who earn a good salary, and enjoy spending it, are 30 over-consuming the world's resources. But I'm afraid it's just not realistic to expect people to stop doing what they like doing. I just wish everyone knew that alternative, less damaging, ways of doing things exist – and that these can be fun too.'

35 C Laura Field, primary school teacher

'I started off by moving close enough to my work so I could cycle, walk or use public transport. Then I realized I could live without the car. I began taking my young 55 daughter Freya to school on my bike, but now we walk. I 40 have to rely on friends to do our recycling. Shopping was also a big problem at first, but now I shop locally. At home I have reduced my fuel usage a lot by putting plastic on the windows and only heating rooms when we're in them. I recycle paper, glass and cans, so our dustbin is only 45 about one quarter full each week. I know that our water is polluted, that the climate's changing. The Government is afraid of doing anything about it because they think people don't want to change their lifestyles. But we're intelligent enough to try to avoid an environmental crisis 50 and I think it shows a total lack of moral courage not to face it.'

D Danny Richardson, student

'I first got involved in direct action during the battle to stop them building that bypass, which was when the press and TV really began to take notice of us. It meant living in a very damp and cold tree-house, with no hot meals and the ever-present risk of a fall, but a real sense of community developed among us. Since then there must have been dozens of campaigns against motorway 60 building and the movement has built up tremendous force. We've had so many successes and it's clear that so many millions of people support us that we know we're unstoppable now. If you ask me it's all come about because people see the decision-making process as 65 remote, and realize the political parties only listen to the rich and big business. But now it's ordinary people who are setting the pace, and if governments don't listen they'll be left behind.'

② Would you consider doing any of the things mentioned?

GRAMMAR: past modals

Since then there <u>must have been</u> dozens of campaigns against motorway building and the movement has built up tremendous force.

1 We use the form *modal + have + past participle* to talk about the past. Match each pair of examples 1–4 below with one of uses a–d.

a   for things that were possible but did not happen
b   for things that possibly happened but we aren't sure if they happened or not
c   for things we are sure happened or did not happen
d   for things we expected to happen but did not happen, or to criticize a past action

1   They should have thought before they destroyed it.
    You shouldn't have made the same mistakes again.
2   She must have been tired after such a long journey.
    You can't have enjoyed seeing such awful destruction.
3   You might have been killed in that forest fire.
    We could have saved a lot of the animals that died.
4   I suppose there's a chance they could have survived.
    He may (*or* might) have gone there, though nobody's seen him.

2 Think about the situation in section D of the Reading text when Danny was living in a tree-house, and match the beginnings 1–6 of these sentences with their endings a–f.

1   In the trees in winter it must have   a   been left to grow.
2   At any time he could have   b   been happy all the time.
3   He thought the planners shouldn't have   c   increased public support for them.
4   He felt that the trees should have   d   fallen and been badly injured.
5   In those conditions he can't have   e   decided to build a road there.
6   TV film of the protesters might have   f   been very uncomfortable at times.

COMMON ERRORS

They must have found her, haven't they?
What is wrong with this sentence? Why? See the Grammar Reference on page 183.

3 1   In pairs, look at picture **a**. Exchange opinions about what people might, must or can't have done to create that situation, and what they should or shouldn't have done to avoid it happening.

2   Look at picture **b**, which shows the same scene some years later. Say what may or could have happened, and what people might or must have done to improve the situation so much.

GRAMMAR: *wish/if only*

I just <u>wish</u> everyone <u>knew</u> that alternative, less damaging, ways of doing things exist.

1 We use *wish* (or the stronger *if only*) with the past simple when we'd like something in the present to be different. This may be improbable or impossible.

Examples:
I wish we lived on a Pacific island.
If only I was (or were) taller.

To express a wish about ability, we can use *could*: *I wish I could change the way people think.*

For Questions 1–6 opposite, complete the second sentence so that it has a similar meaning to the first sentence. Use *wish* (or *only*, as part of *if only*) and other words to complete each sentence. You must use between two and five words.

Example:

It's a pity I haven't got a bike.

I ..*wish I had*.. a bike.

1   It's a shame you don't have time to help.

I .... time to help.

2   It's sad that city life is so unhealthy.

I .... more healthy.

3   It's a terrible pity I can't go there with you.

If .... there with you.

4   I'm sorry you're not here.

I .... here.

5   It is most unfortunate that you cannot attend.

We .... attend.

6   I'm fed up with having to pick up this rubbish.

If .... to pick up this rubbish.

2 For a wish about the past – often something we regret – we use the past perfect, or *could have* (for ability):

I wish they hadn't built that airport.
If only we had been there to prevent it.
I wish I had protested about it, too.
If only I could have done something.

Do these questions in the same way as 1–6 above, but this time using the word given.

Example:

I wish I had told you.

sorry

I'm ..*sorry I didn't tell*.. you.

1   I wish people had taken their advice.

pity

It's a .... their advice.

2   I wish you hadn't thrown that out.

silly

It was .... that out.

3   If only I had warned them in time.

regret

I really .... in time.

4   I bet they wish they had never started that fire.

sorry

I bet they .... that fire.

5   I wish I'd told the others about this.

mistake

It was .... the others about this.

6   We wish you had been able to come to the meeting.

shame

It was .... not come to the meeting.

3 To express irritation or frustration about something happening now, we use *would*:

I wish it would stop raining.
I wish you wouldn't keep on moaning!
If only he would listen to me.
I wish you wouldn't interrupt!

(*I wish you didn't interrupt all the time* is also possible, but for something that generally happens.)

Do these questions in the same way as in activity 1 opposite, using *wish* or *only*.

Example:

I don't often hear from him.

I ..*wish (that) he would phone*.. me more often.

1   Why does he always tell the same old jokes?

I .... tell the same old jokes.

2   When are you going to change your socks?

I .... change your socks.

3   I so much want her to come back.

If .... come back.

4   Please don't push other people.

I .... pushing other people.

5   His behaviour is awfully childish.

I .... grow up.

6   Why do you keep on making the same mistakes?

If .... on making the same mistakes!

4 What would you say in the following situations? Use *wish* or *if only* plus different verbs to write sentences.

Example:

It's early in the morning and you don't want to get out of bed.
'I wish I'd gone to bed earlier.'
'I wish I didn't have school today.'
'If only I could stay here all morning!' etc.

1   You want to buy something new to wear but it is very expensive.

2   On the first day of your summer holidays you have a stomach upset.

3   You're visiting a country where you can't speak a word of the language.

4   Someone is talking all the time while you and your friend are watching a film at the cinema.

5   You're just about to get on the bus when you realize you've left all your money at home.

6   Your brother or sister is always 'borrowing' things from your room.

7   There is one subject that you really hate having to study.

8   You left some valuable things in the car and they were stolen.

> **COMMON ERRORS**
>
> *It's time we find a solution to this problem.*
>
> What is wrong with this sentence? Why? See the Grammar Reference on page 183.

VOCABULARY: the environment

1️⃣ All these jumbled expressions relate to the environment. Find five positive and thirteen negative expressions. The first letter of each word is underlined.

> t̲fsoer e̲fsri   d̲aic n̲ria   d̲welifli troneoptci   b̲golla a̲wgrinm   l̲oi i̲lsck
> h̲extusa mes̲fu   c̲nesrnavtioo   o̲reifhsignv   o̲rditavaciyit   r̲gehenoeus fe̲fcet
> n̲ccnoer o̲fr l̲naiam ea̲wlfer   s̲dentrctiuo fo̲ i̲rna r̲fosste   m̲ndugpi a̲west t̲a a̲es
> er̲lwo r̲enyeg c̲mtnoosunpi   r̲cbano n̲modoiex   d̲seiutnctro fo̲ t̲eh n̲ooze y̲lare
> n̲geer n̲aaswrees   p̲sesiec caig̲fn n̲etxinocti

2️⃣ Look again at the positive expressions. Which of them do you think are effective and which are not? Why?

3️⃣ Look at the negative expressions. Which of them do you think are a serious danger and which are not? Why? What can we do about the most dangerous ones?

LISTENING

1️⃣ In Listening Part 3 you may hear people giving their opinions. Look at the instructions and the questions below and for each of A–F note down one possible cause of each problem.

2️⃣ Follow the exam instructions.

You will hear five people talking about environmental problems. For Questions **1–5**, choose which of the subjects **A–F** each speaker is talking about. Use the letters only once. There is one extra letter which you do not need to use.

A	air pollution		
B	pollution of the sea	Speaker 1	1
C	climate change	Speaker 2	2
D	new illnesses	Speaker 3	3
E	nuclear radiation	Speaker 4	4
F	loss of forests	Speaker 5	5

3️⃣ Listen again and note down:
(Speaker 1) two kinds of victim.
(Speaker 2) two things that are rising.
(Speaker 3) two words for things that have been thrown away.
(Speaker 4) three kinds of thing that have disappeared; three parts of the world where this has happened.
(Speaker 5) two things that cause the problem; at least two results of it.

WRITING: a discursive composition

1️⃣ In Writing Part 2 you may be able to choose an 'opinion' composition. If you do so, it is important to link your arguments together well. Study the linking expressions below and decide what is the purpose a–d of each group 1–4.

a   To add information, often to reinforce a point.
b   To indicate the order of points or reasons.
c   To contrast or give another point of view.
d   To say something happens because of something else.

1   to begin with, first of all, firstly, first, secondly, next, then, finally, lastly, to sum up, to conclude.
2   so, therefore, consequently, as a result, hence, thus (these last two words are quite formal).
3   also, too, as well as, besides, on top of that, apart from that, furthermore, moreover (these last two words are also quite formal).
4   but, (al)though, however, while, even though, even so, yet, nevertheless, in spite of, on the other hand.

2 Write a suitable sentence to precede each of 1–6, as in the example.

We have made a certain amount of progress.. Even so, a lot more work will be needed.

1	....	Therefore, things have been getting worse.
2	....	As well as that, they kept it secret.
3	....	However, I think there is a solution.
4	....	Firstly, because the figures prove it.
5	....	All of them, though, have failed.
6	....	So we must do something about it now.

3 Look through this outline text without completing any of the sentences.

Which of the following questions does it answer?

a   What do you think are the biggest dangers to the world's environment?
b   What should we do about the biggest dangers to the world's environment?
c   What do you think is the biggest danger to the world's environment and what should we do about it?

Our planet is under attack. On land, in the air and in the water there is a greater threat to the continued existence of life on Earth than there has been for many millions of years.

Firstly, ...
....

As a result, ...
....

A further problem is ....
....

As well as that, ...
....

Finally, there is ....
....

In spite of this, ...
....

To sum up, all this is doing tremendous harm to the world: above, on and below the surface. The fact that these are often international problems makes them even more serious.

4 Complete the text above, explaining why you think these dangers are serious and giving examples where you can. Try to use some of the notes you made in Listening 3 on page 142.

5 Now answer Question **c** in activity 3. When you plan your composition, think about these questions:

- What are the two main differences between Question **a** and Question **c**?
- Do you want to write about one of the topics from the Listening, or one of your own?
- How are you going to organize your composition into paragraphs?
- In what style is it best to write compositions like this?
- What reasons and examples can you include to justify your choice of biggest danger?
- What suggestions can you think of for appropriate action?

When you write your composition, try to include some or all of the following:

- a short opening sentence that should interest the reader, within an introductory paragraph that gives the background and outlines your opinion.
- different ways of saying 'biggest danger', to avoid too much repetition.
- forms like *should have done* if you think mistakes have been made in the past.
- the verb *wish* plus the correct tense if you feel strongly about what people should do.
- linking expressions from activity 2 above.
- expressions from Vocabulary opposite.
- a short summary or conclusion at the end. Here you can give your opinion again, but in different words and reinforced by the arguments you have used in the middle paragraphs.

Remember to check your work when you have finished!

VOCABULARY and SPEAKING

1 Work in groups. Put each of the following into one of categories 1–5.

goldfish rabbit bee snake whale hen ant bear ox wolf lizard wasp

goldfish   rabbit   bee   snake   whale   hen   ant   bear   ox   wolf   lizard   wasp
sardine   mosquito   frog   dolphin   shark   pigeon   crocodile   camel   rat   goat
eagle   toad   salmon   fox   donkey   cockroach   tortoise   goose

1   Mammals:

....

2   Birds:

....

3   Fish:

....

4   Reptiles / amphibians:

....

5   Insects:

....

2 Add at least three examples of your own to each of 1–5.

3 Think about all the creatures in 1–5 in the context of your country. Which of them are:

a   common?   b   rare?   c   only found in captivity?   d   kept as pets?
e   eaten?   f   used as working animals?   g   hunted?   h   destroyed as pests?

Why are the creatures in category b rare?

Do you disagree with the way any of those in c–h are treated? Why?

4 Choose one or two creatures that you associate with these words:

Example: paws: *rabbit, bear*.

tail   wings   claws   shell   sting   horns   hump   fins   beak   poison   fur   hair

LISTENING

1 In Listening Part 1 there may be questions about people's opinions, or whether the speakers agree with each other or not. As in Part 4 (and in real life), people sometimes change their minds during a conversation, so you need to be careful not to decide on your answer too quickly. Read the instructions, the example question and the transcript of the text, then answer these two questions:

1   Which answer, A, B or C, seems correct if you only concentrate on the part of the text in italics?
2   Which answer, A, B or C, is right if you think about the whole text?

You will hear people talking in eight different situations. For Questions **1–8**, choose the best answer, **A**, **B** or **C**.

Example: You are out walking in the country when you hear two people talking. What have they just seen?

A   a wolf
B   a fox
C   a dog

Man: *Did you see that? Moving over there? It was a wolf! I heard they're making a comeback in this part of the world but I didn't really expect to see one that close!*
Woman: Oh don't be silly, Steve. It was the wrong colour and anyway it was no bigger than next door's dog. It's much more likely to be a fox, and a young one at that.
Man: Well now you mention it, I suppose it was a bit on the small side. You're right – that's what it was.

1   You are in the country when you overhear a conversation about a bird. What does the man say about it?
   A what kind it is   **B** where it lives   **C** what kind he thinks it is | **1** |

2   You hear two people arguing about animals kept in zoos. What do they disagree about?
   A how long they live   **B** the kind of food they are given   **C** the amount of space they have | **2** |

3   You hear a woman talking about dogs that bark a lot. What solution does she suggest?
   A a noise   **B** a punishment   **C** a reward | **3** |

4   You hear this woman talking on the radio. What is she protesting about?
   A the killing of animals   **B** the import of live animals   **C** the export of live animals | **4** |

5   You hear this young man interviewed on the radio. What is he angry about?
   A horse riding   **B** dog fighting   **C** fox hunting | **5** |

6   You hear this conversation about looking after pets. What are they discussing?
   A birds   **B** fish   **C** cats | **6** |

7   This girl is talking about the pets she likes most. Which does she have?
   A a rabbit   **B** a dog   **C** a mouse | **7** |

8   You hear these people choosing a pet for their grandmother. What do they decide to get?
   A a cat   **B** a little dog   **C** a big dog | **8** |

SPEAKING

In Speaking Part 3, the examiner might ask you to do a problem-solving task like this:

> Imagine you have been asked to find a good home for these abandoned animals.
> Discuss which of these people would be the best owner for each of the animals.

Before you begin, do the following:

- Look back at the advice on page 43.
- Listen again to the last conversation in the Listening for useful language.
- Think about all the ways you have heard in this Unit of giving opinions and making suggestions.

  While you are doing the task you might want to:

- start the conversation with a suggestion like '*Shall we look at this picture first?*'
- keep it moving by saying '*Now, what do you think about ...?*', '*So we've decided so far that ...*', or '*We haven't talked about this one yet, have we?*'
- use question tags like '*don't you?*' and '*isn't it?*' to check whether your partner agrees and encourage him or her to comment.
- Finish with '*So we agree that ... , but ...*'. Remember that there is no 'right' answer, and that you can agree to disagree.

Read the Use of English Part 1 instructions below, and then follow this advice:

- Revise the linking expressions in Writing activity 1 page 142.
- Look back at the information about Paper 3 Part 1 on page 21.

For Questions **1–15**, read this text and decide which word **A**, **B**, **C** or **D** best fits each gap. There is an example at the beginning **(0)**.

Example: 0 A in (**B**) on **C** by **D** at

Entertainment for dogs

What do dogs really like to watch **(0)** …. television? Peter Neville, who studies animal behaviour, thinks he knows and as a **(1)** …. he has made a video called *Cool for Dogs*. It is not quite *Baywatch*, but it is **(2)** …. to keep pets amused when you leave them at home.

Many owners think their four-legged companion is highly intelligent and **(3)** …. needs constant mental stimulation. A recent **(4)** …. of Britain's dog owners found that over a third of them were **(5)** …. that their pet was as clever as a nine-year-old child. There are even owners who think some dogs are brighter than the average university student, **(6)** …. may say more about our education problems than about our dogs. These are presumably just the **(7)** …. of people who feel their pets need an entertaining dog video when they are out at **(8)** …. .

So what is *Cool for Dogs* like? Basically it consists **(9)** …. a series of short clips: rocky coastlines, soppy music, sunsets, lots of dogs running around and things **(10)** …. that. It is not what Hollywood would call a big production and **(11)** …. it lacks something – a plot. But dogs, **(12)** …. Dr Neville, are keen TV-watchers and they particularly like nature programmes. **(13)** …. we tested it on Laila, our dog. The result? It took several dog biscuits to get nine-month-old Laila to sit in **(14)** …. of the television, and five minutes into the film her eyes had not moved off the last dog biscuit in my hand. Not a huge success, but who's to say it won't **(15)** …? It has, after all, been passed as suitable viewing for pets of any age: not even Parental Guidance is required.

1	**A** conclusion	**B** cause	**C** result	**D** product
2	**A** regarded	**B** supposed	**C** told	**D** considered
3	**A** therefore	**B** however	**C** owing to	**D** because of
4	**A** measurement	**B** judgement	**C** survey	**D** revision
5	**A** reasoned	**B** convinced	**C** proved	**D** influenced
6	**A** what	**B** that	**C** which	**D** whom
7	**A** make	**B** sort	**C** brand	**D** set
8	**A** job	**B** work	**C** office	**D** employment
9	**A** on	**B** of	**C** in	**D** with
10	**A** like	**B** such	**C** as	**D** though
11	**A** moreover	**B** firstly	**C** however	**D** despite
12	**A** following from	**B** relying on	**C** stated by	**D** according to
13	**A** While	**B** So	**C** Although	**D** Yet
14	**A** face	**B** opposite	**C** front	**D** view
15	**A** get over	**B** catch on	**C** take up	**D** bring about

STUDY CHECK

1 Complete these sentences with your past, present or future wishes. Think of as many wishes as you can for each sentence. Talk, for example, about places you would like to be, what you don't like having to do and things other people do or say that you are fed up with.

1 I wish I was ....
2 I wish I had ....
3 I wish I didn't ....
4 I wish I could ....
5 I wish I had done ....
6 I wish I hadn't ....
7 I wish I could have ....
8 I wish .... would ....

Now think again about your answers to Questions 5 and 6. Write two sentences about each saying what might or might not have happened if you had or hadn't done that.

2 You have received this letter from a penfriend, asking for information about the environment in your country. Read the letter carefully and use some of the notes you have made on it to reply, answering all her questions. Write your **letter** in an appropriate style.

a lot of us are worried

now more recycling

Greenpeace? Green Party?

new laws against pollution

what my friends and I do!

less waste! fewer cars!

Just one last thing: I'm writing an international report for Life on Earth magazine so I wonder if you could help me? What I'd like is a brief outline of what people in your country feel about the environment and what is being done there to protect it. What steps are the government and big companies taking? Which environmental organizations are active there, and how effective are they? What are ordinary people – particularly young people – doing about it? And, finally, what else do you think should be done?

Looking forward to hearing from you.

EXAM STUDY GUIDE

1   When you are **revising**, which of these are good ideas and which are not? Why?
    If an idea is bad, write what you should do next to it.

    a   Look back through the book and your notes, highlighting the main points.
        ....

    b   Read and listen to anything in English that interests you. ....

    c   Practise talking only to native English speakers. ....

    d   Leave most of your revising until the day before the exam. ....

    e   Talk to other students about any worries you might have. ....

    f   Memorize whole sentences or paragraphs to use in Speaking and Writing.
        ....

    g   Shortly before the exam, look again at the points you marked in **a** above.
        ....

2   Look at this list of grammar points. Mark those you think you need to revise most, numbering them from 5 to 1 (the one you need to revise most of all).

☐ present forms	☐ modal verbs	☐ articles	☐ participle adjectives
☐ *wish / if only*	☐ future forms	☐ *do / make*	☐ *too / enough*
☐ frequency adverbs	☐ comparatives	☐ past forms	☐ contrast links
☐ phrasal verbs	☐ zero conditional	☐ 1st conditional	☐ 2nd conditional
☐ 3rd conditional	☐ mixed conditionals	☐ *unless*	☐ relative clauses
☐ prepositions	☐ *wh*-questions	☐ present perfect	☐ *so / such*
☐ un/countables	☐ adjective order	☐ past perfect	☐ time links
☐ question tags	☐ the gerund	☐ the passive	☐ *hardly / no sooner*
☐ past modals	☐ *in case / so that*	☐ reported speech	☐ the infinitive
☐ expressing purpose	☐ *used to*	☐ short replies	☐ *have something done*

3   A   Use the Index of Grammar and Functions (page 190) to find the section(s) in this book that explains your 'number one' grammar point. Study it and write a question about it, noting the page number alongside. Write the answer on a separate piece of paper.

        Example: Point 1: The infinitive.
        Question: What's the difference between *start to do* and *start doing*? (page 116)
        Answer: The meaning is the same.

        Now do the same with points 2–5.

    B   Give your five questions to your partner, who should try to answer them.
        They should check the answers on the pages you have indicated.

15 Doing your best

SPEAKING

1 Work in groups. Think back to when you were at primary school.

What can you remember about your classmates, teachers and classrooms?

What differences would you notice if you went into a typical primary school classroom now?

2 The pictures above were taken several years ago. Look at the four people.

Which of them, do you think, is nowadays a model? a footballer? a politician? an actor?

3 Imagine yourself in twenty years' time. What do you think you will remember about the classroom where you are now, the teacher and your classmates?

4 Look around at the people in the classroom and imagine them in twenty years' time. What kind of work do you think they will be doing?

READING: multiple matching

1 Read the instructions opposite for Reading Part 1 and study example sentence H and paragraph 0. Before you do the exam task, underline the part(s) of paragraph 0 which each of these covers:

a   *Anne's aim was*
b   *to let them know about*
c   *her achievements*

Notice that the information in the summary is not always in the same order as in the paragraph.

You are going to read a newspaper article about school. Choose from the list **A–H** the sentence which best summarizes each part (**1–6**) of the article. There is one extra sentence which you do not need to use. There is an example at the beginning (**0**).

A They were more interested in the school's past than its present.
B In many ways they behaved just as they had done 20 years earlier.
C Despite all that had happened, everyone seemed quite content.
D Many of the women said that they would attend.
E They were doing jobs that the school had not expected them to do.
F The head teacher met them to welcome them back to the school.
G Once they had eaten it was as if they were schoolgirls again.
H Anne's aim was to let them know about her achievements.

COMMON ERRORS

She came the old school photo across.
What is wrong with this sentence? Why?
See the Grammar Reference on page 184.

BACK TO SCHOOL

Nicolette Jones attends a school reunion and finds that though times change, people do not.

0   H

When Anne Bechar set out to find the 80 or so women – myself included – who were at Leeds Girls' High School with her until 1979, it was, she admits, because she had lots of good news she wanted to tell
5 them. 'I wasn't very academic at school, and I felt I was a nobody,' she says. 'Now I have lived for two years in Paris and eight years in the Middle East, I have a family and I run a successful business. I feel that I am *somebody*.'

1

10 Anne's detective work, and that of our school tennis champion, Rosemary Fenton, resulted in the tracking-down of all but a dozen of our ex-classmates. Then we received our invitations and 44 of us, astonished by the realization that we had been
15 old girls for 20 years, agreed to show up for a lunch. Another 20 sent news, good wishes and apologies.

2

So, once we'd had our hair done – and wondering whether we would recognize each other – we assembled in a dining hall that made us think of
20 cabbage and sponge pudding. By the end of lunch it could have been 20 years ago; it was like a bad episode of a soap opera in which everything that had happened since was a dream.

3

It was not simply that in our own eyes we were
25 unchanged, or that the pretty girls were still pretty and the funny ones still funny. It was that we had gone back to the roles of two decades ago. Bryony, our head girl, who is now a doctor, asked kind questions of our sixth-form guide with exactly the
30 grace towards younger girls that made her popular then. Anne was told off by her friend Ruth for

talking down to her, exactly as she had done at school. I showed off. By the time a group photograph was taken, the photographer found it
35 hard to impose order. We had become 14-year-olds in 37-year-old bodies.

4

The school, whose authorities had arranged a tour of the new buildings, found us uncooperative. We did not want to see the new language labs and the new
40 music block. Anne and Heather wanted to see the toilets they had flooded by turning all the taps on. Others wanted to see the desks they had cut names on. We all walked along the corridors we had regularly raced down and talked in, and
45 remembered. We wanted to meet the ghosts of our childhood selves.

5

We were amazed, though, at the well-stocked careers room. In our day, careers advice was a teacher who mostly suggested nursing and secretarial work. Her
50 limited imagination had not had much effect. Among us were doctors, lawyers, accountants, pharmacists and laboratory technicians. Diane, who was enough of a rebel at school to break the rules about wearing make-up, is now a beautician. Mandy
55 is now a school governor. And I became a journalist.

6

Helen took the prize for having the largest family in the group: four children. Most of us have two. Half a dozen are unmarried and as many childless. We had our share of sadnesses – divorces and deaths in
60 the family, for instance – but the great thing was, it didn't show. It was clear we were all more sure of ourselves than at 16 or 18. And we were old enough to realize that there is something special about friends who have known you for a long time.

2   What do the expressions in each of 1–4 have in common?

1   *ex-classmates* (line 12)   *old girls* (line 15)
2   *head girl* (line 28)   *sixth-form* (line 29)
3   *head teacher* (sentence F)   *authorities* (line 37)   *school governor* (line 55)
4   *language lab* (line 39)   *music block* (line 40)   *careers room* (line 47)

VOCABULARY: education

1 Which of the following are for those aged:
a 10 and under? b 11–18? c 18 and over?

secondary school   primary school   junior school
university   nursery   infant school

In which of them would you find these people, and
what would each of them do there?

a pupil   an undergraduate   a lecturer   a student
a teacher   a professor   a postgraduate

What is the difference between a *public school* and a
private school?

2 How many words can you put in each of these
categories?

1   arts subjects
2   science subjects
3   social sciences

Which are the most popular subjects at university in
your country? Why?

3 At what age, usually, do students obtain these
qualifications?

GCSEs   'A' Levels   BA or BSc   MA or MSc   PhD

What are the equivalents in your country, and how old
are people when they get them?

4 Explain these:

take an exam   sit an exam   do an exam
fail an exam   pass an exam   have an exam
resit an exam   retake an exam

GRAMMAR: expressing purpose

*The head teacher met them to welcome them back to
the school.*

To show the purpose of an action, we can use *to* plus
the infinitive, or the slightly more formal *in order to*
and *so as to*:

He studied every day in order to get good marks.
She worked extremely hard so as to get her degree.

In the negative, *in order not to* or *so as not to* can be
used:

*He took the exam six months later in order not to / so
as not to risk failing.*

We can also use *so*, *so that* or *in order that* with a
modal + infinitive, or a subject + verb:

We both chose Latin so (that) we could study together.
*Answer sheets are checked twice in order that they
receive a fair assessment.* (more formal)

When we do something to avoid a possible future
problem, we use *in case* plus an appropriate tense.
*Don't talk to anyone during the exam in case they
think you're cheating.*

To refer to the past, *in case* plus the past simple or the
past perfect is used:

*I bought a bikini yesterday in case I wanted to go
swimming.*
*I looked through my work once again in case I had
missed anything.*

1 Imagine a friend is going away to university. Give
him or her some advice by completing these sentences.
The first one has been done as an example.

1   In the first week, go to all the meetings to *get to
know other students.*

2   When you meet the staff, ask lots of questions to
    ....

3   Go for a walk around the university campus, so
    ....

4   Find out what your timetable is, so as not to ......
    ....

5   Make lots of notes in every lecture, so that ....
    ....

6   Do as much work as you can now in case ....
    ....

7   Buy all the recommended books straight away in
    case ....

8   The first time I had an exam I took an extra pen in
    case ....

2 Now imagine that you are writing an official guide
for students. Give them advice by completing the
following:

1   Read our prospectus and visit our website in order
    to ....

2   You should follow all advice from members of
    staff, so as to ....

3   You are advised to live near your place of study in
    order not to ....

4   Please read the college regulations carefully in
    order that ....

5   You are requested to inform us of any change of
    address in case ....

6   Last year's new students photocopied all
    documents in case ....

COMMON ERRORS

You'll get a good grade in case you work hard.
What is wrong with this sentence? Why?
See the Grammar Reference on page 184.

3 Answer these questions using the above forms.

Why do people:
• write shopping lists?
• go to university?
• do sports?
• have insurance?
• learn languages?
• make friends?

Why do you:
• take notes?
• speak to your partner?
• have a dictionary?
• do homework?
• need a spare pen?
• study English?

Grammar: *have something done*

1 Look at **a**, from the Reading text, and **b**. What is the difference in meaning between them?

a we'd had our hair done   b we'd done our hair

2 Match sentences 1–3 with meanings a–c. Which tense is used in each case?

1 We have our work marked by the teacher.
2 We had our work marked by the teacher.
3 We'd had our work marked by the teacher.

a The teacher marked our work.
b The teacher had marked our work.
c The teacher marks our work.

3 Answer questions 1–9, using *to*, *in order to* or *so as to* to express purpose, plus one of the verbs below. To help you, the first three have an object suggested in brackets.

Example:
Why do people take their car to a garage?
To have it repaired.

> check (teeth) cut (grass) test (eyes) educate
> fix deliver ~~take~~ paint make

Why do people:
1 contact a decorator?
2 pay a dressmaker?
3 ring an electrician?
4 employ a gardener?
5 visit an optician?
6 go to the dentist?
7 pay a photographer?
8 phone for a pizza?
9 send their children to school?

4 For 1–10, write a sentence saying whether:
a you do it yourself.
b a member of your family does it for you.
c you have it done.

Examples:
shoes / clean – *I clean my shoes myself* or *I clean my own shoes*; iron / shirts – *my mother irons my shirts*; hair / cut – *I have my hair cut.*

1 cook / meals
2 wash / socks
3 mend / shoes
4 shampoo / hair
5 photocopy / important papers
6 clean / room
7 make / bed
8 correct / homework
9 dry clean / clothes
10 repair / electrical equipment

Now rewrite those you answered **c**, saying who does them for you.

Example: *I have my hair cut by the hairdresser.*

USE OF ENGLISH: key word transformations

These Part 3 questions all practise the grammar you have just studied. Follow these instructions:

> Complete the second sentence so that it has a similar meaning to the first sentence, using the word given. **Do not change the word given.** You must use between two and five words, including the word given.
>
> _____
>
> 1 I started revising earlier so I could do more work.
>
> **order**
>
> I started revising earlier .... do more work.
>
> 2 During the Speaking exam, the examiner fills in your mark sheet.
>
> **have**
>
> You .... in by the examiner during the Speaking exam.
>
> 3 He invented an illness in order to avoid having to go to school.
>
> **so**
>
> He invented an illness .... to go to school.
>
> 4 I'd better do this exercise now because there might not be time later.
>
> **case**
>
> I'd better do this exercise now .... time later.
>
> 5 He arranged for them to send him the book by post.
>
> **had**
>
> He .... to him by post.
>
> 6 He was offered a job but rejected it so that he could carry on with his studies.
>
> **turned**
>
> He was offered a job but .... order to carry on with his studies.
>
> 7 My watch needs to be mended before I take the exam.
>
> **must**
>
> I .... before I take the exam.
>
> 8 They mark our written work in Cambridge.
>
> **marked**
>
> We .... in Cambridge.
>
> 9 Read the instructions first in order to save time later.
>
> **as**
>
> Read the instructions first .... waste time later.
>
> 10 A member of your family can collect your certificate.
>
> **have**
>
> You .... by a member of your family.

LISTENING

1 Work in groups. Look at the six sentences in activity 2. Say whether you agree or disagree with each of the ideas in A–F, and why.

2 Follow these Listening Part 3 instructions:

You will hear five people talking about language learning. For Questions **1–5**, choose from the list **A–F** the idea which each speaker **disagrees** with. Use the letters only once. There is one extra letter which you do not need to use.

A	The younger you start, the better you learn.	
B	Teachers should correct all errors immediately.	Speaker 1 1
C	Good language learners are always good at other school subjects.	Speaker 2 2
D	Students only learn what they are taught.	Speaker 3 3
E	We learn our first language entirely by imitation.	Speaker 4 4
F	Students copy each other's spoken errors.	Speaker 5 5

3 What do you think makes a good language learner? What can make it difficult for somebody to learn a language?

WRITING: set books

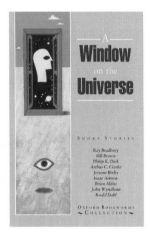
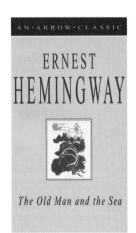
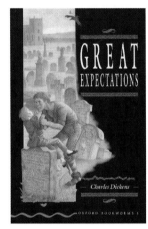

1 Look at these books. Have you read any of them in English, or in your first language? If you have, tell you partner briefly about them. If you haven't, tell him or her which you would most like to read, and why.

2 Read this text about Writing Part 2. As you do so, complete the fifteen key words that have the second half missing, as in the example (0).

Question 5 in Writing is (0) hea.*ded* 'Background reading texts'. It is also known as the 'set books' question, because to answer it you need to have read one of a (1) num...... of books listed in the exam (2) regul...... . Each book is normally on the exam paper for two years and may be the original or (3) simpl...... versions of novels, plays, biographies or (4) collec...... of short stories.

You do not have to read any of them – or answer Question 5 – if you do not want to, but there are a number of (5) advan...... if you do. Firstly, you have a wider (6) cho...... in Part 2 (even more so if you have read two or three books!). Secondly, you know what the (7) sub...... of one question will be and you will be writing about something (8) fami...... to you. Finally, the reading it involves is good for your (9) vocab...... , your grammar and of course your reading skills.

On the exam paper, Question 5 consists of two possible titles and you can choose one or the other – or (10) nei...... of them. Both are (11) gen...... enough to apply to any of the books, and they may be like other Part 2 tasks such as (12) compos...... , reports, letters and articles. You do not have to write a literary appreciation or go into great (13) dep...... about the text, but you should have a good (14) over...... knowledge of it and be able to discuss important aspects such as the (15) chara...... , their relationships and the main events.

3 If you are preparing for Question 5, try to read your book at least three times:

1   from beginning to end, quickly;
2   more carefully;
3   quickly again, just before the exam.

Look at a–j. When would you do each one?

Examples: a – *between 2 & 3;* b – *during 1.*

a   See a film or theatre version and compare it with the book.
b   Get an overall impression of the characters and story, and when and where it happened.
c   Write down possible exam questions about your book.
d   Talk to other people about the title, the story, the characters and the background.
e   Underline any key words you don't understand and look them up in the dictionary.
f   Refresh your memory about the people in the story, the events and the setting by re-reading the book and looking at your notes.
g   Practise answering exam questions, bearing in mind the advice for other kinds of writing.
h   Make a note of your feelings about the main events, the characters and the setting.
i   Note down any quotations that are significant to the story. Ideally, each should be a short, single sentence that you can remember fairly easily.
j   Make notes under headings such as *Events, Characters, Relationships, Ideas* and *Places.*

4 Here are six things you should NOT do in the exam. Expand the notes to make complete sentences.

Example:
Don't spend / time / Question 5 than / other writing task.
Don't spend more time on Question 5 than on your other writing task.

1   **Don't** misspell / title / book / name / author.
2   **Don't** write / other books / written / same author.
3   **Don't** / Question 5 / if / don't like / even if / read / book.
4   **Don't** / irrelevant quotations / just because / memorized.
5   **Don't** / 'prepared' answers / may / studied / before / exam.
6   **Don't** pretend / read / book if / haven't!

5 Look at these exam questions. For each one, decide:

a   what the topic is. Is it the book in general, the story, an event, a character, a relationship the setting – or more than one of these?
b   what the task type is. Is it an opinion, narrative or descriptive composition? Is it a letter, an article or a report? Or is it more than one of these?

1   A friend has written to you asking about the book you have read. Write a letter back saying what you enjoyed most and least about it.
2   In what ways is the time and place where it is set important to the story of the book you have read?
3   Explain how a relationship between two characters starts and how it develops. How does it affect the story of the book you have read?
4   Describe the events that lead up to an important incident in the story of the book you have read.
5   You have been asked by your school magazine to write about a famous book. Write an article, explaining why the book you have read is so popular.
6   Describe a main character in the book you have read and explain why you like or dislike this person.
7   A well-known producer has asked you if it is possible to shorten the book you have read to make it into a film. Write a report, saying which parts of the story and which characters you would include, and why.

6 Think about your set book, or – if you are not preparing one – any book you have read in English or your first language, especially one you have enjoyed. Choose one of questions 1–7 above and write your answer in 120–180 words.

VOCABULARY: First Certificate

1 When are you given the following papers? In each case answer a, b or c. What are they for?

a before the exam   b during the exam   c after the exam

answer sheet   results slip   marks sheet   certificate   entry form   question paper

2 What do these mean? Why is it important that you know?

booklet   Candidate Number   blank page   turn over   soft pencil   eraser additional materials   Centre Number   printed pages   approx.

Centre Number   Candidate Number

0100/4/1
0101/4/1
0102/4/1

Approx. 40 minutes

Additional materials:
Answer sheet
Soft clean eraser
Soft pencil (type B or HB is recommended)

TIME   Approx. 40 minutes

INSTRUCTIONS TO CANDIDATES
Do not open this booklet until you are told to do so.

This question paper consists of 7 printed pages and 1 blank page.

[Turn over]

3 Apart from *approx.*, you may see other abbreviations in First Certificate materials. Match each of these with one of the meanings below:

e.g.   etc.   info.   esp.   i.e.   NB   max.   PS   No.   incl.   min.

information   especially   minimum   and so on   including   for example   note well
that is   maximum   number   postscript (added to the end of a letter)

LISTENING

1 Explain these words, which are in the Listening Part 2 text you are about to hear:

fairness   standard   perform   confidence   award

2 Work in pairs. What similarities and differences are there between First Certificate and other exams you have taken, for example at school? Think particularly about tests of reading, writing and grammar, and any listening or speaking tests in another language.

3 Follow the exam instructions below.
Notice the expressions of purpose in questions 5, 9 and 10.

You will hear a radio talk by a language teacher. For Questions **1–10**, complete the sentences.

Modern exams tell students how, for whom and [1] they should write.
Candidates nowadays spend less time talking to [2]
Marking used to be more concerned with [3] than what a student did well.
In the past, a lot of reading comprehension texts were [4]
Nowadays, a writing exam is used to test only [5]
Some people think the exam is [6] in December.
When the standard of work improves, the number who [7] goes up, too.
The questions are no easier or harder, whatever a person's [8]
To ensure fairness, exam papers are always marked by [9] examiner.
To pass, the best thing a student can do is think about [10]

4 Is there any part of the First Certificate Listening Paper that you are not sure about?
If there is, see the Index of Exam Task-types on page 189.

Reading Room

SPEAKING

1 In pairs, follow these Speaking Part 3 instructions:

Your school or college has suggested providing students with some of the things in the pictures. Talk to each other about how they might help people study the subjects below and decide which you think would be the **three** most popular and useful suggestions. Which, if any, would students not want, or not need?

- maths
- art
- music
- science

- modern languages
- environmental studies
- history
- geography

2 In Speaking Part 4, the examiner will ask you questions about things connected with the topic of Part 3. For example, if the topic is *Education* and you have been discussing history, maths and so on, he or she might ask you:

a Can you think of any other subjects that schools should also teach?
b What do students in your country like least about school? What do they like most?
c Should lessons be more about things that young people are really interested in?
d What makes a school lesson interesting? What makes it boring?

Look at these statements about Part 4. Without telling your partner which ones you are thinking about, ask him or her suitable questions. He or she must reply by choosing the right answers.

Example: 5 – You say: *What is this part of the test for?* or *What is the purpose of Part 4?* Your partner answers: *To show how well you can exchange opinions.*

1 You speak to the examiner and Candidate B.
2 Usually about four minutes.
3 Ask the examiner to clarify or repeat them.
4 So that the examiners can hear what you say.
5 To show how well you can exchange opinions.
6 No, you can disagree if you like.
7 If you don't speak you can't get any marks!
8 Listen carefully to his or her opinions.
9 About the same amount of time as Candidate B.
10 They'll just say 'thank you' and 'goodbye'.

3 Work in groups of four, Students A, B, C and D.

Student A: You are the Interlocutor. Encourage the candidates to talk together about *Education* by asking them questions. Make sure they both have an equal opportunity to speak. You can ask a–d in 2 above and think of your own questions.

Student B: You are the Assessor. Listen to the candidates and for each one write down a provisional mark out of ten. Take into account their fluency, pronunciation, grammar, vocabulary and success in communicating with the others. Do not tell the candidates their mark or make any comment on their performance at this stage.

Students C & D: You are the candidates. Listen carefully to the examiner's questions and discuss the topic of *Education* together. Think about points 1–10 in 2 above and, where necessary, ask each other questions to help the conversation to flow smoothly.

4 Form pairs.

Students A & B: Discuss the candidates' strong and weak points, and decide on their marks.
Students C & D: Discuss your feelings about your performance in the 'exam'.

5 Re-form groups.

Students A & B: Tell the candidates their marks and comment on their performance.
Students C & D: Tell the examiners about any difficulties you had.

USE OF ENGLISH: word formation

You have already practised answering Use of English Part 5 using affixes, spelling changes and participles, but there is another possibility: compound words. Compounds can be one word, two words joined by a hyphen or two separate words, but in Part 5 the answer must be one word with no hyphen, such as *classroom*, *schoolteacher* and *handwriting*.

Look at example 0. Here, the word given in capitals is HOME so the answer is the compound *homework*.

Now follow the exam instructions, watching out for the kinds of changes mentioned above.

For Questions **1–10**, read the text below. Use the word given in capitals at the end of each line to form a word that fits in the space in the same line. There is an example at the beginning **(0)**.

Example: | **0** | homework |

THE BIG DAY ARRIVES

At last it's here: tomorrow is Exam Day. There's no more **(0)**	**HOME**
to do, you have done lots of **(1)** .... and you've had plenty of	**REVISE**
(2) .... practice with past papers. You've finished the course.	**USE**
So what should you do now? Probably the least **(3)** .... course	**ADVICE**
of action would be to carry on **(4)** .... late into the night, trying	**STUDY**
(5) .... to learn things you should have learned long ago and	**DESPERATE**
waking in the morning with an awful **(6)** .... A far better idea is	**HEAD**
to practise, as a singer or a **(7)** .... does, what you already know.	**MUSIC**
In order not to feel **(8)** .... the next day, go to bed early and	**SLEEP**
get up at your usual time. You may be a little bit **(9)** ...... , but	**NERVE**
that is probably just a sign of your **(10)** .... to do well in the exam.	**DETERMINE**

In the Listening (Paper 4) and Speaking (Paper 5), **timing** is not a problem because in both these parts of the exam you follow the instructions on the recording or from the examiners. In the other three papers, however, you will have to decide how to divide up your time in the best way possible. Look at this list of things you need to do in Papers 1, 2 and 3, the number of questions and the marks available. Then look at the time allowed for the whole paper and note down how many minutes you think you should spend on each.

Paper 1 Reading   Time allowed: 75 minutes

Part	Task type	No. of questions	Marks	Minutes
1	Multiple matching	6 or 7	12 or 14	....
2	Multiple choice	7 or 8	14 or 16	....
3	Gapped text	6 or 7	12 or 14	....
4	Multiple matching	13–15	13–15	....

Paper 2 Writing   Time allowed: 90 minutes

Part	Stage	No. of questions	Marks	Minutes
1	planning your work	1	20	....
1	writing			....
1	checking for mistakes			....
2	choosing a question	1	20	....
2	planning your work			....
2	writing			....
2	checking for mistakes			....

Paper 3 Use of English   Time allowed: 75 minutes

Part	Task type	No. of questions	Marks	Minutes
1	Multiple-choice cloze	15	15	....
2	Open cloze	15	15	....
3	Key word transformations	10	20	....
4	Error correction	15	15	....
5	Word formation	10	10	....

Before the exam, use past papers or practice tests to practise your timing in Papers 1, 2 and 3.

① Ask your partner about his or her plans for the exam. Talk about practical aspects such as how to get there, what time to leave home and arrive at the exam centre, having lunch and things to take. Explain why in each case.

Example:
I'll go on my bike to get some exercise before I start the exam.
I'm going to leave at eight o'clock in case the traffic is bad.

Then discuss what you'll do when it is all over!

② Follow these instructions.

1   Write a **report** about yourself. Using the third person, describe your progress during the course under each of the following headings: *Reading*, *Writing*, *Use of English*, *Listening*, *Speaking*, *Grammar* and *Vocabulary*.

2   Exchange reports with your partner. Check for common errors and tell him or her which of the comments you agree with, which you disagree with, and why!

Fill in the one-word gaps in the instructions and answer the questions. Check your answers by referring to the *Index of Exam Task-types* on page 189.

PAPER 1 READING

Part 1 multiple matching

Choose the most suitable summary sentence from the list A-H for each part (1–6) of the article. There is one ...... sentence which you do not need to use. There is an example at the ...... (0).

1. What three things should you read before you look at the text? ....
Why? .... What should you write at the top of paragraph 0? ....

2. How should you read the text the first time you go through it? .... Why? ....
What should you cross out:
   a after you have read the text once? ....
   b as you read the text again? ....
   Why? ....

3. Fill in the gaps: A good way to improve both your multiple matching and your more general reading skills is to write your own .... at the top of each .... as you read.

4. Fill in the gaps: You should not expect headings or summaries always to reflect the .... in which things actually happened in a narrative. There may be .... to earlier events.

Part 2 multiple choice

For Questions 7–14, choose the answer (A,B,C or D) which you think fits .... according to the ....

1. When you first read the text, why should you not spend too much time on any expressions you don't know? ....

2. What should be your first aim if the text is from a novel? ....

3. There may be questions that ask *What does X mean in line ...?* What do these test?

4. Fill in each of gaps 1–10 with one word:
Begin by looking at the first line of each question, but not the (1) .... because some may mislead you. Draw a (2) .... against the relevant part of the text and make up your own (3) .... what the text says. Now see which of A, B, C or D is (4) .... to your understanding of what the text says, and then try to find clear (5) .... that it is right and that the others are not. Remember that one common kind of (6) .... answer suggests ideas that are not in the (7) ....; another type (8) .... what it really says. If all else fails, improve your chances by (9) .... out any that are definitely wrong, and then (10) ....!

Part 3 gapped text

Seven paragraphs have been .... from the article. Choose from the paragraphs A–H the one which .... each gap (15–20). There is .... extra paragraph which you do not need to use. There is an example at the beginning (0).

1. What should you look for in each paragraph? .... What should you decide next? ....

2. Fill in the gaps: A missing sentence may have structure and .... like that in the parts of the text which go before or .... it. Other possible clues include linking expressions of .... , ... and ....

3. What should you underline as you read:
   a a narrative text with paragraphs missing?
   ....
   b a text with sentences missing?
   ....

4. Write down six common reference words: ....
....

Part 4 multiple matching

For Questions 21–35, ... from the places A–G. The places may be chosen more than .... When more than one answer is required, these may be given in .... order. There is an example at the beginning (0).

1. 1 Study answers 1–10 and write a suitable question for each using the prompts in brackets.
   1 (consist) *What does Part 4 consist of?* A text in sections and 13, 14 or 15 questions.
   2 (first) ....? Look at the instructions, title and headings.
   3 (how) ....? Quickly, for gist.
   4 (underline) ....? The key words in each question.
   5 (example) ....? To show you how the task works.
   6 (read again) ....? You should think about the underlined words.
   7 (section) ....? Yes, it can be the right answer several times.
   8 (question) ....? Yes, it can have answers in two or three sections.
   9 (can't find) ....? Quickly go on to the next question.
   10 (marks) ....? Just one. In Parts 1–3 you get two.

2 Fill in the gaps: In Part 4 the questions tell you what to .... for and successfully completing the task depends on your ability to .... these details quickly. In the text these details will probably be expressed in different .... from those in the questions. You should .... this part of the text as soon as you find it, preferably in pencil.

Part 1 transactional letter

1 Part 1 consists of one task which everyone .... to do. On the exam paper there are between one and .... short texts which give you all the .... you need to write your letter. In this letter you may need to .... information, request information, ... complaints, corrections or suggestions.
You do not need to write either your .... or that of the person you are writing to, and you should .... copy large parts of the text to use in your letter.

2 These notes give advice on what to do before you start writing. Expand them into sentences.
1 study / instructions / materials / decide / style / aim
....
2 highlight / key words / text / notes
....
3 plan / purpose / paragraph
....
4 note / expressions
....

3 Look at the instructions, the advertisement and the notes in Question 1 and fill in the details in categories a–f.
a Number of texts: ....
b Notes: ....
c Text type(s): ....
d Text by: ....
e Your writing style: ....
f Your writing aim: ....

4 Add one word to complete these suggestions for answering Part 1 questions.
1 Start with a beginning like *Dear* and finish with *Yours sincerely*, or a similar suitable ....
2 Organize your letter into a number of suitable ....
3 Include in your first one the reason why you are ....
4 Although the texts may use note form, you should write in complete ....
5 The style you use will depend on the purpose, the content and the ....
6 You can use expressions from the texts, but in general write in your own ....
7 Try to cover all the main points in the texts and in the ....
8 Add your own suggestions, details or requests only if they are ....
9 If you can, use a wide range of language for both vocabulary and ....

10 When you finish, check for mistakes and that you have followed the ....

5 Now look at the sample answer for Question 1. For each of 1–10, decide whether the writer has followed the suggestion and, where possible, highlight or underline the relevant part of the text. Write the number of the suggestion alongside, too.

QUESTION 1
Transactional letter: Giving information

An international health and fitness magazine is compiling a survey on tablets designed to help people lose weight. They have asked readers to write and tell the editor about their personal experiences with the tablets.

Read the advertisement for the tablets and the notes you have made. Then write your letter to the magazine editor.

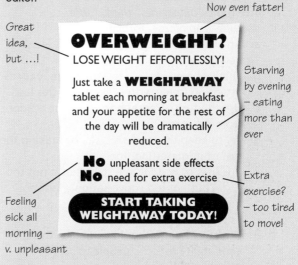

Write a letter of **120–180** words in an appropriate style. Do not write any addresses.

Dear Sir/Madam,

In response to your request for information about Weightaway tablets, I am writing to tell you about my experience.

I am always looking for ways to lose weight and the advertisement for Weightaway made it sound ideal for me. I eat too much but I hate exercise and I found the idea of losing weight just by taking tablets very attractive.

So far, however, I seem to have lost no weight at all. After I take the tablet with my breakfast I feel sick for the rest of the morning. This certainly reduces my appetite, but I consider it to be a very unpleasant effect. Furthermore, by about 6 o'clock in the evening I am extremely hungry and sometimes eat even more than usual. As for exercise, the tablets make me too tired to move at all.

I have nearly finished the tablets I bought and I think I am even more overweight than before. I strongly advise your readers not to waste their money on this product.

Yours faithfully,

Part 2

1. Fill in the gaps with the correct numbers:
   In Part 2 you can choose from .... questions, ... of which offers a further choice between .... tasks based on the set books. As in Part 1, you must write between .... and .... words, and the marks are divided between the two parts: .... per cent each, so it is a good idea to spend the maximum possible .... minutes on both of them.

2. Fill in the gaps using a *wh-* word in each case:
   In all Part 2 questions, you are told .... will be reading what you have written, ... you are writing it and .... it should contain, although the exact contents are more for you to decide than in Part 1. Begin by underlining the words in the instructions .... answer these three points.

3. 1 Fill in the gaps in sentences a–h using each of these words once only:
   attention magazine think title
   describe opinions formal involve
   a An **article** will probably be for a .... or newsletter.
   b Think of a good .... to attract the reader's attention (some writers like to do this last).
   c Use the first paragraph to .... the reader from the start.
   d Try to keep the reader's .... by making the rest of it interesting, too.
   e It is best to write it in a style that is not too .... but not too conversational, either.
   f You can include your own ideas and .... as well as facts.
   g Use any opportunity there may be to show your ability to .... people, places or objects.
   h Try to end by making the reader .... about what he or she has read.

   2 Look at the instructions for the article opposite and underline the key words as suggested in activity 2.

   3 Now look at the sample answer. Which of suggestions b–h has the writer followed?

QUESTION 2
Article

An international music magazine has asked for contributions on stars whose careers have had a big influence on pop music.

Write your **article**.

'The King' is dead – long live 'The King'!

They called him 'The King', but was this title justified? How much influence did the career of this fifties singing star really have on the development of pop music?

Elvis Presley became, during the 1950s, the idol of teenagers everywhere. He sold millions of records and by the early sixties he had had a string of No 1 hits. Not only was he a successful pop star, but he also made many popular films. And although his popularity decreased during the sixties, he made a comeback in the early seventies. The music world was shocked by his early death in 1977 and some people still refuse to believe he is really dead.

What was so special about Elvis? The rock'n'roll age probably began with Bill Haley, but Elvis made pop music sexy. Parents were horrified but teenagers loved everything about Elvis – his hairstyle, his clothes and, above all, his music. He was young, energetic and different and he helped teenagers to find a new identity.

Elvis the man died in 1977, but Elvis the idol lives on.

4. 1 Look at these notes on writing a plan for a **report**. For each set of notes, write a complete sentence. Then put suggestions a–d in the order you think you should follow them.
   a Note / ideas —> headings.
   b Decide / order / sections.
   c Think / heading / section.
   d Divide / report —> sections.

   2 Study the instructions for Question 3 on page 161 and underline the key words as suggested in activity 2.

   3 Read the sample answer and think of a suitable title for it.

   4 Look back at the twelve techniques on page 56 (activity 1). For those that are used, highlight and number an example of each in the sample answer.

QUESTION 3
Report

An international charity is investigating the living conditions of elderly people around the world and has asked for a report from your country.

Write your **report** for the charity.

INTRODUCTION

This report looks at the living conditions of elderly people in this country. A large number of these people, especially those over 80, are women.

WHERE DO MOST ELDERLY PEOPLE LIVE?

Many old people live alone or in special retirement homes, rather than with their families. While this is often from choice, because they prefer to be independent and do not want to cause problems for their families, it may also be because their children and grandchildren have small houses with no room for grandparents.

WHAT CONDITIONS DO THEY LIVE IN?

Although old people may prefer to live in their own homes, these are often old-fashioned and inconvenient. For example, it may be difficult for an elderly person to go upstairs. They may also be lonely. On the other hand, if they live in a retirement home or with their family, they may have little privacy and have to get rid of treasured possessions.

RECOMMENDATIONS

● Accommodation should be suitable for elderly people.

● There must be regular visits for those living alone.

● Those living with others need to have privacy.

---

5 1 Read these suggestions for writing a **short story** and write in these missing words:

an explanation   time links
the first or the third   main stage of the story
a good title   the reader want to
a given beginning or ending   where and when
direct speech   the stages in the story
too many events   the main characters

a Check whether there is a title or
   ....

b Decide whether you have to (or wish to)
   write in .... person.

c Make a plan, with a list of
   .... that you want to
   include.

d Don't include .... or you
   may go over the number of words allowed.

e Start with a sentence that will make
   .... carry on reading.

f Give some background details, perhaps
   saying .... the story takes
   place.

g Introduce .... and indicate
   the relationship between them.

h For each .... , use a
   different paragraph.

i You may want to use some
   .... to make your characters
   more real.

j Join the events with ....
   and use a variety of past tenses.

k Try to use a surprise, a mystery or
   .... to finish the story.

l Give your story .... , if
   possible one that will catch the reader's eye.

2   Look at the instructions for Question 4 and answer **a** and **b** on page 161. What is your reason for writing?

3   Read the sample answer and think of a title for it.

4   Highlight and number any examples of points e–k on page 161 in the sample answer.

QUESTION 4
Story

You have decided to enter a short-story competition. The competition rules say that the story must begin or end with the following words:

The police arrested them as they got in the car.

Write your **story** for the competition.

Philippa and Ned had always had a very successful partnership and they had made a lot of money. Now they were planning one more job before they retired.

That morning, Philippa drove her partner to the bank, but no sooner had he disappeared inside than she remembered she had to collect her new glasses from the optician's. She would just have time before Ned came out of the bank and she quickly parked the car. 'It'll be nice to see clearly again,' she thought happily.

Ned came out and looked round, then hurried towards the car. Meanwhile, Philippa came out of the optician's and ran to join her partner. At that moment, the alarm began to ring in the bank and men and women in uniform rushed out of the building where the car was parked.

The hold-up in the bank had been as successful as usual, but Philippa's poor eyesight had let them down. She had parked the car in front of the police station and the police arrested them as they got in the car.

6   Fill in these details about writing a **non-transactional letter**.

1   Write two ways of ending an informal letter.
    e.g. *Regards* ....
    ....

2   Write two ways of ending a formal letter.
    ....

3   Write five formal expressions you could use in a job application letter.
    e.g. *Dear Sir or Madam* ....
    ....
    ....

4   Write five kinds of information you might give in such a letter.
    e.g. *Your reason for writing*
    ....
    ....
    ....

5   Write three kinds of language you would expect in an informal letter but not a formal one.
    e.g. *phrasal verbs* ....
    ....

6   Look at the instructions in Writing activity 2 on page 26. Why, what and to whom must you write? ....

7   Study the letter in the same activity and highlight examples of each of the four points from 5 above.

7   Answer these questions about writing a **composition**.

1   What kind of composition is the example opposite?
    ....

2   What can you do if you have to write arguments you disagree with?
    ....

3   Why is it not a good idea to go through every point, giving reasons for and against each one?
    ....

4   How, then, should you divide up a 'for and against' composition?
    ....

5   What style should you write in? ....

6   What should you try to avoid repeating too often? ....

7   How many linking expressions in each of these categories can you think of?
    a   Sequencing: e.g. *next*
        ....
    b   Adding information: e.g. *also*
        ....
    c   Contrasting: e.g. *although*
        ....
    d   Resulting: e.g. *therefore*
        ....

8 Read the sample answer to Question 5. How is it organized? What style is it written in? Highlight the linking expressions it uses and say what kind each one is.

QUESTION 5
Discursive composition

Your teacher has asked you to write a composition on the following question.

In the future, people will probably be living on the moon. Will it be the ideal place to live?

Write your **composition** giving points for and against.

The idea of living on the moon is no longer science fiction. However, there will be drawbacks to living there as well as advantages.

On the positive side, people will be able to escape from earth's overcrowded cities and live in an environment where everything is carefully controlled by technology. In addition to this, they will have wonderful clear views of the earth and stars, besides being able to explore the mountains and craters of the moon.

On the other hand, the moon is an unfriendly place for humans. First of all, people will have to wear special suits whenever they go outside and if their equipment fails, they will probably die. Secondly, they will have to get used to being weightless or living in artificial gravity and to using recycled air and water. Finally, they will probably miss the plants and wildlife that exist on earth.

To sum up, the moon might be the ideal place for a holiday or for scientists to carry out research, but not for ordinary people to live there all the time.

9 If you have prepared a **set book**, sit with a partner who has read the same book. On a piece of paper, write down ten questions about it that you think he or she should be able to answer. Your questions could be based on some of the following: the title, the main characters, the plot, the background, the atmosphere, the main events and relationships between the characters. Then exchange questions with your partner and write your answers.

PAPER 3 USE OF ENGLISH

Part 1 multiple-choice cloze

For Questions 1–15, read the .... below and decide which answer A, B, C or D best fits each .... There is an example at the beginning (0).

1 Match the phrases in italics on the left with types 1–4 on the right:

She had a *narrow escape* in the accident.	1 verb + noun / noun + verb collocation
You have to *take turns* in Speaking Part 2.	2 preposition collocation
This dress has been very *badly made*.	3 adjective + noun collocation
He's always been *keen on* tennis.	4 adverb + verb collocation

2 Choose the best word (A, B, C or D) to complete the collocation, and say what type it is:

1 On this beach, ... tide will be at 6.52 am.
   A top   B high   C big   D tall
2 Success depends .... how hard you work.
   A on   B of   C from   D to
3 I've always been interested .... grammar.
   A of   B to   C in   D about
4 We .... a flat near the university.
   A rented   B hired   C paid   D charged
5 He left .... early today.
   A business   B task   C duty   D work
6 This book is .... known.
   A good   B very   C too   D well

Part 2 open cloze

For Questions 16–30, read the text below and think .... the word which best fits each space. Use only .... word in each space. There is an example at the beginning (0).

1 Fill in the gaps, in each case using the initial letter as a clue:

The first thing to do is look at the i............ , the t............ and the e............ . Then, before you fill in any g............ , read right through the t............ in order to get the g............ of it. Start reading again, until you come to the first m............ word. Decide what it is, if necessary reading on to the e............ of the sentence for c............ . If you know the answer, write it on the a............ s............ next to the appropriate number. It is probably best to p............ the word in capitals rather than use your ordinary h............ , particularly if this is not very clear. If you don't know the word, leave the space b............ for the moment, but don't forget to put the n............ answer against the following number. When you have looked at all the q............ , go back to any you couldn't do, see if they are any e............ now and, if so, write them in. If all else fails, g............ . Remember to c............ through the whole text when you have finished to ensure that everything m............ sense.

2 Some of these statements are factually correct and some are not. Correct those that are wrong.
1   There are usually twenty questions in Part 2.
2   Contractions like *isn't* are common as answers.
3   It is more a test of grammar than vocabulary.
4   It is worse to make a mistake than put nothing.
5   The answer is never a word with a hyphen.
6   Correct spelling is essential.
7   The texts are often 500 words long.
8   You get two marks if two words fit one gap.
9   Reference words are never tested.
10 Part 2 has the most marks in Paper 3.

Part 3 key word transformations

In every First Certificate Use of English Part 3 there are ten transformation questions. You may fill in the space with two, three, four or five words but you are not in any circumstances permitted to use more. For the purposes of the exam, contracted forms such as *she's* or *isn't* are regarded as two words, while those containing an apostrophe of possession, for example *a day's work*, are considered to be one word. You are not allowed to change or leave out the key word, or make changes to any of the words already given. Accurate spelling is essential throughout. To obtain both marks the answer must be completely correct, as questions always test more than one item of grammar or vocabulary. One mark may be given for partially correct answers.

*For Questions **31–40** complete the second sentence so that it has a .... meaning to the first sentence, using the word given. **Do not** .... **the word given**. You must use between two and .... words, including the word given.*

1 Read the text above and write down three things you must never do in Part 3:
1   ....
2   ....
3   ....

Write down two things you should always try to do in Part 3:
1   ....
2   ....

Ask and answer two more questions about the information in the text:
1   *How many* ....
   .... ?
2   *If an answer* ....
   .... ?

2 In a Part 3 answer, how many words do these count as?
1 *he's*   2 *can't*   3 *student's book*

3 Sometimes there are inverted commas in the sentence you have to transform. What does this indicate? ....
What should you also look for? ....

Part 4 error correction

*For Questions **41–55**, read the text below and look carefully at ..... line. Some of the lines are correct and ..... have a word which should not be there. If a line is correct, put a ..... (✓) by the number **on the separate answer sheet**. If a line has a word which should **not** be there, write the ..... **on the separate answer sheet**. There are ..... examples at the beginning (**0 and 00**).*

1 Write a reason for each of the following:
1   Begin by reading right through the text.
....
2   Read both the example lines.
....
3   Never change any words in the text.
....
4   Look for clues on the next line or lines.
....
5   Only write one word at the end of a line.
....
6   Avoid putting six or more ticks in total.
....
7   Do not put more than twelve words in total.
....
8   Look right through your corrected text at the end. ....

2 Underline the error in each of these sentences and say what kind of mistake it is:
1   He never speaks to nobody else.
....
2   The thief was sent to the prison for ten years.
....
3   The school secretary telephoned to his mother.
....
4   I tried a little of the food and so did she too.
....
5   She went out of straight after breakfast.
....
6   She walked herself all the way there.
....
7   They can have made a very big mistake.
....
8   That's the one what I want to buy.
....
9   He kept playing despite though his injury.
....
10 He was one person I didn't want to see him.
....

Part 5 word formation

For Questions 56–65, read the text below. Use the word given in ..... at the end of each line to form a word that fits in the space in the ..... line. There is an example at the beginning (0).

1 1 When you have looked at the instructions and the title, what should you do?
....

2 When you come to a gap, what two things should you decide? ....
....

3 When you look at the word given, what should you note down? ....

4 If you add a suffix, what should you check?
....

5 What should you do if you have no idea which word to use? ....

6 What do you need to do when you have written all your answers? ....

2 Write as many words as you can beginning or ending with the following affixes:

dis...
inter ....
re...
over ....
mis...
....less
....ist
....able
....ness
....ful

3 Write down all the words you can form from these base words:

use ....
appear ....
do...
build ....
help..
direct ....
friend ....
child ....

4 Write down six emotions you have felt this week, using participle adjectives ending in *-ed*.
Then say why, using the *-ing* form. Example:
Surprised. The ending of the film was surprising.

1 ....
2 ....
3 ....
4 ....
5 ....
6 ....

5 Match the words on the left with those on the right to form compound nouns:

tea	hair	break		step	down	quake
tooth	loud	door		speaker	table	paste
hand	sight	time		cut	ache	fall	child
earth	head	rain		seeing	cup	writing
school	birth	set		day	back	

PAPER 4 LISTENING

Part 1 multiple choice

You will hear people talking in ..... different situations. For Questions 1–8, choose the ..... answer, A, B or C.

1 Write down three ways in which Part 1 is made a little easier for you. Think about both what you read and what you hear.

1 ....   3 ....
2 ....

2 Complete these statements:

1 Read the introduction, question and options to ....

2 While you are listening, imagine
....

3 Always be sure you know which number text
....

4 Remember that you do not have to understand
....

5 Don't choose an answer just because you hear
....

6 While you listen, you may want to change
....

3 Match types of question 1–5 with what you should particularly listen for (a–e).

1 *Who ...?* questions   a   Factual information. Descriptions.

2 *Where ...?* questions   b   Mood, attitude and feelings. Tone of voice and emphasis.

3 *What ...?* questions   c   People changing their minds. Agreement and disagreement.

4 *How ...?* questions   d   Roles and relationships. Register and pronouns. Descriptions.

5 Opinion questions   e   Demonstratives and expressions of place. Descriptions.

Part 2 note taking / blank filling

You will hear a radio discussion about music. For Questions 9–18, ... the sentences.

1 For each of these answers, write a question about the Listening paper:

1 Yes, because you cannot ask questions once the recording has started.
....

2 No, there isn't time before it starts and there is no link between the four parts anyway.
....

3 Yes, so that you are prepared for the possible content.
....

4 No, it is essential to concentrate throughout, both times it is played.
....

2 How many texts are there? ....

How many words do you write in each answer? ....

3 Expand these notes to form complete sentences giving exam advice:

1 study / questions / idea / likely / hear

....

2 underline / words / might hear / recording

....

3 listen / information / same order / questions

....

4 if / hear / key words / attention

....

5 if / spend / too long / one question / may miss

....

6 not try / use different words / hear

....

7 never / more / one answer / question

....

8 stop listening / writing / answers

....

9 write quickly / ready / next point

....

10 check / answers / grammar / spelling

....

Part 3 multiple matching

In Listening Part 3, you will hear five separate pieces which are related in some way. They are all played once and then you hear them all again. They are not spoken by the same person but there is always a link between them: for instance they may all involve people apologizing or requesting information; or they might deal with the same subject, for example moving house, or painting.

To form an idea of what they will be talking about and what kind of language they might use, you should look at the introduction and the six possible answers. As in Paper 1 Reading multiple matching, there is always one extra answer that you do not need to use. You are advised to wait until you have heard the extracts twice before you finally decide on your answers.

You will hear .... people speaking about their jobs. For Questions 19–23, ... from the list A–F what they are talking about. Use the letters only ..... . There is one extra .... which you do not need to use.

1 Read the instructions above. For each of prompts A–F, write six words you think you might hear:

A doctor ....

....

B chef ....

....

C farmer ....

....

D judge ....

....

E pilot ....

....

F teacher ....

....

2 Study the text in the previous column. Using the prompts in brackets, write five questions about it. Then, using both the information in the text and your experience, write the answers, as in the example:

(texts) *How many texts do you hear?*
You hear five separate texts.

1 (second time) .... ?

....

2 (connection) .... ?

....

3 (introduction) .... ?

....

4 (extra answer) .... ?

....

5 (when / decide) .... ?

....

Part 4 selection from two or three answers

Before you listen to Listening Part 4 for the first time, look at the instructions, as they will contain useful information about who you will hear speaking or the situation in which they are speaking, or possibly both. The seven questions may also give clues to the content of the dialogue. Remember that people may change their opinions during the three minutes, approximately, of the recording.

While the recording is being played, you should concentrate on listening all the time, even when you are noting down your answers. This is easier than it might seem, however, as what you are listening for will always be in the same order as 24–30 on the question paper, and you only need to note down the initial letter. Remember always to do this: even if you have no idea of the correct answer you should guess and write T or F, or whatever letter the question type requires.

Instructions will be in one of the following forms:

1 *For Questions 24–30, decide which of the statements are .... and which are .... .*
2 *For Questions 24–30, decide whether the idea was stated or not and mark Y for ... , or N for .... .*
3 *For questions 24–30, choose the .... answer, A, B or C.*
4 *Answer Questions 24–30 by .... P for policeman, W for Mrs Williams and S for Sam.*

Underline six key words or phrases in the text above. Then write a question and answer for each.

1 .... ?

....

2 .... ?

....

3 .... ?

....

4 .... ?

....

5 .... ?

....

6 .... ?

....

PAPER 5 SPEAKING

Part 1 interview

1 Fill in each of the gaps with one suitable word:
In Part 1 you speak to the (1) .... for about (2) ....
minutes. The examiner begins by (3) .... you and
asking for your (4) .... sheets. He or she then tells
you his or her (5) .... , as well as that of the other
(6) .... , who will not be taking (7) .... in the
conversation. The first examiner will then check
your name and that of the other (8) .... , before
asking you some (9) .... about yourselves. The aim
of this part is to help you (10) .... by letting you talk
about a familiar subject: yourself. You may be
asked about your (11) .... life and current
circumstances, your (12) .... experiences and your
(13) .... intentions, so be ready to use various verb
tenses, including both the present (14) .... to say
what you usually do and the present (15) .... for
temporary things.

2 Write down five possible topics of conversation in
Part 1:

1 ....
2 ....
3 ....
4 ....
5 ....

3 Put a ✓ or a ✗ against each of these suggestions for
Part 1:
1 Greet the examiners when you go in. ....
2 Address your answers to the examiner, not the
other candidate. ....
3 Answer simply *Yes* or *No* ....
4 Make prepared speeches. ....
5 Ask for repetition or clarification if something
isn't clear. ....

Part 2 individual long turn

1 Fill in the numbers: In Part 2, which lasts about ....
minutes, each candidate talks about ...... pictures.

2 Which of these do you NOT have to do in Part 2?
1 Talk for a full minute about your pictures.
2 Speak about the other candidate's pictures for a
full minute.
3 Let the other candidate see your pictures.
4 Describe every detail in the pictures.
5 Discuss the similarities between your pictures.
6 Talk about the differences between your
pictures.
7 Give some personal reaction to your pictures.
8 Tell the other candidate to talk about his or her
pictures.
9 Make brief comments about the other
candidate's pictures.
10 Comment on the other candidate's
performance.

3 1 Write down three expressions you can use to
describe similarity in the pictures:
....
....
....

2 Write down three expressions you can use to
describe differences between the pictures:
....
....
....

3 Write down three ways of saying what you
think is in the picture if you are not sure:
....
....
....

4 Write down three ways of expressing your
preferences:
....
....
....

5 Write down three expressions you can use if you
need to paraphrase:
....
....
....

Part 3 collaborative task

1 In sentences 1–3, put a suitable word in each space.
1 In Part 3 you speak mainly to the other .... for
about .... minutes.
2 Task types include .... solving, ... plans
and ....
3 The examiner will give you a .... , a .... or a
.... , or something similar, to look at.

2 For questions 1–4, decide which is the best thing to
do, A, B or C.
1 If you're not quite sure what you have to do,
you should:
A ask the examiner.
B ask the other candidate in your first
language.
C pretend you understand.
2 When the other candidate speaks to you, you
should reply to:
A the examiner.
B the other candidate.
C the assessor.
3 When you speak to the other candidate, your
questions should:
A encourage him or her to talk.
B only require one-word answers.
C be difficult to answer.
4 If you can't think of a word, you should:
A say nothing.
B say what it is in your first language.
C use other words that mean the same.

3 Write down five more things you should and shouldn't do using these prompts.

1 Study materials:

....

2 Take turns:

....

3 Interrupt:

....

4 Silence:

....

5 Agree:

....

Part 4 three-way discussion

1 What is the connection between Part 3 and Part 4?

....

2 For each of 1–7, fill in the two missing words at the beginning and then answer the question.

1 .... you speak to in Part 4?

....

2 .... does Part 4 last?

....

3 .... you do if you don't understand something?

....

4 .... have to agree with what the other person says?

....

5 .... you do while the other candidate is speaking?

....

6 .... should you speak for?

....

7 .... the examiners say at the end?

....

3 Write down two questions you can ask if you want your partner to repeat something.

1 ....

2 ....

Write down two questions you can use to encourage your partner to speak.

1 ....

2 ....

4 For each of 1–6, write in the key word and then give yourself a mark out of five for how well you do these things.

1 When you speak, use a variety of grammatical .... accurately. 1 2 3 4 5

2 Use the appropriate .... to talk about any of the topics you have covered in this book. 1 2 3 4 5

3 Organize what you say in a logical way and .... it together well. 1 2 3 4 5

4 .... well in English with other students. 1 2 3 4 5

5 Successfully carry out .... like comparing photos and solving problems. 1 2 3 4 5

6 Speak .... , at a natural speed and with good stress and intonation. 1 2 3 4 5

Grammar reference

GRAMMAR REFERENCE UNIT 1

Present tenses

1 Present simple

The present simple is most often used:

a   to refer to situations which are permanent.
    *Maria **lives** and **works** in the centre of Barcelona.*

COMMON ERRORS

Where are you from, Nikos? I'm coming from Athens.

The correct form is: *I come from Athens.*

---

b   to refer to habits or to things which happen
    repeatedly.
    *In the summer I **drink** a lot of lemonade.*
    *I **get up** every morning at 9 o'clock.*
    *Maria sometimes **goes** to parties, but she almost
    never **dances**.*

c   to refer to natural or scientific laws.
    *Water **boils** at 100° C.*

d   to say when things will happen in the future
    according to a timetable or programme.
    *The concert **starts** at 8 o'clock in the evening.*
    *What time **does** our boat **leave?***

e   instead of *will* after words and expressions such as
    if, when, until, before, as soon as, while when we
    are referring to the future.
    *What will you do when you **leave** school?*
    *Can you telephone me as soon as he **arrives**?*

2 Present continuous

The present continuous is most often used:

a   to refer to something which is happening while we
    are speaking.
    *I'm afraid you can't talk to Sonia now – she**'s doing**
    her aerobic exercises.*

b   to refer to situations which are temporary in a
    given time period.
    *Chris **is teaching** this class for the time being
    because the regular teacher is ill.*
    *My exams are next week, so I**'m studying** hard at
    the moment.*

c   to refer to changes, development and progress.
    *Even though he still needs to stay in bed, his health
    is improving.*
    *Unemployment **is increasing** in many countries.*

d   to refer to future arrangements.
    *Next Saturday, our team **is playing** in the semi-
    finals.*

e   in the structure *always / continually / forever /
    constantly + present continuous* to refer to other
    people's habits which we find irritating.
    *You **are always talking**! Be quiet!*

The present continuous is **not** usually used with verbs
such as:

•   *see, hear, taste* and *smell* (= perception)
•   *seem, appear* and *sound* (= appearance)
•   *realize, remember, believe, imagine, know,
    suppose, understand* (= thinking)
•   *like, hate, dislike, love, prefer, admire, need, want,
    wish* (= likes and dislikes)
•   *belong, possess, keep, have, own* (= possession)

Occasionally some of these verbs are used in the
continuous form but there is a change in meaning.
    *Some animals can **see** well in the dark.*
    *I'm seeing** the dentist on Monday. (seeing =
    visiting)*
    *Jack **has** a new car.*
    *Sarah **is having** a good time, isn't she? (having =
    experiencing)*
    *What's the matter with Tom? He **appears** very
    nervous.*
    *My favourite singer **is appearing** on BBC2 this
    evening. (appearing = performing)*

Countable and uncountable nouns

Words used before countable nouns	Words used before uncountable nouns	Words used before both
a / an each every many few a few a large number of a lot of	these much little a little a great deal of a large amount of large amounts of	the my some this any lots of plenty of all a lot of

1 Countable nouns

Countable nouns are nouns which can be counted.
one **table**, three **books**, a hundred **people**

2 Uncountable nouns

a   Uncountable nouns are nouns which cannot be
    counted, so they do **not** have a plural form. We
    also never use the indefinite article (*a / an*) with
    uncountable nouns.
    *Rice** is a staple food in China.*
    *The **information** he gave him is extremely
    important.*

b In order to talk about an uncountable noun in the singular we can sometimes use a countable noun which has a very similar meaning.
*Tell me about the **accommodation** – will I have a **room** with a shower?*
*It is rather difficult to find **work** in this town – I've been looking for a **job** for three months.*

c Where no such word as in **b** exists, we use expressions such as *a piece of*, *a bit of* and *an item of*.
*I don't need a lot of paper – just give me a **piece of paper**.*
*Charles gave me a **bit of advice** yesterday, which I found very useful.*
*A shawl is an **item of clothing** which covers the shoulders.*
Precise expressions are sometimes available.
*a **loaf of** bread, a **slice of** bread, a **drop of** water, a **pinch of** salt, a **spoonful of** sugar, a **grain of** sand*

3 Nouns which can be both

Many nouns can be either countable or uncountable – there is usually a change in meaning, though.
*This antique paperweight is made entirely of **glass**.* (the material)
*We need to buy six new **glasses** for the dinner party.* (something you drink out of)
*There is no **room** on my desk for any more books.* (space)
*All the **rooms** have a lovely view of the sea.* (rooms in a house)

GRAMMAR REFERENCE UNIT 2

Articles

1 The indefinite article *a / an*

If a noun begins with a vowel sound we use the indefinite article *an*. If it begins with a consonant sound we use *a*. It is the sound which is important, not the spelling.
an apple, an elephant, an honest man, a hobby, an uncle, a university
The indefinite article is most often used:

a when we mention a countable noun for the first time.
Yesterday a policeman wanted to ask me some questions.
I think I've broken a tooth.

b when we want to classify things / people or say what they are like.
He is a very talented actor.
Platinum is a valuable metal.

c to name a person's job.
Maria is a doctor.

d before certain numbers and in certain 'number expressions'.
She is going to pay a hundred / a thousand / a million pounds for it.
He was driving at sixty miles an hour.
I work forty hours a week.

2 The definite article *the*

The definite article is most often used:

a when we refer to something that has been mentioned already.
To make a Spanish omelette, take three eggs and a large potato.
Cut the potato into small cubes and …

b when we mention something that the listener knows about or something that has already been defined.
By the way, I went to see the film you recommended.

c when there is only one (often in a particular context).
The sky is rather grey today.
Can I speak to the headmaster, please?
The view from this window is really lovely.

d with superlatives.
She is the best teacher at our school – we are the naughtiest students!

e with musical instruments.
I play the piano and my sister plays the violin.

f with means of transport.
I think we should take the bus to Athens, rather than the train.

g with inventions.
The computer has dramatically changed the way we live and work.

h with species of animal in the singular.
The brown bear has almost disappeared in certain parts of the world.

i when we use an adjective (as a noun) to classify or to describe a group of people.
Winter is particularly difficult for the old and the sick.

The definite article is also used:

j with the names of oceans, seas, rivers and mountain ranges.
the Atlantic, the River Thames, the Carpathian Mountains

k with the names of certain countries or groups of countries.
the USA, the UK, the European Union

l with the names of certain state organizations of a country.
the army, the navy, the police

m for nationalities.
the English, the French, the Swiss, the Germans, the Dutch

3 No article

No article is used:

a when we use a countable noun in the plural to talk about something in general.
Dolphins are very intelligent animals.

b when we use an uncountable noun to talk about something in general.
Water has recently been discovered on the moon.
c when we use an abstract noun to talk about something in general.
Love makes the world go round!
d with the names of most streets, cities and countries.
Oxford Street is one of the most famous streets in London.
e in a large number of common expressions.
to go: home / to bed / to school / university / hospital / prison
to be: at home / in bed / at school / at university / in hospital / in prison
by: car / train / plane / bus

COMMON ERRORS

The thief was sent to the prison for ten years.

The definite article is used when referring to the building itself. To refer to prison as a punishment, we do not use the article.

The correct form is: *The thief was sent to prison for ten years.*

Participle adjectives

Many verbs can form adjectives from their present and past participles.
a Adjectives formed from past participles end in *-ed* and usually describe <u>how</u> people feel.
*Yesterday I was so **bored** and **depressed**.*
b Adjectives formed from present participles end in *-ing* and usually describe <u>the cause</u> of people's feelings.
*What an **exciting** film that was! It had such a **surprising** ending!*

GRAMMAR REFERENCE UNIT 3

The future

The following tenses can all be used to refer to the future.

1 Present continuous

The present continuous is used to refer to definite arrangements we have made for the future.
*I'm afraid I can't see you on Thursday because I'**m having** dinner with Chris.*
*Sandra has won a scholarship to Oxford – she **is starting** there next year.*

2 *Going to* future

Going to + infinitive is used:
a to refer to things we intend or plan to do in the future.
*After school I'**m going to go** for a coffee.*
*What **are you going to do** when you finish the course?*

b to refer to things we are sure will happen because of what is happening now.
*The car's out of control! Oh no! It'**s going to crash**!*
*Look at that big black cloud – it'**s going to rain**!*

3 Present simple

The present simple is used:
a to say when things will happen in the future according to a timetable, programme or schedule.
*We must wait for another 20 minutes – the bank **opens** at 9 o'clock.*
*Hurry up! The meeting **starts** in five minutes!*
b to refer to the future after words and expressions such as *if, when, until, before, as soon as, while.*
*Before **you go**, will you turn out the light?*
*When **you meet** Katerina in London, give her my love.*

4 *Will* future

The *will* future *(will* or *'ll* + infinitive) is most often used:
a to make predictions about the future based on what we think or believe, <u>not</u> on what is happening now.
*John **will** probably **be** a very good teacher one day.*
*What do you think life **will be** like in the year 2050?*
*I'm sure I'**ll do** well in the exams.*
b when we make a decision at the time of speaking, without any planning or preparation.
*It's very cold in here, isn't it? I'**ll close** the window.*
*We can't get out this way! We'**ll have to** jump out of the window!*
*I **won't tell** you what he said because you already look angry.*
*Your glass is empty. **Will you have** some more wine?*

5 Future continuous

The future continuous *(will I'll + be + -ing)* is used to refer to something which will be happening at a future point in time.
*This time tomorrow we'**ll be flying** over the Atlantic.*

6 Future perfect

The future perfect *(will I'll + have + past participle)* is used to refer to something that will happen before a future point in time.
*By the year 2050, man **will have travelled** to Mars.*
*Do you think Steven **will have finished** the report by tomorrow?*

7 Future perfect continuous

The future perfect continuous *(will I'll + have + been + -ing)* is used to refer to something which will continue for some time before a future point in time.
*Do you realize that in June I'**ll have been working** here for twenty years?*

Enough

a   *Enough* means *sufficient* or *sufficiently* and is usually used after an adjective / adverb or before a noun.
*Your work is not good **enough**, I'm afraid.*
*Does your boss think that you can type fast **enough**?*
*Have we got **enough** food for the weekend?*

b   *Enough* is very often followed by a full infinitive or by *for* + object (+ full infinitive).
*Do you have **enough money to buy** what you want?*
*Is this pullover big **enough for Jerry**?*
*Is there **enough work for you to do** here?*

Make and do

A large number of expressions include the words *make* and *do*. Generally speaking, we use the verb *do* to talk about some kind of work or task, while the verb *make* is used to refer to something we are building or creating.
Make and *do* also collocate with specific words to form a number of common expressions.

do	make
a lot of / some / a little damage	better
a lot of / some / a little harm	a mistake / an error
a test / an exam	a discovery
your best	a decision
well	a promise
an experiment	a suggestion
some work	certain / sure
the washing-up	an attempt
the housework	a choice
some / the shopping	a plan
an exercise	a meal
your homework	progress
someone a favour	a list / notes
some research	an excuse
good	someone angry
	someone laugh
	an effort
	a noise
	friends with someone
	a phone call
	a complaint
	a model
	a cake
	the tea

Frequency adverbs

Frequency adverbs such as *always, sometimes, regularly, never*, etc. are usually placed:

a   before the main verb of the sentence.
*I **always** read in bed before going to sleep.*

b   after whatever form of the verb *be* is used.
*Paperbacks are **usually** very cheap.*

c   after a modal verb but before the main verb of the sentence.
*I can **never** find the book I want in this bookshop.*

Modal verbs: *must, have to, should*

All of these modal verbs are used to express a sense of obligation or necessity, which may be 'strong' (i.e. it is essential that you or someone else do something) or 'weak' (i.e. it would be a good idea).

1   *Must* and *have to*

a   *Must* is used when there is a strong obligation imposed <u>by the speaker</u>.
*You **must** come to the meeting tonight.*
*I **must** lose some weight – I am far too fat!*

b   *Have to* or *have got to* is used when there is a strong obligation imposed <u>by someone other than the speaker</u> or <u>by a rule or law</u>.
*I'm afraid I **have to** finish this report tonight – my boss wants it tomorrow.*
*James **has got to** wear a uniform at his new school.*

c   *Must* can only refer to the present or the future. When we want to refer to the past we use *had to*.
*I **had to** lose some weight because none of my dresses fitted me.*

d   When we want to say that there is <u>no</u> obligation to do something we cannot use *mustn't* (because this means that something is prohibited or not allowed), so we use *don't have to* or *haven't got to* or *don't need to* or *needn't*.
*What a relief! **We don't have to / haven't got to** do the homework after all!*
*Sophia will take a taxi from the airport, so we **don't need to / needn't** go and meet her there.*

e   The negative form, *mustn't*, expresses prohibition (i.e. something is not allowed).
*You **mustn't** use the office phone to make personal calls.*
*'Jimmy you **mustn't** play in the road!'*

2   Should

a   *Should* is used to express a strong suggestion or some advice. An alternative is *ought to*.
*You **should** have music lessons if you want to learn to play the guitar well.*
*You **ought to** go to the doctor if the pain in your foot continues.*

b The negative form, *shouldn't*, is used for a strong suggestion or piece of advice <u>not</u> to do something.
   *You **shouldn't** eat that meat. I think it's gone off.*

Comparatives and superlatives

1 Comparative and superlative forms

We can compare people and things by using the comparative form of a particular adjective followed by *than*, or by using the superlative form.
   *My sister is **taller than** I am.*
   *Costas is the **oldest** student in the class.*

COMMON ERRORS

You're a better musician than I.

If there is no verb after the pronoun, the object pronoun is normally used. The correct form is: *You're a better musician than me / I am.*

The comparative and superlative forms of a <u>regular one-syllable adjective</u> are made:
a by adding *-er* and *-est*.
   young   younger   the youngest
b by adding *-r* and *-st*, when the adjective ends in *-e*.
   strange   stranger   the strangest
c by doubling the final consonant and adding *-er* and *-est*, when the adjective ends in a vowel and a consonant.
   hot   hotter   the hottest
d by changing the *-y* to an *-i* and adding *-er* and *-est*, when the adjective ends in a consonant followed by *-y*.
   dry   drier   the driest
e The comparative and superlative forms of <u>regular adjectives of two or more syllables</u> and <u>the majority of adverbs</u> are made by putting *more* and *most* in front.
   *beautiful   **more** beautiful   the **most** beautiful*
   *quickly   **more** quickly   (the) **most** quickly*
f <u>Irregular adjectives and adverbs</u> use different words for their comparative and superlative forms. Some adjectives and adverbs share the same comparative and superlative forms.

good	better	the best
bad	worse	the worst
well	better	(the) best
badly	worse	(the) worst

• The determiners *little* and *much / many* also have irregular forms:

little	less	the least
much / many	more	the most

2 Comparisons using *less ... than* and *as ... as*

a When we want to say that something has less of a certain quality than something else we can use *less* + adjective / adverb + *than* (or *the least* + adjective / adverb when we are referring to several things).
   *This book is **less interesting than** the film.*
   *It was **the least expensive** car I could find.*

b When we want to say that something has the same amount of a certain quality as something else we can use *as* + adjective / adverb + *as*. Words and phrases such as *not, almost, nearly, three times*, when put in front, change the meaning accordingly.
   *This exercise is **almost as** difficult **as** the last one.*
   *This coat is **five times as** expensive **as** the other one.*

3 Qualifying comparisons

We can qualify comparisons made with a comparative form + *than* by adding words and expressions such as *a little, a bit, slightly, rather, a lot, far* and *even*.
   *You're **even more intelligent than** I thought you were.*
   *This recording is **slightly better than** the one you already have.*
   *My father is **a lot older than** my mother.*

GRAMMAR REFERENCE UNIT 5

Past tenses

1 Past simple

The past simple is most often used:
a when we refer to actions or events which happened at a particular time in the past.
   *I **cut** my finger yesterday and it still hurts today.*
   *We **left** the house at 4 o'clock.*
b when we refer to completed actions, events or situations which lasted for a period of time.
   *I **worked** for two years as a postman.*
   *I **was** unemployed for a long time and **felt** very unhappy.*
c to refer to habits or things which happened repeatedly in the past.
   *When I was a child, we **had** breakfast at 8 o'clock every morning.*
   *I always **got** good marks when I was at school.*

The past simple is also used after certain words and expressions to refer to the present or future.
   *Look at the time! It's time we **left** for the airport.*
   *I'd rather you **didn't smoke** in here.*
   *I wish I **was / were** rich.*

2 *Used to* and *would*

a *Used to* is commonly used to refer to past habits and situations.
   *He **used to smoke** heavily, but now he can't even stand the smell of a cigarette.*
   *When he was a student, he **didn't use to study** very much.*
   ***Did you use to live** by the sea?*

COMMON ERRORS

These days, I use to stay with friends.

There is no present form of *used to*, so the correct form is:
These days, I usually stay with friends.

b *Would* is not so common in conversation and can only be used to refer to <u>past habits</u>, not past situations.
   *When we were children, we **would go** for a picnic every Sunday.*

3 Past continuous

The past continuous is most often used:
a to refer to something which was already happening before another past event.
   *We **were watching** TV when the police arrived.*
b to refer to temporary activities or situations in the past.
   *John feels so tired because he **was working** hard in the garden all morning.*
c to refer to activities or situations which were going on at the same time in the past.
   *While I **was looking round** the house, Jane **was talking** to the landlord.*

The past continuous is also used in stories to set the scene.
   *It **was raining** heavily and the wind **was howling** in the trees. Sean was on his own, **feeling** rather lonely. Suddenly the telephone rang …*

Contrasting ideas

There are several different words and expressions which can be used to contrast ideas. We can:
a use the conjunction *but*.
   *I have a good job **but** I cannot afford to buy a house.*
b use the conjunction *although* or *though / even though*, followed by a subject + verb.
   *He still lives with his parents **although** he is in his forties.*
   *(**Although** he is in his forties he still lives with his parents.)*

c use the preposition *in spite of / despite*, followed by a noun or gerund.
   *Jane did well in her exams **in spite of / despite** not studying at all.*
   *(**In spite of / despite** not studying at all, Jane did well in her exams.)*
   Alternatively, we can use *in spite of / despite*, followed by *the fact that* + a clause.
   *Johnson still won the elections, **in spite of / despite the fact that** he was unpopular with a great many people.*
   *(**In spite of / despite the fact that** he was unpopular with a great many people, Johnson still won the elections.)*

d contrast ideas in <u>two</u> sentences by using the word *however*.
   *She went to a very good school and did well at university. **However**, she could not convince herself that she was as good as other people.*

GRAMMAR REFERENCE UNIT 6

Conditional sentences 1

Conditional sentences always contain a conditional clause, which is often (but not always) introduced by the word *if*. This conditional clause may be put before the main clause / at the beginning of the sentence, or it may be put <u>after</u> the main clause.

1 First conditionals

When we want to refer to something in the future which is likely or probable, we can use:
a *If* + present simple … *will* future.
   *If you don't do **your homework tonight, Dad will be** angry.*
   *If you ask **her to marry you, she'll probably think** it's a joke!*
   *We'll go out **and celebrate this evening if you pass your driving test.***
b *If* + present simple … modal verb (e.g. *must, could, might*) + infinitive.
   *If you go **to the party, you may see** Anna there.*
   *You must stay **with us if you come** to Athens.*
c Other words and expressions may be used in place of *if*. The most common are *unless, as long as, provided / providing, on condition that*.
   *Unless **you improve, you'll probably fail the exam.** (= If you don't **improve, you'll probably fail the exam.)**
   *As long as **you are careful what you eat in India, you'll have no problems.***
   *Eating out in New York won't be so expensive, **providing** you don't go to top restaurants.*
   *I'll lend you the money, **on condition that** you give it back to me at the weekend.*
d The expression *even if* can be used for emphasis, or to suggest a contradiction.
   *Even if **you offer her the money, she won't accept** it.*
   *Even if **they win this match, they won't be** champions.*

2 Second conditionals

When we want to refer to something in the future (or the present) which is either possible but not probable <u>or</u> unreal or imaginary, we can use:
a *If* + past simple … *would / 'd* + infinitive
   *If you went **to the Golden Lamb to eat, you'd spend** all the money you earn in a week. (= but you probably will <u>not</u> go!)*
   *If I was / were **rich, I'd buy** a huge house by the sea. (= but I am <u>not</u> rich)*
   *Where **would you choose** to live **if you could** live anywhere in the world?*
   (= but you cannot live anywhere you want)

b If + past simple ... modal verb (e.g. *could, might*) + infinitive
*If you spoke to the manager personally, he **might give** you a job.*
*I **could buy** a new car if I got this job.*

Instead of the word *if* we can also use:
Supposing.
***Supposing** we left for New York now, what time would we arrive?*

No matter

No matter is usually followed by *what, when, where, why, who* and *how*. It means that something is always true or always happens whatever the circumstances are.
*He could not find what he wanted, **no matter** how hard he tried.*
When *no matter* refers to the future it is followed by the present simple.
***No matter** what happens, I'll always love you.*
***No matter** where you go, you'll find people who speak English.*

COMMON ERRORS

No matter if I eat a lot, I'm always hungry.

The correct form is: *No matter how much I eat, I'm always hungry.*

GRAMMAR REFERENCE UNIT 7

Modal verbs: *can, could, may* and *might*

These modal verbs are often used to express a sense of possibility. This sense of possibility may be 'strong' (i.e. we are certain about something) or 'weak' (i.e. we are not so sure).

1 Can

Can is used:
a to show that someone has an ability to do something, or senses something.
*Helen **can** cook really well.*
*Did you turn off the cooker? I **can** smell something burning!*
b to show that a certain effect is possible.
*Skiing **can** be really tiring.*
*Smoking **can** damage your health.*

2 May, might and *could*

May, might and *could* are used:
a to show that there is a chance that something will happen in the future.
*Don't drive so fast – you **may / might / could** have an accident.*
b to show that something is possibly true now. (The continuous form should be used where the present continuous would be appropriate.)
*Jane is not at home – she **might** be at work.*
*This painting **could** be extremely valuable – why don't you ask an expert?*

May not and *might not / mightn't* are used:
to show that something is possibly <u>not</u> the case.
*Speak slowly and clearly because he **may not** understand you.*
*You can ask him, but he **might not / mightn't** help you.*

3 Can't and *couldn't*

Cannot / can't or *could not / couldn't* are used when we are almost certain that something is <u>not</u> the case – it is impossible. (We never use *mustn't*, because this means that something is prohibited.)
*She **can't / couldn't** be so young – she has three children!*
*What you tell me **can't / couldn't** possibly be correct – I'll have to check it.*

Relative clauses

A relative clause gives more information about something or someone in the main clause. It comes just <u>after</u> the person or the thing you are referring to, and often (but not always), begins with a relative pronoun such as *who, which, that* or *whose*.

1 Defining relative clauses

a A defining relative clause makes it clear who or what you are talking about. Without this information the sentence is not clear or makes no sense.
*Do you want to speak to the man **that telephoned earlier**?*
*Here is the book **that tells you everything you need to know about tennis**.*
b Commas are never used to mark off a defining relative clause.
c The relative pronoun *that* can refer <u>both</u> to people and to things. We could use the relative pronouns *who* and *which* instead.
  • *Who* gives more information about a person or people.
    *Do you want to talk to the man **who** telephoned earlier?*
  • *Which* gives more information about a thing or things.
    *Here is the book **which** tells you everything you need to know about tennis.*
d In each of the examples in **a** and **c**, the relative pronoun – *that, who* and *which* – is the <u>subject</u> of the relative clause. It is also possible, however, for *that, who* or *which* to be the <u>object</u> of the relative clause. (It is very common in spoken English to leave out the pronoun when it is the object of the relative clause.)
*What's the name of the old woman **(that / who)** I saw selling flowers outside the church?*
*Have you got the books **(that / which)** I ordered last week?*

COMMON ERRORS

Give it back the ball you borrowed.

The object of the sentence has been included twice.

The correct form is: *Give back the ball you borrowed.*

---

e The relative pronoun *that* (not *who* or *which*) is usually used after superlatives and after the following words: *all, every(thing), some(thing), any(thing), no(thing), none, little, few, much, only.* (If the relative pronoun is the object of the relative clause it may be left out.)

> Have you done **anything that** has upset her?
> 'Help!' … it was the **only thing (that)** I could say at that moment!
> 'Titanic' is **the best film (that)** I've ever seen.

f The relative possessive pronoun *whose* can also be used to introduce a defining relative clause. Like *that*, it gives more information about <u>both</u> people and things, and is used in the place of the words *his, her, its* or *their.*

> What's the address of the young man **whose** name is not on our list?
> (= What's the address of the young man? **His** name is not on our list.)
> He was wearing a suit **whose** jacket matched the trousers.
> (= He was wearing a suit. **Its** jacket matched the trousers.)

2 Non-defining relative clauses

a A non-defining relative clause adds extra information. This information is not essential to identify who or what we are talking about. If we left out the relative clause the sentence would still be clear and make sense.

> John Jackson, **who comes from America,** is the winner of this year's competition.
> Paros, **which is an island in the Cyclades,** is one of Greece's top tourist destinations.
> Mrs Hendry, **whose daughter you've already met,** is going to be at the party.

b A non-defining relative clause must always be introduced by a relative pronoun – it can never be left out. The pronouns used are: *who* (referring to a person or people), *which* (referring to a thing or things), and *whose. Whose* can refer to <u>both</u> people and things and is used in the place of *his, her, its* or *their.*

c *That* is never used to introduce a non-defining relative clause.

d The relative pronouns *who* and *which* in each of the examples in **a** are the <u>subject</u> of the relative clause. *Who* or *which* may also be the <u>object</u> of the relative clause.

> Mr Conners, **who** nobody likes, is going to be the next headmaster.
> My computer, **which** I bought last month, has started having problems.

e A non-defining relative clause must be marked off from the rest of the sentence by commas.

3 The relative pronouns *why, where* and *when*

Why, where and *when* are often used to introduce relative clauses (both non-defining and defining) in order to give more information about a reason, place or time.

> She doesn't want to go to a school **where** there are lots of rules.

> Spring is the time **when** most people visit Paris.
> First I went to Oxford University, **where** I met my wife, and then I joined the army.
> The reason **(why)** I'm writing to you is to give you some good news.

4 Relative clauses and prepositions

Prepositions usually come at the end of relative clauses (both non-defining and defining). In more formal English, however, they are sometimes put before the relative pronoun.

> The man **(that / who)** I gave the package <u>to</u> is sitting in the corner.
> (= **The man <u>to whom</u> I gave the package** is sitting in the corner. Formal)
> Java is a place **(that / which) I've not heard very much** <u>about</u>.
> (= Java is a place <u>**about which**</u> I've not heard very **much.** Formal)
> John Kell, **who we all want to speak <u>to</u>,** is coming to the meeting tonight.
> (=John Kell, **<u>to whom</u> we all want to speak,** is coming to the meeting tonight. Formal)

5 The relative pronoun *whom*

Whom is sometimes used instead of *who* or *that* when it is the <u>object</u> of the relative clause (either defining or non-defining). It is not very common in conversation – it is used much more in formal written English. It must be used when the relative pronoun comes after a preposition.

> To whom it may concern.
> Sir Richard, **whom** I have never met, has invited us to dinner.

Prepositional phrases with *in*

A prepositional phrase usually consists of preposition + noun or preposition + noun group. For example, *in danger of, in half* and *in common with* are phrases which all start with the preposition *in.*

a Prepositional phrases often come after the verb or object of the verb.

> The Olympic Games are **in danger of** becoming just another huge business concern.
> She tore the letter **in half** and threw the two pieces into the fire.

b For emphasis, they are sometimes put at the beginning of the clause or sentence.

> **In common with** many film stars, Cecilia Black has far too much money and little talent.

GRAMMAR REFERENCE UNIT 8

The present perfect

1 Present perfect

The present perfect is used:

a to refer to something which started in the past and continues in the present.
He's worked as a doctor for many years.
I've lived in the same house since I was born.

b to refer to something which happened in the past but in a period of time not yet finished.
I have studied for three hours this morning – I'll study for another two hours after lunch.
So far this year I have been to the dentist five times.

c to refer to recent events which are directly related to the present.
Where's my wallet? Oh no! Someone has stolen it!
Why is your hand covered in blood? Have you cut yourself?

d to refer to something which happened in the past but we don't know when.
I've been a couple of times to France – it's a beautiful country.
The government has promised to reduce unemployment.

2 Time-expressions

The present perfect is often used:

a with time-expressions which mean at any time up to now.
ever, never, already, before, yet, still, so far, up to now, recently, lately, this year

b with the word *for* when we want to say how long something has lasted.
I've been a teacher for 10 years.

c with the word *since* when we want to say when something started.
He has had that book since he was a child.

d with the word *just* when we want to say that an event was very recent.
Where's John? Oh, he's just gone out.

3 Present perfect continuous

The present perfect continuous is used:

a to refer to activities or situations which began in the past and which are still continuing.
You've been working so hard recently, why don't you have a rest?
The police have been asking people lots of questions all this week.

b to emphasize the continuity, repetition or duration of an action or situation.
Are you still reading that book? You've been reading it for the last three weeks!

c when you can see the results of a recent activity or situation.
Your clothes are covered in paint! Have you been painting the house?
My eyes are red because I've been chopping up onions!

The present perfect continuous is <u>not</u> usually used with verbs such as *know, like, seem,* etc. For more examples refer to present tenses 2 on page 170.

GRAMMAR REFERENCE UNIT 9

The past perfect

1 The past perfect

a We often use the past perfect when we mention two actions or situations in the past, and we want to show that one happened before the other.
The door opened and a tall woman walked in – Richard suddenly realized that she was the woman he had seen on the plane.
The telephone rang – it was Alex. I remembered that I had promised to help him with his English homework.

b The continuous form is used if we want to emphasize the continuity, repetition or duration of an action or situation.
He was furious! Apparently he had been waiting for her for over two hours!
Maria was so dirty because she had been cleaning out the cellar all morning.

c After expressions such as *it / this was the first time* and *it / this was (one of) the most* we usually use the past perfect.
He was so nervous because it was the first time he had played the piano in public.
It was the best film she had ever seen – she went to see it three times.

2 Narrative time links

a Time links make clear the order of events or situations in a story. The past perfect is very often (not always) used with words and expressions such as *till, until, (just) before, (just) after, when, by the time, once,* and *as soon as.*
By the time the police arrived, the hooligans **had all disappeared.**
When he had finished his homework, he went out to see his friends.
Once he had understood the rules, Dimitri found the card game easy to play.

b To show that one thing happened immediately after another, we can use *hardly ... when* or *no sooner ... than* together with the past perfect.
She **had hardly arrived** home when the phone rang.
She **had no sooner got** out of the bath than the lights went out.

In more formal and literary English these expressions may be used with inverted word order.
Hardly had she arrived home when the phone rang.
No sooner had she got out of the bath than the lights went out.

c The past perfect is <u>not</u> usually used when the order of events is obvious or one action is the immediate result of another.
When she **saw** the mouse she screamed!
Once he **heard** the shots he started to run towards his car.
Janet decided to go by bus – so as soon as one **arrived** she got on it.

d The time links *after that, afterwards* and *then* can be placed before the second action to show the order of events. Once again, it is not usually necessary to use the past perfect because it is now obvious which event happened first.
The thieves drove in the getaway car as far as the airport. **After that,** they took the first flight out of the country.
He took out a knife and put it on the table. **Then** he put his hand into his pocket and brought out a gun.

Common prepositional phrases with *by, in* and *on*

Many prepositional phrases with *by* describe different ways of travelling from one place to another.
by train, by plane, by ship, by bus, by taxi, etc.
If the means of transport (*train, car, bus,* etc.) is part of a noun group, however, the preposition changes.
in my father's car   **on** the express train
on the number 9 bus

GRAMMAR REFERENCE UNIT 10

The passive

1 Forms of the passive

The passive is made by using the appropriate form of the verb *be* followed by the past participle.

• present simple	Blue jeans **are worn** everywhere.
• present continuous	A new look **is being planned** for next season.
• present perfect	Your application for employment with this firm **has been received.**
• past simple	I'm afraid the wrong measurements **were taken.**
• used to past	Clothes **used to be made** in places like Manchester.
• will future	Many new jobs **will be created** by the fast-growing fashion industry.
• going to future	That tiny little mark **is not going to be noticed.**
• past continuous	The matter **was being considered** when the incident occurred.
• past perfect	The health risks **had been known** about for years.
• modal verbs	McQueen's new creations **might be worn** by a top model.

2 Uses of the passive

When we use the passive we <u>only</u> mention the agent (i.e. who or what is responsible for something) if it is important to the meaning of the sentence.

The passive is usually used:
a when we want to make a sentence sound formal.
*Smoking **is not allowed** in the reception area.*
b when we don't know / don't care or it is obvious from the context who or what is responsible for something.
*My jewellery **has been stolen!***
c when we don't <u>want</u> to say who or what is responsible for something.
*I'm sorry but your letter of application for the job **was thrown away** accidentally.*
d to describe processes.
*Water **is added** to the mixture, which is heated.*
e when we want to put particular information at the beginning or the end of the sentence.
*We know that the theft **was committed by** someone sitting in this room!*
*Olga was born in London. She **was brought up** by foster parents in Edinburgh, though.*

People should be let do what they want.

Let is not normally used in passive sentences – *allow* is usually used. The correct form is: *People should be allowed to do what they want.*

The passive is also used with verbs such as *think, believe, consider, say* and *expect* followed by the infinitive of a verb (for the present) or *to have* + past participle (for the past).

> He **is thought to be** the best designer in the world.
> They **were expected to have arrived** by 10 o'clock last night.
> (But: **It is said that** you cannot judge a person by their clothes.)

The gerund /-*ing* form of the verb

See also the Infinitive form of the verb on page 180.

The *-ing* form of the verb is used:

a as part of a continuous verb form.
   *She was **wearing** a lovely satin dress.*

b as an adjective.
   *There's a really **exciting** film on TV tonight!*

c after prepositional phrases.
   *Charles is very good at **making** furniture from pieces of old wood.*
   *I insisted on **paying** for the damage I had caused.*

I'm looking forward to see you soon.

The word *to* is a preposition in this sentence and not part of an infinitive. The correct form is: *I'm looking forward to seeing you soon.*

d as a noun which is the subject of a clause or sentence. (gerund)
   ***Reading** is one of my favourite pastimes.*

e as a noun which is the object or complement of a clause or sentence. (gerund)
   *One of my duties was **washing** the dishes.*

f after certain verbs. (gerund)
   *Have you finished **doing** the housework?*
   *I enjoyed **listening** to her sing at the concert.*

The *-ing* form (gerund) <u>as well as</u> the infinitive can be used with no difference in meaning:

a after verbs such as *begin, continue* and *start*.
   *He began **crying** is the same as He began **to cry***

b after verbs such as *hate, like, love, prefer* and the expression *can't stand* (with a small difference in meaning).
   *I **like singing**.* (i.e. in general)
   *I **like to sing.** when I'm happy* (i.e. more specific)

c The *-ing* form (gerund) <u>as well as</u> the infinitive can be used after certain verbs (with an important change in meaning). The most common verbs of this type are *mean, stop, remember, forget, try, regret* and *go on*.

- *Carrying out the survey **meant talking** to a lot of people.* (meant = involved)
  *I **meant to talk** to you but I'm afraid I forgot.* (meant = intended)

- *I've **stopped smoking**.* (stopped = no longer do)
  *He was tired of driving, so he **stopped to have** a rest.* (stopped = stopped one thing in order to do another)

- *Do you **remember going** to the Louvre when we were in Paris?* (remember = recall something from the past)
  *Remember **to go** to the dentist tomorrow, won't you?* (remember = not forget to do something in the future)

- *Oh dear, I think I've **forgotten to lock** the door!* (forgotten = not done something I had to do)
  *I'll never **forget coming** home to find my house had been burgled.* (forget = cannot recall a memory)

- ***Try using** less milk in the recipe next time.* (try = experiment with)
  *I **tried to reach** the top shelf, but had to get a ladder.* (tried = attempted something to see if it is possible)

- *I **regret telling** my girlfriend not to be so stupid.* (regret = I'm sorry about what happened)
  *I **regret to tell** you that your application was not successful.* (regret = I'm sorry for what I have to say)

- *How long are you going to **go on playing** that awful music!* (go on = continue an activity)
  *After the meeting we **went on to play** a game of squash.* (go on = proceed to do something different)

GRAMMAR REFERENCE UNIT 11

Reported speech

We use reported speech when we say what someone said or thought but do not use their exact words. A reporting verb (such as *say* or *tell*) is used, and changes are made to the verb tenses, pronouns and sometimes to the word order. Words which refer to time and place may also need to be changed.

1 Verb tense changes

In most situations we make the following changes to verb tenses when reporting speech.

Direct speech	Reported speech
• present simple 'I **want to live** in America,' he said.	➜ past simple He said that he **wanted** to live in America.
• present continuous '**He's talking** on the phone,' she said.	➜ past continuous She said that he **was talking** on the phone.
• present perfect 'I **have had** a little accident,' she said.	➜ past perfect She said that she **had had** a little accident.

- present perfect continuous
  '**We've been waiting** for over an hour,' they said.
  → past perfect continuous
  They said that they **had been waiting** for over an hour.
- past simple
  '**I saw** Francis,' he said.
  → past perfect
  He said that he **had seen** Francis.
- past continuous
  'They **were talking** about the money,' he said.
  → past perfect continuous
  He said that they **had been talking** about the money.
- past perfect
  'I thought I **had missed** my flight,' she said.
  → past perfect
  She said that she had thought she **had missed** her flight.

Although *would, should, could* (and *must*, for strong possibility) in direct speech do <u>not</u> change in form in reported speech, other modal verbs do change.

can → *could*	*may* → *might*
will → *would*	*must* → *had to* (for obligation)

'**I can** go,' he said.	He said that he **could** go.
'**You'll** be late,' she said.	She said that I **would** be late.
'It **may** rain,' they said.	They said that it **might** rain.
'**You must** leave,' she said.	She said that I **had to** leave.

2 Other changes

Very often changes need to be made to:

a the pronouns which were used by the original speaker.
'**I** will give it to **you**,' he said.
He said that **he** would give it to **me**.

b words such as *this, these, that, those*, which normally change to *the*.
'**This** book should help you with your grammar,' she said.
She said that **the** book should help me with my grammar.

c words and expressions which tell us <u>when</u> and <u>where</u> things happened.
today → *that day*
tomorrow → *the next / following day*
yesterday → *the previous day / the day before*
2 days ago → *2 days before / earlier*
now → *then*   *here* → *there*   *come* → *go*
'He'll **come** to school **tomorrow**,' Martin's mother said.
Martin's mother said that he would **go** to school **the next day**.

d the order of the words in questions (see **3d**).

3 Reporting verbs

a When we report statements or thoughts we choose an appropriate verb such as *say, tell, think, assure, swear, claim, complain*, etc. followed by *that*. (In conversation, *that* is sometimes omitted.)
'This book was a waste of money!'
She **complained** that the book had been a waste of money.

'The manager will be able to answer all your questions.'
He **assured** me that the manager would be able to answer all my questions.

The reporting verb is occasionally put at the end of the sentence, after a comma.
The manager would be able to answer all my questions, he **assured** me.

b When we report requests, orders, advice or warnings we use a verb such as *advise, ask, tell, order*, etc. followed by an infinitive.
'I don't think you should go on this holiday.'
He **advised** me not to go on the holiday.

'Get off the plane at once!'
He **ordered** them to get off the plane at once.

c *Wh*-questions are often reported by using a reporting verb such as *ask* or *enquire* followed by *what, why, who, where*, etc.
'Where are you going on holiday?'
They **asked us where** we were going on holiday.

'Who was responsible for the accident?'
He **asked me who** had been responsible for the accident.

> ### COMMON ERRORS
>
> *I asked her where was she going.*
>
> The word order of the sentence is not correct.
>
> The correct form is: *I asked her where she was going.*

d *Yes / no* questions are reported using a reporting verb such as *ask* or *enquire* followed by *if / whether*. Word order may also change.
'Have we missed the train?'
She **asked me whether / if** we had missed the train.

'Do you know what our flight number is?'
She **asked me whether / if** I knew what our flight number was.

e Suggestions can most easily be reported by using the verb *suggest* followed by *should*.
'Why don't we go to the cinema?'
She **suggested that we should** go to the cinema.

The infinitive form of the verb

See also the Gerund /-*ing* form of the verb on page 179.

a We often use the full infinitive (with *to*) to express purpose.
*Several teams of doctors went to Africa **to help** the victims of the famine.*

b   A large number of verbs are usually followed by a full infinitive: *afford, agree, appear, arrange, attempt, decide, expect, forget, help, hope, learn, manage, mean, offer, prepare, pretend, promise, refuse, seem, swear, want.*
    *I have **arranged to have** dinner with Mary tonight.*
    *Have you **managed to finish** this exercise?*

c   The full infinitive follows the object of some verbs, particularly reporting verbs such as *ask, encourage, order, permit, persuade, remind, request, tell, warn,* etc.
    *They persuaded us **to go** with them to the theatre.*

d   Some verbs can be followed by either a full infinitive <u>or</u> a gerund. For examples, see points **a** and **b**, on page 179.

e   With the verbs *mean, stop, remember, forget, try, regret* and *go on* there is a big difference in meaning. For examples, see point **c** on page 179.

f   We always use the <u>bare</u> infinitive (without *to*) after modal verbs and after the verbs *let* and *make* in the active voice.
    *You **must go** to a doctor about that cough.*
    *Mr Jones **made** me **write** my composition again.*
    *(But: I **was made to write** the composition again.)*

g   Verbs of perception such as *feel, hear, notice, see* and *watch* can be followed by either a bare infinitive or an *-ing* form. The meaning, however, is slightly different.
    *I **saw** him **kiss** her.* (i.e. I saw the whole kiss, from start to finish!)
    *I opened the door and **saw** him **kissing** her.* (i.e. they were in the middle of kissing.)

GRAMMAR REFERENCE UNIT 12

Conditional sentences 2

In conditional sentences, the conditional clause (*if* …) may be put either before the main clause or after it.

1   Zero conditionals

a   When we want to refer to something which always happens or is always true, or to a scientific law, we can use *If* + present simple + present simple.
    *Maria is very sensitive – **if you get** angry with her **she starts** to cry.*
    *Water **freezes if the temperature drops** below zero.*

b   *If* + present simple + imperative is also possible.
    ***If you want** to start this machine, **press** this button.*

2   Other kinds of conditionals

The following conditionals are all possible:

a   *If* + present continuous + modal verb + bare infinitive
    *Who are you talking to on the phone? **If you are talking** to Anne, **could I talk** to her afterwards?*

b   *If* + present continuous + *will* future
    ***If you are doing** something illegal, you'**ll get** into trouble with the police.*

c   *If* + present continuous + imperative
    ***Leave** the room **if you are not paying** attention!*

d   *If* + present perfect + modal verb + bare infinitive
    ***If you have finished** your work, **you can go** home.*

e   *If* + present perfect + *will* future
    ***If you have read** the book, you'**ll love** the film!*

f   *If* + present perfect + imperative
    ***Put up** your hand **if you have been** to America.*

3   Third conditionals

We use third conditionals when we refer to things which happened (or perhaps didn't happen) <u>in the past</u>. We often use them, for example, when we want to express regret about something. Obviously, we cannot change the past, so all third conditionals describe things which are impossible.

a   If something happened in the past, and this resulted in something else happening in the past, we use:
    *   *If* + past perfect … *would* / *'d* + *have* / *'ve* + past participle
        ***If he had spoken** to her she **would have given** him some advice.*
        ***If I had told** her I loved her, she **would have stayed** with me.*
        ***If I hadn't eaten** that fish, I **wouldn't have been** sick.*
        *We **would not have gone** to that club **if we had known**.*
    *   *If* + past perfect … modal verb + *have* / *'ve* + past participle
        ***If she had seen** him at the party, she **might have spoken** to him.*
        *I **could have phoned** her **if it had not been** so late.*
        ***If you'd touched** the bomb, you **could've been killed**.*

b   If something happened in the past, but has a result in the present, we use:
    *   *If* + past perfect … *would* / *'d* + bare infinitive
        ***If we'd left** an hour earlier, **we'd be** there by now.*
        ***If I hadn't stolen** that money, I **wouldn't be** in so much trouble now.*
    *   *If* + past perfect … modal verb + bare infinitive
        ***If you had listened** to his advice, you **might be** happier now.*

Short replies

1 Using *so* or *neither*

One way of showing that we feel the same way as someone else is to reply to a statement using *so* (for positive statements) or *neither* (for negative statements) followed by an auxiliary verb.

I love that painting.	**So** *do I.*
I'd really love to go to Brazil.	**So** *would I.*
He won't lend me any money.	**Neither** *will I.*
Sonia is not coming tonight.	**Neither** *is Olga.*

2 Using *so* or *not*

a We can avoid repetition when we reply to certain questions by using *so* after verbs such as *believe, expect, guess, hope, imagine, suppose, think, be afraid*, etc.
 Do you think you'll win the competition?
 Well, I hope **so.**

 Have you understood everything?
 I think **so.**

 It'll probably rain, won't it?
 Yes, I expect **so.**

b The negative is formed by using *so* or *not*, depending on the verb.
 I don't think / imagine / expect / suppose / believe **so.**
 I hope / guess / am afraid / suppose / believe **not.**

> **COMMON ERRORS**
>
> *I think so that I've met him before.*
>
> *So* is used only in short replies. The correct form is: *I think that I've met him before.*

GRAMMAR REFERENCE UNIT 13

So and *such*

We can use these words to give emphasis to what we are saying.

1 *So*

a *So* is often just followed by an adjective or an adverb.
 It's **so cold** *in here!*
 You are **so kind!**
 He paints **so well!**

b The adjective or adverb after *so* is sometimes followed by a *that* clause.
 The weather today is **so good that** *nobody wants to do any work.*
 She sang **so beautifully that** *everyone stopped talking to listen to her.*

c *So* is also used in front of the words *much, many, little* and *few*.
 We have **so much** *work to do!*
 What are you going to do with these books? There are **so many!**
 There are **so few** *people here that we'll have to cancel the meeting.*
 There is **so little** *time left.*

2 *Such*

a *Such* is often just followed by a noun / noun group. The indefinite article *a / an* must be used with singular countable nouns.
 Mr Smith is **such a genius!**
 Let's go for a picnic – it's **such a lovely day** *today!*
 We had **such bad weather** *on holiday!*
 These are **such wonderful paintings** *– where shall I put them?*

b The noun / noun group after *such* is sometimes followed by a *that* clause.
 It was **such a rainy day that** *we had to stay at home.*
 It was **such delicious food** *that we couldn't stop eating!*

Order of adjectives

a When we put more than one adjective before a noun, the order of the adjectives is important. The order is normally as follows:

Opinion	*nice awful*
Quality	(size, age, shape, temperature)
	big old round cold
Colour	*red black*
Origin	*Greek English Spanish*
Material	*leather stone wooden*
Purpose	*sports dining writing*

a lovely, big, wooden, dining table
a fantastic, new, Italian, racing bike.
an old, black and white, English sheepdog

b Normally, we put no more than three adjectives before a noun. More information can be added by using:
- *made of;*
 a beautiful, old, writing desk **made of** *mahogany.*
- *from;*
 an expensive, black, leather coat **from** *Italy.*
- *with;*
 a new, dark blue jeep **with** *four-wheel drive.*
- a relative clause;
 She was wearing a large diamond ring, **which was extremely valuable.**

Using *be* and *feel* for sensations

English usually uses the verbs *be* and *feel* to describe sensations such as feeling cold, hot, hungry, thirsty, scared, etc. The verb *have* is <u>not</u> used.
 I'm / feel scared – what do you think will happen to us?
 She's / feels really hungry – she hasn't eaten anything for days.
 I am / feel so tired – I just want to go to bed!

> **COMMON ERRORS**
>
> *Open the window, please, I have hot.*
>
> The correct form is:
> *Open the window, please, I'm (or I feel / I'm feeling) hot.*

Referring to the past: modal verbs

We use an appropriate modal verb + *have* + past participle when we want to refer to the past – to describe things that:

a were possible but did not happen.
   *What a terrible risk you took – you **might have been killed**!*
   *We **could have done** more to help those people, but we didn't.*

b possibly happened, but we are not sure if they happened or not.
   *I wonder where Andrew is? He **could have missed** the bus I suppose.*
   *Do you think they are alright? They **may have had** an accident or something.*

c we are sure happened or did not happen.
   *Jenny: There is no doubt about it – you **must have seen** a ghost!*
   *Fred: It **can't / couldn't have been** a ghost – they don't exist!*
   *Roger didn't answer the phone, so he **must have gone out**.*
   *It **can't / couldn't have been** Angela you saw yesterday – she is in America.*

d we expected to happen but did not happen; or to criticize a past action.
   *They **should have been** at the airport to meet us – why didn't they turn up?*
   *You **shouldn't have said** that to him – it was very rude!*
   *You **oughtn't to have gone out** if you were feeling ill.*

Wishes

1 Present situations

When we would like a situation in the present to be different, we may use:

a *wish / if only* + past simple
   *I **wish / If only I lived** in France (but my wife refuses to leave England).*
   *I **wish / If only it was** Friday (but it's Monday).*
   *She **wishes she didn't have to** go to school (but by law she has to).*

b *wish / if only* + *could* (to talk about an ability) + bare infinitive
   *I **wish / If only I could swim** (but I cannot).*

2 Past situations

When we regret a situation in the past – which obviously cannot be changed – we may use:

a *wish / if only* + past perfect
   *I **wish / If only I hadn't lost** my temper (but I did).*
   *I **wish / If only she had worked** a little harder for her exams (but she didn't).*
   *She **wishes we had taken** the dog with us (but we didn't).*

b *wish / if only* + *could have* (to talk about ability) + past participle
   *My father **wishes he could have done** more to help.*

3 Using *would*

When we are annoyed, frustrated or unhappy about a situation in the present we may express our feelings by saying *I wish / If only* + *would* + bare infinitive.
   *I **wish / If only he would stop** being so rude.*
   *I **wish / If only you wouldn't drive** so fast.*
   *I **wish / If only the weather would improve**.*

It's (high) time …

This expression means that something ought to happen or be done <u>now</u>. As with *wish*, however, we do not use the present tense – we use the past simple.
   *Good heavens! It's 11 o'clock! **It's high time we left**.*

Expressing purpose

To show the purpose of an action, we can use:

a the full infinitive form of a verb.
   *A meeting was arranged **to discuss** the various proposals.*

b *in order to* (slightly formal), or the negative form *in order not to*, followed by a verb.
   *We are sending this letter to parents **in order to inform** them of the situation.*
   *Please handle this parcel carefully **in order not to damage** the contents.*

c *in order that* (very formal) followed by a modal verb + infinitive or by an ordinary verb.
   *Arrangements need to be made **in order that the exam can take place**.*
   *Her aunt left her a large sum of money **in order that she received** a good education.*

d *so as to*, or the negative form *so as not to*, followed by a verb.
   *They left immediately **so as to catch** the bus.*
   *Cook the food over a gentle heat **so as not to burn** it.*

e   *so / so that* followed by a modal verb + infinitive or by an ordinary verb.
*I'm telling him all this **so (so that) he knows** what to do.*
*I explained the exercises to Costas **so (so that) he could do** them on this own.*

When we do something to avoid a possible problem in the future, we can use *in case* + present simple.
*Make sure you take an umbrella with you **in case it rains**.*
*I've made you some sandwiches **in case you feel hungry later**.*

If we want to mention the precautions we took at some time in the past we can use *in case* + past simple.
*I took some money with me **in case I saw** something I wanted to buy.*

Have / Get something done

a   When we do not do something ourselves – someone else does it for us – we use *have* + noun / noun group + past participle.
*We **have our eyes tested** every year at school.*
*I've just **had my hair cut** – do you like it?*
*William **had two teeth taken out** by the dentist yesterday.*

b   *Get* + noun / noun group + past participle has exactly the same meaning but it is slightly more informal. *Get* is also usually used in imperatives.
*We **are getting the car serviced** tomorrow.*
***Get your hair cut**! It's far too long and untidy!*

c   *Have / Get* + noun / noun group + past participle can also be used to refer to things which are done to us by someone else and which are beyond our control.
*Natasha **got her nose broken** in a fight last week.*
*Charles **had his passport taken away** by the border police.*
*Would you believe it? Robin's just **had his car stolen**!*

Phrasal verbs

Grammatically, there are four main types of phrasal verbs:

a   verb + adverb, with <u>no</u> object. The two parts of phrasal verbs of this type cannot be separated.
*The plane **took off** at 6 o'clock.*
*Put some wood on the fire – otherwise it will **go out**.*

b   verb + adverb, followed by an object. The two parts of phrasal verbs of this type can be separated and, in fact, <u>must</u> be separated if the object is a pronoun.
*They have **put off** the meeting.* or *They have **put** the meeting **off**.*
*Have you **taken down** that picture yet?* or *Have you **taken** that picture **down** yet?*
*What does that sign say? I can't **make** it **out**.*

c   verb + preposition, followed by an object. The two parts of phrasal verbs of this type cannot be separated – the object must always come after the preposition.
*She **takes after** her mother.*
*I **came across** an old friend this morning.*

d   verb + adverb + preposition, followed by an object. Obviously, the parts of phrasal verbs of this type cannot be separated.
*We've **run out of** sugar.*
*I'm **looking forward to** seeing you.*

Irregular verbs

Infinitive	Past simple	Past participle	Infinitive	Past simple	Past participle
arise	arose	arisen	get	got	got
awake	awoke	awoken	give	gave	given
be	was / were	been	go	went	gone
bear	bore	borne	grind	ground	ground
beat	beat	beaten	grow	grew	grown
become	became	become	hang	hung / hanged	hung / hanged
begin	began	begun	have	had	had
bend	bent	bent	hear	heard	heard
bet	bet	bet	hide	hid	hidden
bind	bound	bound	hit	hit	hit
bite	bit	bitten	hold	held	held
bleed	bled	bled	hurt	hurt	hurt
blow	blew	blown	keep	kept	kept
break	broke	broken	kneel	knelt	knelt
breed	bred	bred	know	knew	known
bring	brought	brought	lay	laid	laid
build	built	built	lead	led	led
burn	burnt / ed	burnt / ed	lean	leant / ed	leant / ed
burst	burst	burst	learn	learnt / ed	learnt / ed
buy	bought	bought	leave	left	left
catch	caught	caught	lend	lent	lent
choose	chose	chosen	let	let	let
come	came	come	lie	lay	lain
cost	cost	cost	light	lit	lit
creep	crept	crept	lose	lost	lost
cut	cut	cut	make	made	made
deal	dealt	dealt	mean	meant	meant
dig	dug	dug	meet	met	met
do	did	done	pay	paid	paid
draw	drew	drawn	put	put	put
dream	dreamt / ed	dreamt / ed	read	read	read
drink	drank	drunk	ride	rode	ridden
drive	drove	driven	ring	rang	rung
eat	ate	eaten	rise	rose	risen
fall	fell	fallen	run	ran	run
feed	fed	fed	say	said	said
feel	felt	felt	see	saw	seen
fight	fought	fought	seek	sought	sought
find	found	found	sell	sold	sold
flee	fled	fled	send	sent	sent
fly	flew	flown	set	set	set
forbid	forbade	forbidden	shake	shook	shaken
forget	forgot	forgotten	shine	shone	shone
forgive	forgave	forgiven	shoot	shot	shot
freeze	froze	frozen	show	showed	shown

Infinitive	Past simple	Past participle
shrink	shrank	shrunk
shut	shut	shut
sing	sang	sung
sink	sank	sunk
sit	sat	sat
sleep	slept	slept
slide	slid	slid
smell	smelt / ed	smelt / ed
sow	sowed	sown
speak	spoke	spoken
speed	sped	sped
spell	spelt / led	spelt / led
spend	spent	spent
spill	spilt / led	spilt / led
spin	spun	spun
spit	spat	spat
split	split	split
spoil	spoilt / ed	spoilt / ed
spread	spread	spread
spring	sprang	sprung
stand	stood	stood
steal	stole	stolen
stick	stuck	stuck
sting	stung	stung
stink	stank / stunk	stunk
strike	struck	struck
swear	swore	sworn
sweep	swept	swept
swim	swam	swum
swing	swung	swung
take	took	taken
teach	taught	taught
tear	tore	torn
tell	told	told
think	thought	thought
throw	threw	thrown
tread	trod	trodden
understand	understood	understood
wake	woke	woken
wear	wore	worn
weave	wove	woven
weep	wept	wept
win	won	won
wind	wound	wound
write	wrote	written

Index of phrasal verbs and multi-word verbs

These phrasal verbs all appear in written contexts in the Student's Book. The meaning given in brackets is only a guide and you are advised to check the context on the page referred to. Those highlighted in bold are presented and practised in the Phrasal Verbs sections within the units.

account for (make up a proportion of) 59
add to (increase) 25
add up (increase, form a total) 39
back up (support) 137
branch out (do something different) 39
break into (become involved in) 79
break in[to] (enter building by force) 91
bring about (cause) 101
bring back (remind of memories) 101
bring back (return item) 101
bring forward (do sooner) 101
bring in (introduce sth. new) 101
bring off (succeed) 101
bring out (publish, release) 101
bring round (revive) 101
bring up (raise child) 101
bring up (raise topic) 101
build on (use as a foundation) 85
build up (increase) 10
carry on (continue) 76
carry out (do task) 14
catch on (become popular) 15
catch up on (do after delay) 27
check through (look for mistakes) 137
cheer up (stop feeling depressed) 123
close down (go out of business) 21
come across (find by chance) 149
come back (return) 68
come from (originate in) 8
come in (enter room, house, etc.) 54
come through (survive) 21
come up to (approach someone) 78
cross off / out (remove from list) 8
cut down (reduce) 75
decide on (choose from possibilities) 77
die out (become extinct) 44
divide up (separate into parts) 157
do away with (abolish) 37
draw up (prepare and write out) 31
drift apart (become less close) 119
dry up (lose all its water) 139
end up (do / become unintentionally) 29
fall off (lose contact with a surface) 97
fall over (land on the ground) 70
fill in (complete) 12
fill up with (become full of) 23
find out (discover) 28
get away (escape) 25

get away with (avoid punishment for) 23
get back (return) 27
get back up (return to the surface) 23
get by (manage to survive) 23
get down (descend) 23
get [someone] down (depress) 55
get into (manage to enter) 23
get off (leave bus, train, etc.) 23
get on (enter bus, train, etc.) 106
get on (progress) 23
get on with (have a good relationship) 55
get out of (leave plane, etc) 26
get over (recover from) 23
get rid of (remove unwanted person / thing) 49
get through (succeed in exam) 23
get to (manage to) 109
get to (reach) 114
get together (all meet) 23
get up (rise from bed) 23
get up to (do things disapproved of) 29
get up to (reach) 23
get used to (become accustomed to) 13
give away (give as a present) 75
give away (reveal a secret) 75
give back (return to owner) 75
give in (hand to teacher) 75
give in (surrender) 75
give off (produce light, smell, etc.) 129
give out (distribute) 75
give up (abandon attempt) 75
give up (stop doing habit) 40
go back (date from) 9
go back (return) 8
go off (start operating: alarms, etc.) 51
go on (continue) 116
go on to (do something different) 76
go out (be broadcast) 79
go out (become unlit) 51
go out (leave) 54
go out with / together (form a couple) 49
go through (examine) 8
go through (experience) 118
go up (rise) 154
grow up (become an adult) 79
hand over (give) 78
help out (give / lend money to) 57
hold up (delay) 94
hold up (threaten with a gun) 88
hunt down (look for until found) 25
invite out (offer to take with you) 65
keep away (not go near) 99
keep on [doing] (refuse to stop) 141
keep up (maintain standard) 12
knock down (cause to fall) 68
lead to (result in) 53

lead up to (happen in sequence) 92
leave behind (not take with you) 44
leave out (not include) 25
let down (disappoint) 119
listen [out] for (be ready to hear) 42
live on (survive by eating) 96
look after (take care of) 52
look at (study, consider) 52
look back (read earlier part) 10
look for (try to find) 52
look forward to (want to happen) 52
look into (investigate) 52
look out for (be careful to avoid) 52
look over (inspect) 52
look through (examine one by one) 52
look up (search for information) 52
make for (help create) 71
make out (see with difficulty) 25
make out (write name on cheque) 107
(be) made up of (consist of) 15
move in (start to live in a house or flat) 49
move on (pay attention to sth. else) 52
move out (stop living in a house or flat) 49
note down (quickly record on paper) 17
pass by (go past without stopping) 109
pay in (put money in the bank) 107
phone back (return a call) 11
pick up (take hold of and lift) 25
point out (cause people to notice) 59
pull [yourself] out of (escape from) 123
push in[to] (jump a queue) 115
put away (return to where kept) 64
put in (spend time or make an effort) 123
put off (postpone) 64
put off (stop someone wanting to) 64
put on (cause to start working) 64
put on (cover with clothing) 64
put on (increase weight) 64
put on (organize) 69
put on (write) 107
put out (extinguish) 64
put through (connect by phone) 64
put up (increase) 64
put up with (tolerate, accept) 64
queue up (form a line to wait) 39
ring up (phone somebody) 31
rule out (dismiss idea, possibility) 37
run away (leave, escape from) 55
run into (collide with) 89
run up to (approach at speed) 73
send off (tell to go somewhere else) 25
send off (tell to leave the field of play) 74
set out (start taking action / a journey) 149
settle for (accept as second-best) 123
shake off (get rid of) 29
shout back (reply loudly) 110
show off (display to impress) 10
show up for (attend) 149
speed up (make go faster) 115
spell out (state exactly) 59
start off (begin by doing / going) 139
stick to (keep doing) 39

sum up (make a judgement) 69
swallow up (devour completely) 30
switch over to (change system to) 114
take after (resemble) 96
take away (subtract) 96
take back (return item to shop) 96
take down (make a note of) 96
take in (trick) 96
take in (fully understand) 96
take off (become successful) 47
take off (leave the ground) 96
take off (remove clothing) 96
take on (accept difficult job) 96
take on (employ workers) 96
take out (extract) 91
take out (pay for subscription) 84
take over (gain control of) 96
take to (begin to like person) 96
take up (occupy time or space) 96
take up (start hobby) 96
talk down to (speak in superior manner) 149
tell off (punish by speaking angrily to) 149
think about (consider) 11
think back (remember past events) 57
think of (bring to mind) 61
throw out (force someone to leave) 49
tidy up (put everything in its place) 86
track down (find) 123
try out (test) 69
turn away (refuse admission) 54
turn back (reverse direction) 131
turn down (reject, refuse) 131
turn into (become) 131
turn off (disconnect) 131
turn on (operate) 131
turn out (be found to be) 131
turn over (roll, invert) 131
turn up (arrive unexpectedly / after delay) 131
wake up (end sleep) 50
walk on (not stop) 109
warm up (do preliminary exercise) 13
watch out for (be alert to the danger of) 128
write back (send a letter of reply) 85

Index of exam task-types and advice

Reading:

Multiple matching (headings) Part 1 . . . . 18 / 38 / 59 / 89
Multiple matching (summaries) Part 1 . . . . 8 / 123 / 148
Multiple choice Part 2 . . . . 18 / 24 / 48 / 98 / 118 / 128
Multiple choice (global questions) Part 2 . . . . 24 / 128
Gapped text (missing paragraphs) Part 3 . . . . 14 / 108
Gapped text (missing sentences) Part 3 . . . . 24 / 44 / 78 / 114 / 118
Multiple matching Part 4 . . . . 28 / 68 / 134 / 138

Writing:

Transactional letter (formal) Part 1 . . . . 15 / 84 / 122
Transactional letter (informal) Part 1 . . . . 85 / 147
Article Part 2 . . . . 45 / 62 / 117
Non-transactional letter Part 2 . . . . 26 / 107 / 136
Report Part 2 . . . . 17 / 56 / 74
Discursive composition (for and against) Part 2 142
Discursive composition (opinion) Part 2 . . . . 35 / 87
Short story Part 2 . . . . 93 / 97 / 103
Set books Part 2 152

Use of English:

Multiple-choice cloze Part 1 . . . . 21 / 47 / 146
Open cloze Part 2 . . . . 36 / 57 / 96 / 131
Key word transformations Part 3 . . . . 11 / 41 / 65 / 111 / 126 / 151
Error correction Part 4 . . . . 75 / 107 / 117 / 137
Word formation Part 5 . . . . 30 / 61 / 83 / 156

Listening:

Multiple choice Part 1 . . . . 32 / 86 / 102 / 124 / 144
Note taking / blank filling Part 2 . . . . 22 / 42 / 62 / 72 / 104 / 154
Multiple matching Part 3 . . . . 34 / 52 / 92 / 142 / 152
Multiple choice Part 4 . . . . 13 / 94 / 132
True / false questions Part 4 . . . . 76 / 112
'Who said what?' questions Part 4 82
Yes / no questions Part 4 66

Speaking:

Interview Part 1 . . . . 13 / 53 / 87
Individual long turn Part 2 . . . . 33 / 77 / 112
Collaborative task Part 3 . . . . 23 / 43 / 66 / 105 / 125 / 145 / 155
Three-way discussion Part 4 . . . . 66 / 95 / 133 / 155

Index of grammar and functions

Adjective order 130
Adverbs of frequency 40, 41
Affixes 30, 32, 34
Approximate expressions 56
Articles 20
as long as 64
be / have + adjectives 130
Collocations 21
Communication strategies 66
Comparative and superlative forms 46
Compound words 72, 156
Conditionals: zero 120, 126
Conditionals: first 60
Conditionals: second 60
Conditionals: third 120, 126
Conditionals: mixed 120, 126
Contrast links 55, 57
Countable / uncountable nouns 16
Definite article 20
Direct speech 110, 111
Disagreeing 124
do / make 36
during / for 80
enough 35
Future: *going to* 31
Future: use of present continuous 31
Future: use of present simple 31
Future: *will / shall* 31
Future continuous 31
Future perfect 31
Future perfect continuous 31
Gerund 106
have something done 151
in case 150
in order to / that 150
in the end / at the end 74
Indefinite article 20
Infinitive 116
-ing form of the verb 106
it's time + past simple 141
Linking expressions 142
look forward to -ing 106
Modal verbs 70, 40, 41, 43
Narrative time links 91
no matter 64
Object pronouns: after comparatives 46
Obligation 40
Paraphrasing 133
Participle adjectives 26
Parts of speech 61
Passive 100
Past continuous 50
Past modals 140
Past perfect 90
Past perfect continuous 90

Past simple 50, 83
Phrasal verbs, see Index of phrasal verbs 187
Phrasal verbs: separable / non-separable 149
Possibility 70
Prefixes 30
Prepositional phrases with *in* 74
Present continuous 10
Present perfect 80, 83
Present perfect continuous 83
Present simple 10
provided / providing (that) 64
Punctuation 73
Purpose links 150
Quantifiers 63
Question tags 140
Reference words 96
Relative clauses 70
Relative pronouns 70
Reported questions: word order 110
Reported speech 110
Reporting verbs 110
Sequence links 122
shall / will 31
Short replies 124
since / for 80
so / such ... that 130
so / so that / so as (not) to 150
Stative verbs 10
Stative verbs: continuous use 10
Suffixes 30, 32, 34
Suggesting 125
unless 64
used to / would 50
Verbs followed by the gerund / *-ing* 106
Verbs followed by the infinitive 116
Wh- questions 95
whom 71
wish / if only 140
wish / if only + past perfect 141
wish / if only + *would* 141
Zero article 20

Oxford University Press
Great Clarendon Street, Oxford OX2 6DP

Oxford   New York
Athens Auckland Bangkok Bogotá
Buenos Aires Calcutta Cape Town Chennai
Dar es Salaam Delhi Florence Hong Kong
Istanbul Karachi Kuala Lumpur Madrid
Melbourne Mexico City Mumbai Nairobi
Paris São Paulo Singapore Taipei Tokyo
Toronto Warsaw

and associated companies in
Berlin Ibadan

OXFORD and OXFORD ENGLISH
are trade marks of Oxford University Press

ISBN 0 19 453364 6

© Oxford University Press 1999

Acknowledgements

The author would like to thank all the OUP staff in Oxford, Athens
and elsewhere who worked on this project, as well as the teachers
who trialled the *Knockout* material in various parts of the world. The
author would also like to thank Hermelinda and David May, and of
course Alan May for his contributions to both this book and the
Workbook.

Grammar Reference by Richard Mann.

The author and publisher would like to thank the following for
permission to use adapted material and/or to reproduce copyright
material:

Aitken & Stone Ltd for p49 extract based on an article by Chris
Manby published in *The Times* referring to the author's novel, *Flatmates*
published by Hodder & Stoughton, Copyright © Chris Manby 1997.
The Consumers' Association for p137 article abridged from *Which?*
July 1992, published by The Consumer's Association, 2 Marylebone
Road, London NW1 4DF. Curtis Brown Ltd on behalf of the author
for extract from Lionel Davidson: p54 *The Rose of Tibet*, (Gollancz,
1962), copyright © Lionel Davidson, 1962. The Guardian for
adaptations of articles, p90 'Birdthief caged by parrot that dared
squeak its name' (*The Guardian* 4.9.96); p139 'Change Your World'
special report (The Guardian/WWF, April 1997); by Claude Fancillon:
p129 'Surviving when lightning strikes in the mountains...' (*Guardian
Weekly* 14.8.94); and by Colin Luckhurst: p132 'A weather eye on the
news' (*Guardian Weekly* 12.2.95); all articles copyright © The Guardian.
Guinness Publishing for extract from John Goldman: p9 *Taekwondo,
The Complete Course* (Guinness Publishing Ltd), copyright © John
Goldman, 1991. Phil Healey for p89 adaptation of Healey & Glanvill's
Urban Myths, from *The Guardian* 31.5.97. David Higham Associates
for adapted extract from Michael Asher: p96 *The Last of the Bedu*
(Penguin). The Independent for adaptations of articles, by Alix
Sharkey: p44 'Smash hits of the Sixties, megabores of the Nineties'
(*The Independent* 27.7.93); by Scarlett Chidgey: p69 'Bowled Over'
(*The Independent on Sunday* 2.3.97); by Peggy Speirs: p109 'Your
Holiday Disaster: Trapped, and the hotel manager swore blind it could
not happen' (*The Independent on Sunday* 23.2.97); and film review by
Chris Jones: p25 'Director's Cut' (*The Independent* 8.4.94); all articles
copyright © The Independent/Independent on Sunday, Newspaper
Publishing plc. Milk Marque for diagram p60 of 'Germometer' from
The Dairy Book of Home Cookery (1992). Times Newspaper Ltd, News
International, for adaptations of articles, by Bill Frost: p104 'A Very
Awkward Customer' (*The Times* 15.9.97) © Times Newspapers
Limited, 1997; by Geoff Brown: p29 'Can scientists shake off their
mad media image?' (*The Times* 1.1.96) © Times Newspapers Limited,
1996; by Nick Nuttall: p37 'Tomorrow's world will be a little late' (*The
Times* 7.7.97) © Times Newspapers Limited, 1997; by Robert Young:
p59 'Britain is fast-food capital of Europe' (*The Times* 25.4.97)

© Times Newspapers Limited, 1997; by Ian Murray: p61 'Decline
in pollution blamed for asthma rise' (*The Times* 24.4.97) © Times
Newspapers Limited, 1997; by Ian Murray: p61 'Dieters must plump
for silence to avoid piling on the pounds' (*The Times* 23.6.97) © Times
Newspapers Limited, 1997; by Joe Joseph: p146 'Where's the fast
forward on this thing?' (*The Times* 10.1.98) © Times Newspapers
Limited, 1998; by Nicolette Jones: p149 'Back from the Future'
(*The Times* 11.6.97) © Nicolette Jones/Times Newspapers Limited,
1997; by Louis Rogers: p14 'Live longer with a virgin from Crete'
(*The Sunday Times* 6.4.97) © Times Newspapers Limited, 1997; by
Christopher Lloyd: p18 'All aboard for a ride into terror' (*The Sunday
Times* 13.3.94) © Times Newspapers Limited, 1994; by David Mills:
p39 'Turning over a new leaf' (*The Sunday Times* 22.6.97) © Times
Newspapers Limited, 1997; by Maureen Freely: p123 'EQ versus IQ'
(*The Sunday Times* 1.2.98) © Times Newspapers Limited, 1998; by
Cheryl Holmes Perfect: p13 'Rope Tricks' (*The Sunday Times* 4.5.97)
© Cheryl Holmes Perfect/Times Newspapers Limited, 1997; by John
Brewer: p72 'Pushed to the limit' (*The Sunday Times* 13.4.97) © John
Brewer/Times Newspapers Limited, 1997; and by Christopher
Middleton: p50 'The best rest?' (*The Sunday Times* 20.4.97)
© Christopher Middleton/Times Newspapers Limited, 1997. Time
Out Magazine for adaptation of article by David Elmer: p79 'Sniggers
with attitude' from *Time Out* (London) 21-28 May 1997. X Magazine
(Elixir Magazine) and the author for p57 extract from article on
Homelessness by Jennifer O'Shea Johnston, copyright © 1998.

Although every effort has been made to trace and contact copyright
holders before publication, this has not been possible in some cases.
We apologize for any apparent infringement of copyright and if
notified, the publisher will be pleased to rectify any errors or omissions
at the earliest opportunity.

Illustrations by:

Jeremy Banx: pp36, 53, 81, 97; Rowan Barnes-Murphy pp17, 41, 75,
111, 127, 145, 151, 157; Brett Breckon: pp23, 60, 105, 130, 140, 155;
Stephan Chabluk: p30; Emma Dodd pp10, 70, 101, 116, 121; Adam
Graff: p51; Paul Hess: pp48, 95, 125; Mark Oliver: pp19, 65, 90, 120;
Pierre-Paul Pariseau: pp12, 34, 43, 58, 86, 133, 155; Tina
Ramsbottom: p67.

Commissioned photography by:

Bob Battersby p138; Maggie Milner: pp98, 102

We would like to thank the following for permission to reproduce
photographs:

Action Plus p8 (Tony Henshaw); Allsport p72 (Al Bello), p77 (Shai
Rottervik/football), (John Gichigi/basketball), (Gary M Prior/Grand
Slam tennis)

Bubbles p38 (PB Hercules Robinson/reading home), p118 (Pauline
Cutler/children), p156; Collections p57 (Select), p113 (Dorothy
Burrows/walkers); Columbia p84 (courtesy Kobal/The Wild One); et
archive p82 (Maeght Gallery/Joan Miro), (V&A/Hiroshige); Express &
Echo, Exeter p76 (John Ffoulkes); Fox TV p78 (Frank Spooner/
Gamma/ The Simpsons); Gateshead Borough Council p82 (Colin
Cuthbert/Angel of the North); Hanna-Barbera Productions, Inc p78
(Corbis Everett/ The Flintstones); Robert Harding Picture Library p28
(researcher), p88 (car burglar), p92 (Earl Kogler/girl in cell), p122,
p128 (thunderstorm); Impact Photos p56 (Tony Page), p68 (Chris
Moyse), p77 (Bruce Stephens/tennis), p82 (Martin Black/mural), p113
(Caroline Penn/beach scene), p114 (Ben Edwards), p135 (Robert
Gibbs/backpacker);

MGM p78 (Corbis Everett/Tom & Jerry); MTV/Mike Judge p79
(Rex Features/Beavis & Butthead); Magnum p38 (Harry Gruyaert/
reading/tube); The National Portrait Gallery, London p82 (Elizabeth 1);
Paramount p28 (courtesy Kobal/The Nutty Professor); Rex Features
p38 (PB/reading scooter), (NJ/reading/deckchair), p45 (Magnus/
Rolling Stones), (Beatles), (Sipa/Rod Stewart), (IM/David Bowie),
p118 (PAB/COY/teenagers), p128 (Jamie Jones/snow); Selznick/MGM
p84 (courtesy Kobal/Gone with the Wind), p146 (Sipa), p148
(The Sun/David Beckham), (Kate Winslet), (Sipa/Bill Clinton),
(SLO/Naomi Campbell); Frank Spooner p138 (Stuart Freedman/
demonstration); The Stock Market p62 (Thai food), (Myers
Photography/pizza), p113 (London) and cover; Tony Stone Images
p14 (Charlie Waite), p20 (Tim Flach), p22 (John & Eliza Forder), p33
(Joe Cornish/home office), (Terry Vine/office), (Glen Allison/Sydney),
(Allan McPhai/New York), p62 (Diana Miller/stuffed vine leaves), p63
(Chris Everard/kebab), p88 (Dante Burn-Fort/house burglar), p108,
p113 (John Lawrence/Rome), p128 (Allan Moller/tornado), (Jeremy
Walker/fog), p135 (Brian Bailey/skier), p138 (Ed Pritchard/cyclist),
p139 (David Woodfall/recycling), p142 (Gary Braasch);Twentieth
Century Fox p24 (courtesy Kobal); United Artists p37 (courtesy
Kobal).

Designed by Keith Shaw, Threefold Design.